T5-ASA-550

The Guitar of God

University of Pennsylvania Press

MIDDLE AGES SERIES

Edited by Edward Peters

Henry Charles Lea Professor
of Medieval History
University of Pennsylvania

A complete listing of the books in this series
appears at the back of this volume

The Guitar of God

Gender, Power, and Authority
in the Visionary World
of Mother Juana de la Cruz
(1481–1534)

Ronald E. Surtz

University of Pennsylvania Press
Philadelphia

Copyright © 1990 by the University of Pennsylvania Press
ALL RIGHTS RESERVED
Printed in the United States of America

Library of Congress Cataloging-in-Publication Data

Surtz, Ronald E.
    The guitar of God: gender, power, and authority in the visionary
world of Mother Juana de la Cruz (1481–1534) / Ronald E. Surtz.
        p.   cm. — (Middle Ages series)
    Includes bibliographical references.
    ISBN 0-8122-8225-6
    1. Juana de la Cruz, sor, 1481–1534.   2. Sex role—Religious
apsects—Christianity—History of doctrines—16th century.
3. Authority (Religion)—History of doctrines—16th century.
4. Private revelations—History of doctrines—16th century.
5. Women in the Catholic Church—Spain—History—16th century.
6. Catholic Church—Spain—Doctrines—History—16th century.
7. Spain—Church history—16th century.   I. Title.   II. Series.
BX4705.J726S87   1990
271'.973024—dc20   89-78260
                                                        CIP

Para Nora,
     mujer fuerte bíblica

Contents

Acknowledgments

In the preparation of this book I have received help and encouragement of many kinds. Travel grants from the Princeton University Committee on Research in the Humanities and Social Sciences and a National Endowment for the Humanities Summer Stipend enabled me to carry out research in Spain and Italy. Princeton University also provided a partial subvention for publication. Particular thanks are due to Father Teodoro Alonso Turienzo of the Escorial library and to Father Josef Metzler of the Archivio Segreto Vaticano as well as to the staff of Firestone Library. Father Jesús Gómez López supplied necessary research materials. I am very grateful for the hospitality of Doña Amalia Serrano Camarasa, María del Valle Vaquero Serrano, and María Carmen Vaquero Serrano of Toledo. Edmund L. King took the time to read the typescript and to iron out many stylistic infelicities. I owe a special debt of gratitude to Professors Jodi Bilinkoff, John Fleming, and William Jordan for their advice and encouragement. I would also like to thank my editors at the University of Pennsylvania Press and my work-study students, Aurora Lauzardo and Jessica Hadlow. Last but not least, the affection, good humor, patience, and criticisms of Nora Weinerth made the writing of this study a joyous experience. I dedicate this book to her because she is in a very real sense its second author.

Preface

My first research trip to Spain in 1977 signaled not only the end of the care-free life of the tourist but also my initial encounter with the figure whose visions I discuss in this study. Upon examining *El libro del conorte* in the Escorial library, I was immediately struck by Mother Juana's wild imagination and by her creative rewriting of sacred history. The inherent interest of the manuscript seemed to demand further investigation.

Since one of the objectives of my research trip was to collect data on the early Castilian theater, Mother Juana's Assumption sermon was of particular interest to me, for it contained detailed instructions for the performance of a play. The scenario in the *Conorte* seemed familiar, and upon my return to the United States, I was able to verify that the very play that realized those instructions was to be found in another manuscript (Biblioteca Nacional, Madrid, MS 9661), from which it had been edited by Eduardo Juliá Martínez. Because Juliá Martínez apparently did not know of the relationship between the Madrid and the Escorial manuscripts and because of a few lapses in his transcription, I decided to reedit both the play and the corresponding part of the sermon.[1] Meanwhile, I had learned of Father Jesús Gómez López and of his efforts to reopen Mother Juana's beatification process.[2] Thus, it appeared to me that the late Middle Ages was being reborn in the twentieth century.

El libro del conorte continued to fascinate me, above all for its obvious relevance to the study of late-medieval Castilian spirituality. At first, I intended to analyze the visions from the perspective of popular religion, for it seemed to me that beneath their often eccentric surface lay a set of religious attitudes that was very typical of the late Middle Ages. Since historians of Castilian spirituality have tended to give preference to heterodox figures, the case of Mother Juana appeared to provide a concrete manifestation of the religious mind-set of a more traditional believer. Prior commitments prevented me from carrying out that projected study, and in the meantime, I began to doubt that popular religion was the most appropriate approach to the visions.

At the 1982 meeting of the Modern Language Association, I delivered a brief paper on the problem of authority in Mother Juana's writings.[3] That talk gave me the first opportunity to deal with another aspect of the revelations, namely, Mother Juana's personal voice. By concentrating on those passages in which the nun seemed to reflect self-consciously upon her visions and upon her readers' reception of those visions, I became aware of the ways in which she defended from within the *Conorte* its divine inspiration. Nonetheless, at that time I was not fully aware of the extent to which the problem of authority was related to such other questions as the novelization of sacred history.

When in 1987 I was invited to share with an English-speaking audience the preliminary results of my research on Mother Juana, I chose the guitar vision (see Chapter 3) because its eccentric imagery seemed to lend itself to an oral presentation. Indeed, the audience found the vision both fascinating and shocking, for it appeared that figures like Mother Juana were rare, if they were to be found at all, in other countries. Nonetheless, since the focus of that talk was the analysis of the guitar vision as a synthesis of traditional images, I was still thinking of Mother Juana as a figure more given to juxtaposing commonplace images than to creating new ones. Her originality appeared to consist, above all, in the ways in which she recombined traditional motifs.

Meanwhile, the burgeoning interest in women's studies in the United States had touched Hispanic letters as well.[4] During the same year of 1987 I was invited to contribute an essay to an anthology on women and religion in early modern Spain. I decided to analyze the first part of the Creation sermon (see Chapter 1) because it seemed that the way in which Mother Juana treated Eve would meld well with the focus of the collection as a whole, namely, the reinterpretation of the role of women in religious contexts. Studying the Creation sermon resulted in a sort of epiphany, for there suddenly appeared the image of another Mother Juana whose existence I had scarcely suspected. Indeed, I quickly became aware of the presence of an extremely astute figure who was able to defend her right—and by extension that of all women—to speak and to write about matters considered appropriate only for men. If beforehand I saw a woman who merely re-created traditional images, now I saw a skillful writer who was cleverly able to manipulate her readers and listeners.

That abrupt change of perspective resulted in a frenzied rereading of the visions in an effort to discover the "real" Mother Juana. Not unsurprisingly, the two figures, the one more conservative, the other more daring, appeared juxtaposed and even complementary to each other. Rereading the visions made me realize that alongside the ultraorthodox insistence on such traditional doctrines as the need for repentance and the veneration of the Eucharist could be found a self-conscious preoccupation with problems of power and authority. Indeed, the *Conorte* had both a spiritual and a worldly dimension, for if on the one hand the manuscript was a record of Juana's spiritual experiences, on the other hand it was a very physical object that needed to be defended against the nun's real or imagined critics.

The emergence of Mother Juana as both a chronicler and a defender of her experience of the divine led me to reread her official biography. Not unexpectedly, I found notable parallels between the preoccupations expressed in the sermons and the few known events of her life. Indeed, the questions of power and authority that come through in her writings are dramatically and concretely played out in her life. If, as I will discuss in the Introduction, the brouhaha surrounding the episode of the benefice of Cubas ultimately demonstrated the limits placed on her authority by the ecclesiastical hierarchy, Juana's mystical experiences provided her with an authority that in a sense circumvented that hierarchy. The enormous prestige she enjoyed bears witness to her credibility as a visionary and to her successful bid for power and authority in this world. Indeed, it was Cardinal Cisneros and Emperor Charles V who came to visit her and not vice versa. How was it possible for a woman of such humble birth to achieve such renown? That question was the beginning of my fascination with the ways in which the nun created her own authority and defended her experience of the divine. Those same issues became the point of departure for this book.

Notes

1. See Surtz, *"El libro del conorte" and the Early Castilian Theater* (Barcelona: Puvill, [1982]).

2. Father Gómez López has published "El *Conorte* de Sor Juana de la Cruz y su sermón sobre la inmaculada concepción de María," *Hispania Sacra,* 36 (1984) 601–627, and coauthored (with Inocente García de Andrés) *Sor Juana de la Cruz, mística e iluminista toledana* (Toledo: Diputación Provincial, 1982).

3. I later published a revised version of the talk: "La Madre Juana de la Cruz (1481–1534) y la cuestión de la autoridad religiosa femenina," *Nueva Revista de Filología Hispánica,* 33 (1984) 483–491.

4. My study owes an obvious debt to such studies of medieval women's spirituality as Rudolph M. Bell's *Holy Anorexia* (Chicago and London: University of Chicago Press, 1985); Elizabeth Petroff's *Consolation of the Blessed* (New York: Alta Gaia Society, 1979); and Caroline Walker Bynum's *Holy Feast and Holy Fast: The Religious Significance of Food to Medieval Women* (Berkeley and Los Angeles: Univer-

sity of California Press, 1987). Recent books of interest in the area of Hispanic female spirituality include Jodi Bilinkoff's *The Avila of Saint Teresa: Religious Reform in a Sixteenth-Century City* (Ithaca: Cornell University Press, 1989) and Electa Arenal and Stacey Schlau's *Untold Sisters: Hispanic Nuns in Their Own Works* (Albuquerque: University of New Mexico Press, 1989).

Abbreviations

Casa	*Libro de la casa y monasterio de Nuestra Señora de la Cruz,* Biblioteca Nacional (Madrid), MS 9661.
Conorte	*El libro del conorte,* Escorial MS J-II-18.
Daza 1610	Fray Antonio Daza, *Historia, vida y milagros, éxtasis y revelaciones de la bienaventurada virgen santa Juana de la Cruz* (Madrid, 1610).
Daza 1613	Fray Antonio Daza, *Historia, vida y milagros, éxtasis, y revelaciones de la bienaventurada virgen Sor Juana de la Cruz* (Madrid, 1613).
Migne, *Patrologia Latina*	*Patrologia cursus completus: series latina,* ed. J.-P. Migne, 221 vols. (Paris: Migne, etc., 1841–1864).
Navarro	Fray Pedro Navarro, *Favores de el rey de el cielo, hechos a su esposa la Santa Juana de la Cruz* (Madrid, 1622).
Reparos	*Reparos por el eminentíssimo Señor Cardenal Bona a los Sermones del libro que llaman Conorte, en la causa de beatificación de la venerable sor Juana de la Cruz* (n.p., n.d.).
Vat.	Archivio Segreto Vaticano, Congregazione Riti, MS 3074, *Scripta proc. ord.* [*El libro del conorte*].
Vida	*Vida y fin de la bienabenturada virgen sancta Juana de la Cruz,* Escorial MS K-III-13.

Note on the Text

In transcribing medieval and Golden Age texts, I have resolved abbreviations and added accent marks, punctuation, and capital letters in accordance with modern usage. I have regularized the use of *u/v* and *i/j/y* and transcribed as *r* initial *rr-* and *-rr-* after a consonant. I use *e* to represent the Tironian sign.

Quotations from the Bible are taken from the revised version of the Douai-Rheims English translation of the Latin Vulgate (New York: Edward Dunigan, 1844). I therefore follow the Vulgate numbering of the Psalms.

The Vatican manuscript of the *Conorte,* although recently restored, has suffered the ravages of time. Many folios are missing, and the text is often extremely difficult or altogether impossible to read. This is because the paper has disintegrated completely or the ink has soaked through from the other side of a given folio. Although there are cases of interpolations and omissions, for the most part the Escorial and the Vatican manuscripts coincide, with only occasional differences in wording. Since its deteriorated state makes quoting at length from the Vatican manuscript in most instances impossible, when necessary I offer instead a summary or paraphrase of the pertinent passages in which the two manuscripts differ.

Unless otherwise indicated, English translations of Mother Juana's writings and other medieval and Golden Age Spanish texts are my own.

Introduction

It is a commonplace of Spanish literary historiography that medieval and Golden Age Spain had few women writers. For the Middle Ages only a handful of female authors can be mentioned,[1] and outside of Saint Teresa of Avila and, to a lesser extent, María de Zayas, critics are often hard-pressed to document the presence of women of letters in the Golden Age. And yet, it suffices to leaf through Serrano y Sanz's biobibliography of Spanish women writers to realize that there were hundreds of female authors in the period from 1500 to 1700.[2] To be sure, many of them are known only through the publication of a single laudatory sonnet or a solitary composition entered in a poetry contest. The works of others, the majority of them nuns, were never published and even today are available only in manuscript form. And, needless to say, writing was for these religious women seldom either a vocation or even an avocation. About a third of the nuns wrote because they were ordered to by their confessors so that the Inquisition could determine the orthodoxy of their religious experiences.[3] Saint Teresa's *Life* is the best-known manifestation of this phenomenon, but many other women found themselves subjected to the same pressures, albeit with less notable results.

Mother Juana de la Cruz is one of these all but unknown women writers. Or perhaps we should say forgotten, for she enjoyed considerable fame not only during her lifetime but also for nearly two centuries after her death. She was visited by persons of high social standing, including Cardinal Cisneros, Emperor Charles V, and Gonzalo Fernández de Córdoba (the celebrated hero of the Italian campaigns). In the seventeenth century her renown was enhanced by the publication of several biographies, one of which (Daza's) was translated into French, Italian, German, and English. Her fame extended even beyond the bounds of the Western world, for Franciscan missionaries introduced into Japan the devotion to the rosary beads that people believed had been blessed by God and the Virgin Mary at Mother Juana's request.[4]

Born of peasant stock, Juana was able to achieve such prestige through one of the few channels open to women in her time, the mystical experience.[5] If previous to the late fifteenth century the bellicose religiosity of a Castile devoted to the Reconquest against the Muslims did not provide a congenial setting for mysticism of any sort, the messianic atmosphere of the Spain of Cardinal Cisneros and of the Catholic Sovereigns, Ferdinand and Isabella, was especially propitious for all sorts of extraordinary religious phenomena.[6] Female visionaries in particular enjoyed considerable authority: Cisneros himself, as both archbishop of Toledo and inquisitor-general of Castile, protected these women and sought out their advice.[7] The mysticism of such visionaries embodied the kind of nonintellectual and noninstitutional mediation between God and humankind in which women were traditionally allowed to participate. If the extreme saturation of the religious atmosphere is a general phenomenon in late-fifteenth-century Europe, in Spain it can be related not only to the general messianic climate but also to the dissemination of spiritual writings through the new medium of the printing press and to the reform of the religious orders undertaken by Cisneros and supported by the monarchs.[8] The search for new forms to express this irrepressible longing for the divine resulted in the flowering of a mysticism barely perceptible in the Castile of preceding centuries. The phenomenon of the visionaries would seem to correspond to the needs of those believers who, dissatisfied with the traditional system of mediation with the divine provided by the ecclesiastical hierarchy, sought a more direct way of contacting the supernatural. The visionary functioned as a locus of spiritual power, a channel of grace, a direct pipe-line to the eternal.

A representative sign of the favorable official attitude toward mysticism in general and female visionaries in particular is the prologue to the Castilian translation of a biography of Angela of Foligno. The prologue can be said to reflect the ideas of Cisneros himself, for the translation was commissioned by him and published bearing his coat of arms. It appears, observes the translator, that what is hidden from males blinded by their carnal ways has been clearly manifested through this strong woman.[9] He goes on to remark that for the greater scorn and embarrassment of sinful males, God has sometimes ordained that women should teach men. In this respect Angela resembles the Old Testament prophetess Holda (IV Kings 22:14) to whom the people had recourse, to the shame and disgrace of men and doctors of the law, for because the male sex had broken God's commandments, the gift of prophecy was transferred to the female sex.[10] Cisneros no doubt saw in Mother Juana a figure analogous to Holda and Angela. In any case, the prologue establishes a dichotomy between two types of knowledge: that acquired through formal studies by the lettered, that is to say, by males, and the infused science closely associated with women. This sort of endorsement of female wisdom notwithstanding,

Mother Juana still feels obliged to defend a woman's right to have this kind of unmediated knowledge of the divine.

According to tradition, it was one of Mother Juana's companions, Sister María Evangelista, who wrote the nun's official biography (*Vida y fin de la bienabenturada virgen sancta Juana de la Cruz*).[11] The biography is as sparing in historical facts as it is generous in recording the supernatural happenings of Juana's intense spiritual life. In effect, the *Vida* sets out above all to describe some of the visions and to enumerate the nun's miraculous powers, emphasizing her harsh ascetic practices and the supernatural cures that she effected. But the events recorded in the *Vida* turn out to be so generic that the reader finds few biographical details that could distinguish Mother Juana's life from those described in other such hagiographic narratives.[12] The only parts that seem to belong wholly and uniquely to Juana are the visions and a few scattered episodes in which a personal experience can be glimpsed. It is precisely these episodes that will be highlighted in this introduction.

The historically verifiable incidents in Mother Juana's life are few. She was born in 1481 to farmers of modest means in the small village of Azaña. From an early age she manifested an affinity for the contemplative and ascetic life. When she was fifteen, her relatives sought to marry her off, but she fled from the family home, dressed in male attire,[13] to become a nun in the Franciscan convent of Santa María de la Cruz. The convent is located near the village of Cubas, which is between Madrid and Toledo.[14] It was founded as a result of a series of apparitions (1449) of the Virgin Mary, who ordered that a church be built on the site.[15] In 1464, a group of *beatas*[16] occupied a nearby house, where they lived uncloistered under the rule of the Secular Third Order of Saint Francis. Later in the century, under the auspices of Cisneros the convent became cloistered and adopted the rule of the Regular Third Order of Saint Francis.[17] The trajectory of the regulation of the community is directly linked to Cisneros's reforming efforts and corresponds as well to the more general tendency in the late fifteenth and sixteenth centuries to pressure communities of *beatas* to regularize.[18] Juana's arrival at Santa María de la Cruz thus coincides with the time of the reformation and regularization of the convent; she professed in 1497 and in 1509 became abbess. The *Libro de la casa y monasterio de Nuestra Señora de la Cruz* brings together, in addition to miscellaneous reminiscences of the visionary's life, some poems the nuns sang and plays they performed in the convent under her direction.

Of particular interest for the study of Mother Juana's life is an incident recorded in none of her biographies and known only through a letter written by Father Antonio de Pastrana in 1512. A certain Franciscan friar, whom Pastrana described as "enlightened by the darkness of Satan," believed himself destined to beget a sort of Messiah, and with that purpose in mind, he wrote to Juana, inviting her to be the mother of the future prophet.[19] Juana responded by denouncing the unfortunate friar to the ecclesiastical authorities, who ordered his arrest. The episode demonstrates two important aspects of Mother Juana's status as visionary. The deluded friar, inspired no doubt by the nun's renown as a mystic, believed he had found in her the ideal collaborator for his mission, above and beyond the obvious biological function she was to perform. But Mother Juana remained a loyal daughter of the Church, despite what the extraordinary phenomena she experienced might have indicated. In any case, the woman who enjoyed such divine favors showed herself to be an orthodox believer who did not allow herself to be seduced by the friar's daring, and indeed flattering, proposals.

In time, Juana was dismissed from the position of abbess as a result of an incident that demonstrates dramatically the limits imposed on the authority that women were allowed to exercise within the ecclesiastical hierarchy. Two of the few extant documents associated with Mother Juana are orders written by Cardinal Cisneros and dated March 9 and December 28, 1510. In both orders Cisneros answers a petition by the parish priest of the village of Cubas, who, having secured another parish, requests that the one he is leaving be annexed to the convent of Santa María de la Cruz. Cisneros grants the priest's request, for it turns out to be a convenient way to remedy the convent's precarious financial situation and to ensure that cloistered nuns not have to resort to begging for their sustenance.[20]

According to Cisneros's orders, the nuns would acquire not only the profits from the parish's property but also the privilege of appointing a chaplain to oversee the spiritual well-being of the parishioners. This was an almost unheard-of situation, for the privilege of naming a chaplain involved the question of whether a woman could be empowered to exercise spiritual jurisdiction. There remains as well the problem of whether Cisneros had the authority to grant such a right.[21] In any case, in time certain ecclesiastics tried to take the benefice of Cubas away from the convent, arguing that women, even if they were nuns, were not suited to exercise spiritual care over lay people.[22] Mother Juana, ever concerned with the fiscal well-being of her convent, turned to other ecclesiastics, who advised her to secure a papal bull that would confirm a candidate suitable to occupy the curacy on behalf of the convent.[23] The nun did so, but her action was denounced to the heads of the order by the convent's assistant superior, an enemy of Mother Juana. Mother Juana was accused of having acted without official permission and of having spent too much money in securing the bull. Although the question of patronage does not seem to have been a central issue, the matter was further complicated by the fact that the cleric who was acting as parish priest of Cubas was none other than Mother Juana's brother.[24] The upshot of all this was that Juana was forced to step down, and the nun who had denounced her became the new abbess.

In time Mother Juana's action was vindicated, for the new abbess became gravely ill and, calling together the other nuns and the chaplain, confessed to them how she had unjustly accused Juana (*Vida*, fol. 98v). And so Mother Juana was reinstated as the convent's abbess, a post she held until her death in 1534. Despite its ultimately favorable outcome, the episode of the benefice of Cubas demonstrates the extent to which serious questions were raised by the granting of extraordinary powers to a woman, no matter how extraordinary the woman herself may have been. In effect, the episode boiled down to a question of power, and despite the analogous case of the abbess of the convent of Las Huelgas, who enjoyed a similar privilege,[25] it is evident that it was considered improper for a woman to exercise a jurisdiction deemed the exclusive prerogative of ecclesiastics, that is, of the male sex. The very fact that Cisneros had to send two orders nearly identical in content in the same year suggests that significant opposition to his decision existed.

Furthermore, although the orders signed by Cisneros do not require that the abbess have the chaplain of her choice confirmed by the superiors of the order,[26] it appears that this had been done in the case of the appointment of Mother Juana's brother. In point of fact, her biography tells how the brother already occupied the post in question by the mandate and desire of the superiors because he was suited for the position and the parishioners were satisfied with him.[27] This means that even before the convent's right to the benefice of Cubas had been questioned, and despite the apparent intent of Cisneros's orders, the abbess did not enjoy unrestricted control of the benefice. In any case, it seems evident that despite Cisneros's desires, other ecclesiastics opposed allowing the abbess of Santa María de la Cruz to exercise powers normally reserved for men, and they did all that was possible to limit women's authority in spiritual matters.

Less problematic was Mother Juana's role as visionary, for mysticism was an area in which women were traditionally permitted to act.[28] From an early age Juana experienced raptures and visions.[29] During a period of thirteen years, she believed that God revealed Himself through her, delivering sermons through her mouth. The sermons normally consist of the novelesque retelling of a gospel episode followed by the description of the allegorical pageants that take place in Heaven to celebrate the major feasts of the liturgical year. Juxtaposed with those pageants are such spiritual and tropological interpretations as are relevant to the salvation of humankind. Juana's companions transcribed the sermons corresponding to the liturgical year 1508–1509, the resulting sermon-book forming Mother Juana's principal work, *El libro del conorte* [*The Book of Consolation*].[30] If the episode of the benefice of Cubas demonstrates the limits on the power women could exercise within the ecclesiastical hierarchy, the very existence of a sermon-book is a dramatic reminder of Juana's appropriation of the priestly, and therefore masculine, role of preacher.[31]

The thorny question of the source of Mother Juana's revelations will not be discussed here. It was once quite fashionable to attribute such phenomena to the sublimation of sexual energy or to interpret them as the psychophysiological reaction to extreme fasts. Naturally, Mother Juana and her supporters did not hesitate to ascribe her visions to divine inspiration. Whatever the origin of the revelations, more appropriate to this discussion are the contents of the visions, for as will be seen, they epitomize the visionary's most intimate concerns at the same time that they codify a series of cultural experiences. At a historical moment when the male ecclesiastical hierarchy possesses all the power, it is no accident that Juana should have a series of visions in which women appropriate considerable authority and prestige, sometimes at the expense of male power. Such questions of gender, power, and authority will constitute the principal focus of this study.

The peculiar circumstances of Juana's birth suggest a possible psychological explanation for the nun's preoccupation with socio-religious roles. Her *Vida* recounts that Juana was conceived as a male, but then the Virgin Mary prevailed upon the Lord to change the unborn child into a female:

Y la bienabenturada Juana de la Cruz estava entonçes en el vientre de su madre enpezada a façer varón. Tornóla muger como pudo y puede haçer como todopoderoso. Y no quiso su divina magestad deshazerle una nuez que tenía en la garganta por que fuese testigo del milagro. (*Vida*, fol. 2v)

(And blessed Juana de la Cruz was at that moment in the belly of her mother in the process of becoming a male. He [God] turned her into a woman as He could and can do since He is all-powerful. And His Divine Majesty refused to take away an Adam's apple that she had in her throat so that it might bear witness to the miracle.) [32]

While the knowledge of such an episode can be significant in a psychological sense, it does not necessarily explain the nun's future preoccupations. Nonetheless, a person who leads his or her life conscious that he or she was intended to be of the opposite sex cannot help being conscious as well of the arbitrary nature of God's assignment of sexual identities to people and, by extension, of the arbitrary nature of gender roles in the eyes of God. There is no way of knowing whether the story that God turned Juana from male to female in her mother's womb was revealed to her in a vision or whether it was created by her biographer. It is unlikely, however, that her biographer invented the physiological detail of the prominent Adam's apple that the nun bore throughout her life. The Adam's apple is more than the visible sign of a prenatal miracle: it is also the emblem of a divinely determined androgyny. If Juana displayed a typically masculine physical characteristic, might she not also feel that she had the divinely given right to exercise powers considered befitting only to men? If, by the will of God, Juana was an androgynous figure, did she feel a kinship with the other androgynous figures, including Christ Himself, who appear in her visions? [33] The motif of a God with feminine characteristics, and particularly, of Christ as mother, dates back to the church fathers. Could Juana's interest in that tradition arise, at least in part, from her consciousness of her own androgyny? What is certain, as will be seen in subsequent chapters, is that some of Juana's visions raise a series of questions among which preoccupations with gender and with the sphere of action granted to women compared with that granted to men figure prominently. If sexual identity is something arbitrary, then male power is in turn an arbitrary power. It is possible that Mother Juana's awareness of her own androgyny made her particularly sensitive to the arbitrary nature of both sexual identity and the authority associated with socio-religious roles. In any case, gender and, more concretely, the Lord's indifference to sexual roles in the face of human worry about them are a recurring manifestation in Mother Juana's visions.

It would be of no small interest to discover what Golden Age readers thought of Juana's concern for questions of gender and power. Obviously, one cannot go back in time to read the visionary's *Vida* and sermons with the mentality of a sixteenth-century reader, even assuming that in that century a unanimous reading might be conceivable. Nonetheless, it is possible to approach the mentality of readers chronologically closer to Mother Juana by examining the reception of her writings after her death. Naturally, this reception involves very special readers: the visionary's supporters and detractors. Nonetheless, thanks to their chronological proximity to Juana, such readers furnish an invaluable point of departure for later readings of the texts.

Shortly after Mother Juana's death a certain Ortiz, who possibly can be identified as the celebrated Franciscan spiritual Francisco Ortiz (1496–1547), wrote a series of annotations, mostly approving, in the margins of the Escorial manuscript of *El libro del conorte*. Then, an anonymous Inquisitorial censor, apparently a close relative of Mother Juana,[34] examined critically both the sermons and Ortiz's marginal glosses. He crossed out countless passages and even entire columns and, in the case of the Trinity sermon, obliterated nearly the entire chapter with ink-soaked pieces of cotton. Finally, in 1567–1568 Father Francisco de Torres filled the margins of the Escorial manuscript with annotations intended to defend both Juana's orthodoxy and her status as a female visionary.[35]

At the beginning of the seventeenth century a renewed interest in Mother Juana is manifested in a series of biographies (Daza, Navarro) and in such literary works as Tirso de Molina's dramatic trilogy, *La Santa Juana* (1613–1614). The biographical episodes these authors choose, the ways in which they are treated, and the episodes that are omitted constitute a sort of "reading" of the visionary's life and visions. The two versions of Daza's biography are particularly illuminating, for the second version (1613) was motivated by the Inquisitorial censorship of the first (1610).

In 1621 Mother Juana's beatification process was officially opened in Rome. In 1666–1667 both the *Conorte* and the *Vida* were submitted to the scrutiny of the Congregation of Sacred Rites.[36] The Jesuit Martín de Esparza Artieda (1606–1689) was entrusted with the task of examining the *Conorte,* while Cardinal Giovanni Bona (1609–1674) was to evaluate the *Vida.*[37] These official Roman censors pointed out a series of serious doctrinal errors, which prompted Father Joseph Coppons, procurator general of the Franciscan Order in the Roman Curia, to write a defense of Mother Juana's writings. These opinions, both the negative and the positive, will serve as the basis for an exploration of the reception of the nun's works by specific sixteenth- and seventeenth-century readers. Their readings, although more concerned with delineating the border between orthodoxy and heterodoxy than with addressing questions of gender and authority, nonetheless provide useful pathways for approaching the visionary's spiritual world.

Notes

1. In his survey of women writers in medieval Spain, Alan Deyermond finds only three of particular significance, all of whom belong to the fifteenth century: Leonor López de Córdoba, the author of an autobiographical memoir; Sister Teresa de Cartagena, the author of a devotional treatise and of a defense of her right to write such a treatise; and Florencia Pinar, the author of several love poems. See Deyermond, "Spain's First Women Writers," in *Women in Hispanic Literature: Icons and Fallen Idols,* ed. Beth Miller (Berkeley and Los Angeles: University of California Press, 1983), 27–52.

2. Manuel Serrano y Sanz, *Apuntes para una biblioteca de escritoras españolas desde el año 1401 al 1833,* 2 vols. (Madrid: Sucesores de Rivadeneyra, 1903–1905).

3. Nuns constitute nearly half of the women writers in the period 1500–1700. About a third of the nuns (that is, a sixth of all the women of letters known to Serrano y Sanz) wrote spiritual autobiographies and/or recorded their supernatural experiences. Male suspicion of women's visions focused largely on the question of their divine or diabolical inspiration, for it was believed that the female sex was especially susceptible to false revelations. See Julio Caro Baroja, *Las formas complejas de la vida religiosa* (Madrid: Akal, 1978), 37–42. A classic late-medieval formulation of the question of the discernment of spirits and of the need for careful investigation of alleged visionaries can be found in the writings of John Gerson. Significantly, his *De probatione spirituum* (1415) arose from the controversies surrounding the revelations of Saint Bridget of Sweden. For an edition and commentary on Gerson's treatises on the testing of spirits, see Paschal Boland, *The Concept of "Discretio spirituum" in John Gerson's "De probatione spirituum" and "De distinctione verarum visionum a falsis"* (Washington, D.C.: Catholic University of America, 1959).

4. P. Lorenzo Pérez, "Mártires del Japón en el año de 1622," *Archivo Iberoamericano,* 18 (1922) 171.

5. For a view of the female visionary experience as an alternative to the male authority of office, see Caroline Walker Bynum, *Jesus as Mother: Studies in the Spirituality of the High Middle Ages* (Berkeley and Los Angeles: University of California Press, 1982), 261–262.

6. This messianic atmosphere was created in part by royal propagandists. See Américo Castro, *Aspectos del vivir hispánico* (1949; Madrid: Alianza, 1970), 13–45; and José Cepeda Adán, "El providencialismo en los cronistas de los Reyes Católicos," *Arbor,* 17 (1950) 177–190.

7. Francisco Jiménez de Cisneros (1436–1517) became Queen Isabella's confessor in 1492 and archbishop of Toledo in 1495. In 1507 he became both inquisitor-general and a cardinal. For the relations between Cisneros and the holy women of his time, see Marcel Bataillon, *Erasmo y España,* trans. Antonio Alatorre, 2d ed. (México: FCE, 1966), 68–71; and Alvaro Huerga, OP, "Los pre-alumbrados y la Beata de Piedrahita," in Augustin Fliche and Victor Martin, *Historia de la Iglesia, vol. 17: El Renacimiento* (Valencia: EDICEP, 1974), 523–546.

8. Johan Huizinga studies the phenomenon of the late-medieval intensification of the religious sensibility in chapters 12–14 of his *The Waning of the Middle*

Ages, trans. F. Hopman (1949; Garden City: Doubleday, 1954), 151–200. For spiritual works printed under the aegis of Cisneros, see Pedro Sáinz Rodríguez, *La siembra mística del cardenal Cisneros y las reformas en la Iglesia* (Madrid: Universidad Pontificia de Salamanca and Fundación Universitaria Española, 1979), 43–45, 47–53, 95–111. For an overview of the reform of the clergy under Cisneros, see José García Oro, OFM, *Cisneros y la reforma del clero español en tiempo de los Reyes Católicos* (Madrid: CSIC, 1971).

9. "paresce que en esta muger fuerte claramente se muestra lo que estava abscondido aun a los varones muy especulativos, pero ciegos con sus carnales exposiciones y entendimientos" (*Libro de la bienaventurada Sancta Angela de Fulgino* [Toledo, 1510], fol. 1r).

10. "a la qual recurría el pueblo en oprobrio e denuesto de los varones e doctores de la ley, que por ser quebrantadores e traspassadores de los mandamientos, la prophecía fue trasladada a sexo femíneo" (fol. 1v). Similarly, the Cisneros-sponsored printing of a Castilian translation of Saint Vincent Ferrer's *Tractatus de vita spirituali* omits the chapters in which the saint warns against the temptation to seek after visions and revelations. See Alvaro Huerga, "La edición cisneriana del *Tratado de la vida espiritual* y otras ediciones del siglo XVI," *Escritos del Vedat,* 10 (1980) 297–313.

11. Daza (1610, *Prólogo al letor*) relates that Sister María was illiterate but was miraculously given the ability to read and write in order to compose Juana's biography and to record her visions.

12. Caroline Walker Bynum observes that the biographies of medieval holy women tended to be more stereotypical than those of their male counterparts. See her *Holy Feast and Holy Fast: The Religious Significance of Food to Medieval Women* (Berkeley and Los Angeles: University of California Press, 1987), 83. For a study of stereotypical patterns in the lives of religious women in early modern Italy, see Gabriella Zarri, "Le sante vive. Per una tipologia della santità femminile nel primo Cinquecento," *Annali dell'Istituto Storico Italo-Germanico in Trento,* 6 (1980) 371–445.

13. This is an important variant of the hagiographic motif of the "transvestite saint." See Marie Delcourt, "Le complexe de Diane dans l'hagiographie chrétienne," *Revue de l'Histoire des Religions,* 153 (1958) 1–33; Vern L. Bullough, "Transvestites in the Middle Ages," *American Journal of Sociology,* 79 (1973) 1381–1394; and John Anson, "The Female Transvestite in Early Monasticism: The Origin and Development of a Motif," *Viator,* 5 (1974) 1–32. In more general terms, the motifs of familial opposition and escape in male attire are traditional hagiographic formulas. See Michael Goodich, "The Contours of Female Piety in Later Medieval Hagiography," *Church History,* 50 (1981) 24–25.

14. For a thumbnail sketch of the history of the convent, see Manuel Castro, OFM, *La provincia franciscana de Santiago. Ocho siglos de historia* (Santiago de Compostela: Liceo Franciscano, 1984), 242–243.

15. For a discussion of the apparitions that led to the building of the church and to the eventual founding of the convent, see William A. Christian, Jr., *Apparitions in Late Medieval and Renaissance Spain* (Princeton: Princeton University Press, 1981), 57–87; and Gaspar Calvo Moralejo, OFM, "'Santa María de la Cruz.' Apariciones marianas en el siglo XV y nueva advocación de la Virgen," *Estudios*

Marianos, 44 (1979) 95–113. For the advocation "Mary of the Cross," see Gaspar Calvo Moralejo, OFM, "Santa María de la Cruz," *Antonianum,* 50 (1975) 561–576.

16. In the sixteenth century a *beata* was "a woman who had made a simple (that is, private) vow of chastity, wore a habit, and observed a religious rule of some kind, whether temporarily or permanently, cloistered or in society, or alone or in company of others. Beatas were usually under diocesan supervision and not subject to an order, even if they adopted its habit and rule. . . . Permanent members of formal communities of third-order Franciscan women were also called beatas" (William A. Christian, Jr., *Local Religion in Sixteenth-Century Spain* [Princeton: Princeton University Press, 1981], 16–17).

17. For an overview of the Regular Third Order of Saint Francis in Spain, see T. de Azcona, "La Tercera Orden Regular de San Francisco en España," *Confer,* 21 (1982) 157–183. Isidoro de Villapadierna studies the Third Order in Spain in the fifteenth century in his "La Tercera Orden franciscana de España en el siglo XV," in *III Convegno di Studi Francescani: Il movimento francescano della penitenza nella società medioevale* (Roma: Istituto Storico dei Cappuccini, 1980), 125–144.

18. For pressure to regularize communities of *beatas* in the sixteenth century, see Christian, *Local Religion,* 170–171.

19. Antonio de Pastrana's letter describing the incident is printed in Manuel Serrano y Sanz, "Pedro Ruiz de Alcaraz, iluminado alcarreño del siglo XVI," *Revista de Archivos, Bibliotecas y Museos,* 8 (1903) 2–3.

20. José Luis Domínguez Ruiz, *El cardenal Cisneros y el monasterio de Santa María de la Cruz,* dissertation of the Facultad de Derecho Canónico of the Universidad Pontificia de Comillas, 1974, includes on pp. 25–37 a photographic reproduction of eighteenth-century copies of the original orders. (I wish to thank Father Jesús Gómez López for obtaining a photocopy of this thesis for me.)

21. For the legal aspects of Cisneros's orders, see Domínguez Ruiz, *El cardenal Cisneros,* 70–87.

22. "las mugeres, aunque fuesen religiosas, no heran sufiçientes para ser cura de ánimas de personas seglares" (*Vida,* fol. 77v).

23. "persona sufiçiente para estar en el serviçio del curado por el monasterio" (*Vida,* fol. 77v). There is a copy of the papal bull in the Archivo Histórico Nacional (Madrid), Códices, 1199-B, fols. 51r–54r. The bull is dated "anno incarnationis domini millesimo quingentesimo decimo quarto nonas Iulii," that is, July 7, 1514, but the added indication "anno septimo" corresponds to 1519, the seventh year of the pontificate of Leo X. The Archivo Histórico Nacional manuscript gives Reg. Vat., tom. 184, fol. 64, as its source, but an inquiry at the Vatican revealed that tom. 184 (tom. 1174, according to modern numeration) does not contain the bull in question. The ambiguous dating of the Madrid copy of the bull thus poses a problem for the chronology of the episode of the benefice of Cubas relative to Juana's dismissal from the post of abbess. Daza (1610, fol. 85v) and Navarro (p. 766) recount that the incident that motivated the requesting of the bull, namely, the attempt made by certain ecclesiastics to take the benefice away from the convent, occurred only after the death of Cisneros in 1517. These sources would argue in favor of 1519 as the correct date for the bull. To add to the confusion, Daza (1610, fol. 88v) gives 1527 as the year in which Juana was deposed as abbess.

24. During a conversation with her guardian angel, Juana asks if her sin was

all the greater because the bull was for the benefit of her brother. The angel answers that what counts is her good intention in seeking to procure the well-being of her convent (*Vida*, fols. 85v–85r).

25. See José María Escrivá, *La abadesa de Las Huelgas* (Madrid: Editorial Luz, 1944), 120–121. For an overview of the phenomenon of female spiritual jurisdiction in a European context, see Joan Morris, *The Lady Was a Bishop: The Hidden History of Women with Clerical Ordination and the Jurisdiction of Bishops* (New York: Macmillan, 1973).

26. Concerning this aspect of Cisneros's orders, see Domínguez Ruiz, *El cardenal Cisneros*, 68.

27. "residía en el curado, puesto por mano y voluntad de los perlados, porque hera persona sufiçiente y aparejado a toda virtud, y el pueblo estava contento d'él" (*Vida*, fol. 78r).

28. Question 39, article 1, of the Supplement to Part III of Saint Thomas Aquinas's *Summa Theologica* denies women a role as priests but allows them the role of prophetesses: "Prophecy is not a sacrament but a gift of God. Wherefore there it is not the signification, but only the thing which is necessary. And since in matters pertaining to the soul woman does not differ from man as to the thing (for sometimes a woman is found to be better than many men as regards the soul), it follows that she can receive the gift of prophecy and the like, but not the sacrament of Orders" (St. Thomas Aquinas, *Summa Theologica*, trans. Fathers of the English Dominican Province, 3 vols. [New York: Benziger Brothers, 1947–1948], 3 : 2698).

29. On the question of mystical visions, see Ernst Benz, *Die Vision* (Stuttgart: Ernst Klett Verlag, 1969) and Peter Dinzelbacher, *Vision und Visionsliteratur im Mittelalter* (Stuttgart: Anton Hiersemann, 1981). On women's visions in particular, see *Medieval Women's Visionary Literature*, ed. Elizabeth Alvilda Petroff (New York and Oxford: Oxford University Press, 1986).

30. Daza (1610, fol. 61v) observes that while Sister María Evangelista transcribed most of the *Conorte*, Sister Catalina de San Francisco and Sister Catalina de los Mártires also had a hand in its transcription.

31. Female appropriation of priestly functions was regarded with extreme suspicion. In the course of the Inquisitorial trial (1509) of Sister María de Santo Domingo, Brother Juan Hurtado testified that she had both heard confessions and delivered sermons: "*Interrogatus* si la dicha soror María oye confesiones de algunos, *dixit* que ha oído, y no sabe a quién, que la dicha soror María oye confesiones, pero no *sacramentaliter,* y también ha hecho uno o dos sermones, pero no como a sermonadores, el uno en Viloria y el otro en Piedrahita" (quoted in Vicente Beltrán de Heredia, OP, *Historia de la reforma de la provincia de España (1450–1550)* [Rome: Istituto Storico Domenicano, 1939], 113–114). Years later, during the trial of María de Cazalla (1533), Pedro Ruiz de Alcaraz criticized her explanations of the Scriptures, declaring that "la dicha María de Caçalla se entremetía en hablar cosas de la Sagrada Escriptura que a ella no era líçito hablarlas por ser muger" (Milagros Ortega, *Proceso de la Inquisición contra María de Cazalla* [Madrid: Fundación Universitaria Española, 1978], 188). And in 1575 certain Sevillian opponents of Saint Teresa's reform accused the Discalced Carmelites of appropriating the priestly role of confessor, alleging "que se confesaban unas con otras, tomando ocasión de la

regla que dice la Madre, que las monjas den cuenta a las prioras de su espíritu" (*Peregrinación de Anastasio,* diálogo XIII, in *Obras del P. Jerónimo Gracián de la Madre de Dios,* ed. Silverio de Santa Teresa, 3 vols. [Burgos: El Monte Carmelo, 1932–1933], 3:201).

32. For the context of this episode, see Chapter III.

33. Let us recall Juana's flight from home dressed in male clothing.

34. Perhaps this anonymous censor should be identified with Father Miguel de Medina or with another of the theologians whose negative opinions of the *Conorte* resulted in the Inquisitorial order of November 6, 1568, that all extant copies be turned over to the Inquisition (Archivo Histórico Nacional [Madrid], Inquisición, libro 576, fol. 264r).

35. For an overview of these superimposed readings, see Annie Fremaux-Crouzet, "Alegato en favor de 'las mujeres e idiotas': aspectos del franciscanismo feminista en la *Glosa* de Francisco de Torres a *El Conorte* (1567–1568) de Juana de la Cruz," in *Homenaje a José Antonio Maravall,* 3 vols. (Madrid: Centro de Investigaciones Sociológicas, 1985), 2:101–102.

36. On November 21, 1665, Mother Juana's writings were ordered sent to Rome. On June 26, 1666, they were turned over to Bona and Esparza, who presented their reports to the Congregation of Sacred Rites on August 13, 1667. For the chronology of these events, see *Sacra Rituum congregatione . . . in causa toletana beatificationis et canonizationis ven. servae Dei Joannae de Cruce . . . Super assertis opusculis dictae Servae Dei* (Rome: Typis Reverendae Camerae Apostolicae, 1729), 4.

37. As the author of a treatise on the testing of spirits, Bona was doubtless considered an expert investigator of revelations. For Bona's *De discretione spirituum,* see his *Opera omnia* (Antwerp, 1677), 223–322.

I. The Beard and the Apple

The sermon discussed in this chapter is exceptional in that its subject is an Old Testament story, the Creation, whereas nearly all the rest of the sermons deal with episodes from the lives of Christ, the Virgin Mary, or the saints. This sermon is further anomalous because it lacks any reference to a specific gospel episode, and thus falls outside the basic structuring of *El libro del conorte* around the feasts of the liturgical year. Finally, the Creation sermon stands out in that it ends with an extended defense of the *Conorte*'s divine inspiration. Although the other sermons contain occasional short passages that seek to assert that divine inspiration, the Creation sermon, probably because it occupies the last place in the Escorial manuscript, presents a far more complete defense than any other in the collection.[1]

The Creation sermon has three major sections: an account of the creation of Adam and Eve (see Appendix A), the description of an allegorical pageant inspired by the Creation, and a defense of the divine inspiration of Mother Juana's revelations. The sermon begins with God's abbreviated account of the creation of the heavens, the earth, and the angels. He then creates man to populate the places in Heaven previously occupied by the fallen angels.[2] Woman is created from man, and when God sees that they are living in purity, innocence, and love, He places them in Paradise. But soon Adam and Eve begin to "play" (*jugar*), and this leads to wickedness and spite:

E que estando ellos en esta inoçençia, enpeçaron entramos a jugar, e luego enpeçó a reinar en ellos la maliçia y el desamor. (*Conorte*, fol. 444r)

(And when they were in this innocent state, the two of them began to play, and thereupon malice and enmity began to prevail in them.)

Adam is very much in love with Eve and tries to follow her wherever she goes, but Eve reacts by beating him. Adam complains to the Lord, who counsels him to strike Eve in return, but Adam responds that he cannot do that because he loves her too much. Adam again tries to pursue Eve, speaking to her and "playing" with her, but she continues to beat him. Adam complains once again to the Lord, who tells him to solve the problem by merely avoiding Eve. This, Adam says, he cannot do. God responds by telling Adam to go to sleep, and leave it to Him to find a means for making Adam the master of Eve:

"Pues, no te quieres apartar d'ella, déxame e no me digas esas cosas. Anda, ve, échate a dormir, que yo te faré de manera que te tema e aya miedo de llegar a ti e que tú seas señor sobre ella e no ella sobre ti." (*Conorte,* fol. 444rv)

("Since you refuse to stay away from her, leave me, and don't tell me these things. Get going, leave, go to sleep, for I will transform you in such a way that she will fear you and be afraid to come near you and you will be master over her and not vice versa.")

As Adam sleeps, God creates a beard on his face, and when Adam awakens and seeks out Eve, she is terrified and flees from him. Adam follows her, offering her flowers, apples, and other fruits, but she still refuses to approach him.[3] Adam complains once again to the Lord, asking Him to take away the beard so that Eve will no longer flee from him, but God replies that it is His will that men should have beards and thereby have dominion over women:

"Calla, Adán, que bien estás assí, que mi voluntad es que todos los varones tengan lo mesmo e sean señores sobre las mugeres." (*Conorte,* fol. 444v)

("Be silent, Adam, for you are just fine like that, for it is my will that all men should have a beard and be lord over women.")

The Lord then provides an allegorical interpretation of the beard story. In point of fact, one of the ways in which Mother Juana was able to control the reception of her visions was by incorporating into them an "official" (that is, divine) interpretation. By having God Himself supply the vision with a gloss, Juana could restrict the hermeneutic options of her listeners and readers to a single "authorized" version. In the Creation sermon this official interpretation superimposes a Trinitarian gloss on the beard episode: Adam represents God the Father, Eve represents Christ, and the angels represent the Holy Spirit. Just as Adam has power over woman and the entire created world but is also meek and loving, so the Father is Lord of Heaven and earth but merciful to those who fear, obey, and serve Him. Just as woman is more meek and humble than man, so the Son was humble and obedient to the Father even to the point of undergoing the Crucifixion.[4] And just as prudent women are naturally meek and compassionate, and more ready to pardon than men, so Christ on the cross prayed for those who had crucified Him. Just as woman is astute and clever, so Christ is the wisdom of the Father.[5]

After this gloss, the Lord returns to the beard story to explain how Adam would sometimes make Eve come to him by force and other times by flattery. Finally, He says, Adam ate the apple that Eve offered him because he hoped that by pleasing her he would stop her from fleeing from him.[6]

God then commands the angels and saints to perform an allegorical pageant to express His joy in the Creation. A representation of the earth appears, which consists of four columns that support houses, castles, and entire cities.[7] There is also a flat area populated by plants, animals, and a crowd of human beings. In a gloss God explains that the four columns represent His power, will, mercy, and pleasure, which sustain the world. The human beings there are compared to children because they share the purity and innocence in which Adam and Eve lived before the Fall.[8] God, says Juana, similarly rejoices when He sees us in a state of grace, which He compares to the purity and innocence of children. Suddenly, the children are transformed into grown-up men and women, who begin to strike one another, fighting like cats and dogs. When the Lord sees that they have left the state of innocence and that malice reigns among them, He begins to get angry, but His angels beg Him to have mercy. Suddenly, a galleon, a smaller ship, an ark, and a field appear.[9] The galleon is filled with elegantly dressed lords and ladies and represents the sinners who give themselves over to worldly vices and thereby to sin. The smaller ship is filled with poorly clad people who represent priests, nuns, and penitents. The ark contains people who are suffering: the suffering souls in Purgatory as well as those who have been imprisoned for their sins. Another group of people remains apart in a nearby field. These are those who are outside the Catholic faith. In His anger God punishes everyone for the sins of the few, sending storms, earthquakes, and plagues. Some of those in the ships are converted and begin to pray and to do penance for their sins. Ladders suddenly appear, and the Lord invites the converted to climb the ladders to His heavenly kingdom, which they do, while holding onto the robes of the Virgin and the angels. Those who refuse to be converted fall into a deep lake.

God goes on to remark that no one should marvel that Juana's book relates certain episodes in greater detail than the canonical Scriptures, for the book is inspired by the Holy Spirit, who knows more than do earthly evangelists. Those who wanted God to work miracles in order to prove

His identity are told that His speaking through His servant Juana is the kind of miracle that is appropriate to the times. God will not force conversion upon those who refuse to accept the message of this holy book. Those who ask how it is possible that there are dancing, entertainments, and horses in Heaven should know that if God could create animals on earth, surely He is capable of creating them in Heaven. Furthermore, in the Sermon on the Mount Christ said that those who mourn are blessed, for they will laugh in the kingdom of Heaven.[10]

God then returns to the beard story to observe that when He created Adam and Eve, He formed them with hair on their heads and other parts of their bodies, but their faces were identical: they had the faces of angels. They were like children in that the sexual differences between them were not apparent from their faces. But when Eve tried to dominate Adam and refused to consider him as her equal, God permitted Adam to grow a beard so that Eve would fear him:

Enpero, por quanto la muger le quería sojuzgar e no le quería tener por igual sino por menor que ella, permitió El que le naçiesen a Adán barvas en el rostro por que fuese tenido en veneraçión. (*Conorte,* fol. 451r)

(However, since the woman wished to subjugate him and refused to consider him an equal but, on the contrary, she considered him inferior to her, He allowed a beard to grow on Adam's face so that he would be held in respect.)

God then expounds upon Proverbs 6:20 ("My son, keep the commandments of thy father, and forsake not the law of thy mother"[11]), connecting the affective use of the term *son* with the Holy Spirit's love and relating the paternal discipline to the castigating Father. He likens the Passion to childbirth and Christ to a mother who gives birth. Juana's book is compared to something to eat: no one will savor and understand it who does not love and savor the sweetness of God. If anyone in mortal sin reads from this book, upon finishing he will be in a state of grace. These words were uttered by God, who also commanded that they be written down. In fact, all of the words contained in this text are similarly written on the walls of the heavenly city. Some day even the disbelievers will realize that Juana's book is divinely inspired. The sermon, and with it the entire Escorial manuscript, ends with reiterated affirmations of the *Conorte's* divine inspiration.[12]

Unlike the other sermons, which provide a novelesque embellishment of biblical episodes, here the canonical biblical narrative all but disappears. Instead, Mother Juana incorporates and elaborates upon a noncanonical legend that ultimately melds rather poorly with the Genesis narrative. The story of the creation of Adam's beard is a telling example of the ways in which Mother Juana's creative genius functioned, for although her audience and readers are led to believe that the narrative is a direct revelation from God, in point of fact she is but re-creating a traditional tale.[13] For the purposes of comparison I have selected two other sixteenth-century versions of the beard story: a legend that circulated among the *moriscos* (see Appendix B) and a poem by the Meistersinger Hans Vogel (see Appendix C). The *morisco* text[14] is nearly identical to Mother Juana's version in its narrative outline but is radically unadorned and unembellished in its recounting. The German poem[15] similarly offers a scarcely embellished version but differs in a number of details. Significantly, the presence of at least one child ("Floh Weib und Kind hinauß") indicates that the beard episode takes place after the Expulsion and is thus not directly linked to the Fall. Moreover, in the German poem God takes the initiative by asking Adam whether or not his wife fears him. The beard appears on Adam's face after God tells him to dip his hand into the waters of a stream and to touch his jaw. In a comic epilogue Eve dips her hand into the water, but just then a bee stings her between the legs. When she touches that part of her body with her wet hand, hair grows there.

On one level the beard story is a sort of calque of the canonical biblical narrative: the creation of Adam's beard while he sleeps parallels the creation of Eve from the sleeping Adam.[16] This motif sets the Peninsular versions (i.e., the *morisco* legend and Juana's sermon) apart from the family of versions of which Vogel's poem is a sixteenth-century representative, for the German text and its congeners substitute the water motif. The scene in which the bearded Adam pursues Eve through Paradise, offering her apples and other delicacies, prefigures the later canonical scene in which Eve will offer Adam the forbidden fruit, which tradition, of course, identified with an apple.[17] Of the three versions of the legend under consideration here, Juana's sermon alone includes the episode of Adam's prelapsarian gifts to Eve.

However, there are contradictions in detail between Mother Juana's sermon and the Book of Genesis. For example, Juana states that God gave Adam clothes just after creating him, while Genesis views Adam's and Eve's shame and the subsequent covering of their bodies as one of the consequences of the Fall.[18] In the canonical narrative, Eve's submission to Adam is one of the effects of the Fall; in Mother Juana's version, Eve's refusal to submit to Adam is viewed as the principal cause of the Fall.[19]

Another possible conflict between Juana's version of the beard legend and traditional interpretations of Genesis is the episode in which Adam's and Eve's initial bliss and innocence are ruined when they begin to "play." It seems unlikely that Mother Juana refers to childish games, since such games would on the contrary suggest their continuance in an innocent state.[20] *Jugar* did, however, have connotations of sexual dalliance in the romances of chivalry and in Golden Age erotic poetry.[21] It would appear, therefore, that it was the appearance of sexual love in Paradise that disrupted the idyllic relationship between Adam and Eve. Eve either refused to submit sexually to Adam or did so with great reluctance. Moreover, when the Creation sermon says that Adam made Eve come to him, sometimes through cajolery and other times by force,[22] there is room for speculation that he may have tried to rape her. Does Mother Juana suggest that the Fall could have been Eve's revenge? In any case, if *jugar* does indeed have sexual connotations, then Mother Juana's version of events in Paradise would run counter to received tradition, for it was generally agreed that Adam and Eve did not have sexual relations before the Fall. Saint Augustine, for example, asserts that although they could have done so, the Fall occurred before they actually did the deed.[23]

Adam's beard is both the symbol and the physical manifestation of Adam's and Eve's sexuality, for as Mother Juana herself observes, their angel-like faces (angels being notoriously asexual beings) at first did not betray the sexual differences between them.[24] Juana's narrative underscores the specific role of the beard as symbol of the sexual differences between Adam and Eve. Adam is unable to make Eve do his will through action, but the beard's symbolic masculinity, that is, its authority as a sign, achieves what action could not. In point of fact, God notes how He was pleased that men should be *señalados* ("marked" or "distinguished") by means of the beard (*Conorte,* fol. 444v).

Similarly problematic in Juana's Creation sermon is the official, or divinely inspired, interpretation that is inscribed in the vision. In the first place, traditional modes of scriptural exegesis required that Adam represent Christ and that Eve represent the Virgin Mary or the Church.[25] Mother Juana's identification of Adam as the Father and of Eve as Christ thus runs counter to received interpretations.[26] It does arise logically, however, from Adam's characterization in the beard legend. Like the Father, who is both powerful and merciful, capable of both destruction and love, Adam is characterized as powerful (or so one assumes him to be after the beard adjustment) and loving (a quality he demonstrates from the beginning in his relationship with Eve). The Christ/Eve parallel is not derived from the way Eve actually behaves during the greater part of the beard story, but rather from how she ends up after her forced subordination to Adam. Nonetheless, although God attributes that subordination to the effects of Adam's beard, in the course of the Creation sermon Juana never makes Eve actually demonstrate her newly imposed submissiveness. Moreover, in humbling Eve, Juana ends up exalting her because of the association between Eve's submissiveness and Christ's humility. Indeed, Bynum has pointed out how late-medieval holy women identified strongly with Christ's humanity, specifically, with the suffering and thereby redeeming flesh that submitted to the Passion. Christ's humanity was related to His divinity as female was to male.[27] Thus, in the beard vision submission and humility are not cast in a negative light; rather, they are viewed as valuable qualities because they partake of Christ's "feminine" side, His humanity. Eve's reeducated state could thus be viewed in a positive light because of its association with Christ's humanity.[28]

At first glance Mother Juana's rewriting of Genesis hardly seems radical. She has merely substituted a legendary story about Adam and Eve for the canonical narrative, and the apocryphal material seems to provide an alternate version of the Genesis account of the subordination of female to male. But upon closer examination Juana's substitute narrative and its novelesque elaboration are highly subversive. Her silences become as important as her revelations, for by sidestepping the Genesis account, Juana effectively sidesteps Eve's guilt in the Fall: the serpent is not mentioned, and the apple episode is introduced but obliquely as an example of Adam's desire to bribe and thereby control Eve.

Indeed, if guilt is to be assigned, in Juana's narrative it is Adam and his love (and, as it would appear, his lust) for Eve that are responsible for the Fall.[29] Commentators on Genesis introduced an element of sexuality into the characterization of Eve. She was portrayed as an inherently sexual being, and it was that female sexuality that seduced Adam into sinning.[30] Juana's reworking of the beard legend inverts that scheme: it is Adam who is apparently the victim of his sexual desires, while Eve is merely the unwilling object of those desires. Thus, ironically, in Juana's sermon Adam's fall is brought about by his love, nay, his lust, for Eve. Although the motif of Adam's sinning out of love for Eve appears in medieval literary treatments of the Fall,[31] Juana's Creation sermon is the only version of the beard story to incorporate that motif.

Furthermore, Mother Juana implicitly relates the question of responsibility for the Fall to the question of activity as opposed to passivity. In

Genesis Adam is relatively passive. It is God who finds a suitable mate for him, and Adam has no active role in the creation of Eve, which occurs while he is sleeping. Eve, on the other hand, has a relatively active role. It is she who plays out the temptation scene with the serpent, and it is she who offers the forbidden fruit to Adam.[32] Thus, in Genesis action is associated with guilt, while passivity is associated with absolution from responsibility. In the beard legend there is a reversal of roles, for it is Eve who is relatively passive. Thus, if passivity is to be equated with innocence, then Eve is exonerated, while the more active Adam is implicated as primarily responsible for the Fall.

Further ironies and equivocations in Mother Juana's rewriting of the beard legend serve to undermine its seemingly crystal-clear justification of female subordination. Juana implies that they were originally created in such a way that Eve was naturally master over Adam and Adam was naturally submissive to Eve. Eve's subjection to Adam is brought about almost as if to rectify what Adam perceives to be a flaw in the Creation. It is by divine fiat that Adam's beard is created, a beard that is intended to cause Eve to submit to Adam through fear and that therefore symbolizes man's dominion over woman. Mother Juana seems to be saying that such domination is unnatural and has come about only through an arbitrary act, the literally *ex machina* intervention of *Deus* Himself. Furthermore, contrary to the traditional view that Eve bore primary responsibility for the Fall, Juana redeems Eve by associating her with Christ: Christ and Eve share certain positive "feminine" traits. The power Eve loses through her subordination to Adam is in a sense recovered and perhaps even surpassed as she is exalted through her association with Christ's humility.[33]

In fact, the beard legend is, among other things, a story of power and submission. God is, of course, all-powerful because He is the Creator. Being loved by Adam gives Eve power over him and allows her, at least for a time, to maintain her independence. Adam's love for Eve is a source of weakness and makes him dependent upon her.[34] The portrait of the love-sick Adam pursuing a disdainful Eve all over Paradise is both touching and comical, and constitutes one of Mother Juana's noteworthy amplifications of the beard legend. Indeed, the abject Adam's pursuit of the aloof Eve recalls the courtly love paradigm. Juana's sermon thus depicts a prelapsarian *in illo tempore* in which woman was not only not subordinate to man but was able to enjoy a brief moment of superiority.

The ambiguities inherent in Mother Juana's treatment of Eve and in her concern for problems of power and authority are likewise present in the episode of the Franciscan friar who asked Juana to be the mother of the Messiah he was to father and in the episode of the benefice of Cubas (see the Introduction). In the case of the deluded friar's scandalous propositions, Juana, like Eve, refuses to have sexual relations with a man. But while Eve's refusal appears to arise from her desire to maintain her independence, Mother Juana's response is more ambiguous. She does choose to preserve her virginity, but she also bows to a higher ecclesiastical authority by denouncing the friar to her superiors. This act, it could be argued, serves a double purpose: it demonstrates her orthodoxy and punishes a male for seeking to compromise her reputation. In the case of the benefice of Cubas, the issue of women's independence was more salient. The crux of the case was the nuns' privilege of appointing a chaplain to oversee the spiritual well-being of the parishioners. It was this right that was contested, for it was deemed unsuitable that women exercise a spiritual jurisdiction. Juana's dilemma was thus parallel to Eve's. Just as Eve's initial insubordination to Adam was not to be tolerated, so the nuns' right to appoint a chaplain was viewed as an unseemly usurpation of male power.

Between her deposition as abbess and her vindication and subsequent reinstatement, Juana experienced a vision in which she asks her guardian angel which is the greatest sin of all those she has confessed. Alluding to the episode of the benefice of Cubas, the angel answers that it was the sin like the one Eve committed. Just as Eve destroyed the whole world, so did Juana destroy her own good name and diminish the honor of God:

La bienaventurada preguntó al ángel, diziendo: "Señor, ¿quál es el mayor peccado que yo tengo en todos los que he confesado?" El ángel le respondió: "Aquel que nunca se deviera hazer, que fue como el de Eva, que destruyó todo el mundo. E, ansimesmo, así tú causaste destrución en ti mesma y en tu fama buena que tenías por las virtudes manifiestas a las gentes que Dios te havía dado sin ser tú merecedora d'ellas, pues de la mano de Dios te venían. Y fuiste causa de menoscavo en la honra de Dios y en la consolación y honra de tus hermanas las religiosas de tu compañía." (*Vida*, fol. 83v)

(The blessed woman questioned the angel, asking: "My lord, which is the greatest sin I committed of all those I have confessed?" The angel answered: "The one that never should have been committed, which was like Eve's, which destroyed the whole world. And likewise, you caused the destruction of yourself and of the good name that you earned through the virtues manifested to everyone [and] which God had given to you without your deserving them, for they came from His hand. And you were the cause of the damage to God's honor and to the consolation and honor of your sisters, the nuns of your community.")

That the angel's words were a source of extreme distress to Juana is evident from the fact that they are the point of departure for another vision, which occupies an entire, albeit short, chapter in the *Vida* (fols. 97v–98r). In this second vision Juana expresses her anguish at having committed so grave a sin that her angel compared her with Eve. For her part, she fears being condemned to eternal damnation, but the angel assures her that she will not end up in Hell. The angel then cautions her against seeking to understand the words that God speaks through her, for such matters are better left to the Church authorities. The vision ends with the angel's order to write down all that the two of them have said. Thus, Juana's anguish at being considered an Eve-like figure appears to be tempered by the underscoring of her role as an intermediary for God's revelation.

Eve is a sort of cipher in the Creation sermon. She never speaks. The listener or reader has no access to her inner being but must rely on the indirect portrait furnished by the reactions she causes in God and Adam. Eve's role in the beard story is thus analogous to Mother Juana's role in the reception of her visions. Juana stresses her own passivity; she is merely the vehicle for such divine revelations (see Chapter 3), because the inscribed narrator in the sermons is God Himself. The result of this ingenious narrative strategy is that the beard story appears to be presented from a strictly male point of view. Whatever subversions and ambiguities the text may contain are thus to be attributed to God, the ostensible narrator, and not to Juana. But just as the benefice of Cubas episode demonstrates the limits of female authority in questions of ecclesiastical jurisdiction, so here a limitation is placed upon the role of visionary. Juana is merely a vehicle; the interpretation of the revelations must be left to the male-dominated Church hierarchy. Once again, Juana brings the question of activity as opposed to passivity to the fore: women are permitted to experience visions but not to explicate them. Yet in the case of the Creation vision (and many others as well), Juana does in fact interpret her revelations by incorporating a gloss into the very vision: God Himself becomes the interpreter. The authority that would be taken away with one hand has been restored with the other.

In fact, the very act of writing is authorized by divine mandate, since in the *Vida* the angel orders Juana to write down his revelations. Similarly, the end of the Creation sermon reveals that it is God Himself who has ordered the sermons to be written down.[35] The connection between the act of writing and Genesis is not fortuitous, for Saint Paul relates to the Fall his injunction that women keep silent.[36] Women should not speak, let alone preach, because Eve's words led Adam to sin.[37] But Mother Juana does not keep silent; in fact, she preaches and she writes—or, more precisely, she dictates. It is her rewriting of Genesis that allows her to speak, to deliver and then to write down her sermons, for if Eve's role in the Fall is minimized, then all women are in a sense redeemed and thereby empowered to speak.

Relevant to such questions is a passage found only in the Vatican manuscript of the *Conorte*. After the Trinity simile, which relates woman to Christ, the Vatican manuscript interpolates an intriguing section that, unfortunately, is extremely difficult to decipher and therefore problematic to interpret. The passage begins by recalling that when Adam asked God to take away the beard, He refused because He wished men to be differentiated from women with regard to their bodies. With regard to their souls, however, Adam and Eve were equal.[38] Mother Juana goes on to say that, since woman has a soul that is female (presumably because *ánima* is feminine in gender in Spanish) and man has a soul that is female, then both men and women are in a sense "females." Likewise, since both men and women have a spirit (*espíritu* being masculine in gender in Spanish), both man and woman can be considered to be "males."[39] Therefore, a man can be said to be a "woman," and a woman can be said to be a "man":

E por tanto dezía el poderosso Dios a Adán, cuando le rogava que le quitasse las barvas, que bien estava assí, por cuanto era su voluntad que el honbre tuviesse diferençia alguna de la muger cuanto al cuerpo; enpero cuanto al ánima entramos son iguales e conpañeros. Porque si la muger tiene ánima, la qual se llama fenbra, por semejante tiene tanbién el honbre ánima . . . llamada fenbra, de manera que todo honbre e muger se puede llamar fenbra. E por el contrario[?] puede[?] ser dicho el honbre e la muger[?] varón[?] porque si el honbre tiene[?] espíritu biviente e permaneçiente[?] para sienpre, por semejante[?] tiene[?] la muger espíritu biviente e permaneçiente[?] para sienpre. Assí que honbre[?] e muger todo[?] es una cossa e un espíritu e un ánima en[?] cuanto el honbre puede ser dicho[?] muger e la muger puede ser dicha honbre, pues entramos[?] tienen[?] espíritu e ánima biviente. (*Vat.*, fol. 139v)

(And therefore, when Adam begged Him to take away the beard, almighty God said that he was just fine like that, inasmuch as it was His will that man should be differentiated from woman with respect to his body; however, with respect to the soul, both are equals and compeers. Because if woman has a soul, which is by name female, likewise man too has a soul . . . by name female, so that every man and woman can be called female. And, conversely, man and woman can be said [to be] male, because if man has a living and everlasting spirit, likewise woman has a living and everlasting spirit. Thus, man and woman are of one substance and spirit and soul inasmuch as man can be said [to be] woman and woman can be said [to be] man, for both have a spirit and a living soul.)

However, having made this surprising declaration, Mother Juana appears to trivialize it, recalling the episode in which God tells Adam that if Eve strikes him, he should strike her back, for they were created equal. This observation ends the interpolation, and the passage that follows corresponds with the Escorial manuscript (*Conorte*, fol. 445v): Adam would sometimes approach Eve with cajolery and other times with a show of force (which might carry the connotations of rape), and Adam ate the apple to please Eve so that she would no longer flee from him.

Although Mother Juana appears to put to a trivial use her observations on the equality of men's and women's souls, it could also be argued that in the larger context of the entire sermon such observations bolster the text's defense of Eve and thereby, indirectly, of Mother Juana's right to preach and to have her sermons written down. If God does not care about the differences between the sexes, a point that is also implicit in the Saint Clare sermon (see the end of Chapter 4), then Mother Juana, by virtue of both the *ánima* and the *espíritu* that she shares with males, is empowered to perform what in the eyes of the world is the male task of preaching.

Mother Juana's version of the beard story, her personal experience of the episode of the benefice of Cubas, and the act of revelation of the Creation and other sermon-visions have as their common denominator problems of gender, power, and authority. Juana's appropriation of authority is intimately connected with her visionary experience, since it is from within her sermon-visions that God Himself empowers her to write. Juana and her companions' obedience in writing and thereby "creating" *El libro del conorte* is both a lesson well learned from Eve's example of subordination and an imitation of Christ's obedience to the Father. Juana is a daughter of Eve, but because of the latter's association with Christ, the nun is also the new or second Eve by analogy to Christ as the new or second Adam. Finally, Juana is both "redeemed" through Eve and Eve's "redeemer."

Such ambiguities are part of Juana's overall rhetorical strategy. If the act of writing is an act of Christ-like obedience, then the act of obedience is tremendously empowering. Just as Eve's eventual submission and obedience to Adam are exalted through their association with Christ, so Juana is exalted by her obedience to God's divine mandate to write.[40] In a brilliant display of circular reasoning, Juana argues that if writing is an act of obedience and of submission, then obedience and submission empower her to write. At a time when women were not supposed to speak of theological matters, let alone to write about them, Mother Juana uses the visionary world of the Creation sermon and the ambiguities inherent in her treatment of Eve to create an authority otherwise denied her. Her self-authorizing logic is an act of empowerment that permits her to speak and thus to "create" *El libro del conorte*.

Notes

1. The Vatican manuscript offers a different layout and location of the Creation sermon as well as a number of interpolations and omissions. The sermon proper (*Vat.*, fols. 137r–152r) appears in a more appropriate liturgical order, namely, between the Purification of the Virgin Mary and the Parable of the Vineyard sermons. (The readings in the Roman Breviary for Septuagesima and the week that follows include both the Creation story and the parable of the vineyard.) However, the Vatican manuscript does place the latter section of the defense of the *Conorte* at the very end of the manuscript (*Vat.*, fols. 728v–732r), where it is appended to the Advent sermon. Assuming that the Vatican text preserves the original liturgical order of the sermons, it appears that the scribe of the Escorial manuscript, perceiving the kinship between the two extended defenses of the *Conorte,* welded them together, placing the amplified version of the Creation sermon at the end of the manuscript. What is more important, however, is that in both cases Mother Juana herself, or perhaps her scribes, seeks to control the *Conorte*'s reception by ending the manuscript with a defense of its divine inspiration.

2. This was a widely held belief in the Middle Ages. See, for example, Saint Gregory the Great's *Homiliae in Evangelia,* Book II, Sermon 14; or Saint Anselm of Canterbury's treatise *Cur Deus homo,* Book I, chapters 16–18. The notion was popularized by fifteenth-century Spanish poets, who saw in the Incarnation the means by which man would be able to take the place of the fallen angels in Heaven. In the *Vita Christi* of Fray Iñigo de Mendoza the angels sing: "Estas son las maravillas / que Dios se sabe hazer, / que por reparar las sillas / que trastornó Luçifer / es nasçido de muger" (Fray Iñigo de Mendoza, *Cancionero,* ed. Julio Rodríguez-Puértolas [Madrid: Espasa-Calpe, 1968], 30). In a Nativity poem Juan del Encina writes: "Para aver de reparar / las sillas que se perdieron / de todos los que cayeron, / fue necessario encarnar, / y el Hijo de Dios tomar / carne humana en este suelo, / por nos limpiar y afinar / quísonos acá plantar / para trasponer al cielo" (Juan del Encina, *Obras completas,* ed. Ana María Rambaldo, 4 vols. [Madrid: Espasa-Calpe, 1978–1983], 1:46).

3. In his marginal annotations to *El libro del conorte,* Father Francisco de Torres sees in this episode the antiquity of the custom of offering bunches of flowers to the beloved. Nonetheless, he says that after the Fall, such a practice is illicit if inspired by a love that is base or lustful (*Conorte,* fol. 444v).

4. Cf. "He humbled himself, becoming obedient unto death, even to the death of the cross" (Philippians 2:8).

5. This line of reasoning constitutes a reversal of the medieval misogynist view of women, a view that saw in feminine wiles woman's capacity for deceiving

man. However, since Wisdom (Sapientia) was feminine in gender and therefore personified allegorically as a woman, feminine astuteness could also have positive connotations. For the positive symbolic value of the female figure of Wisdom in the "sapiential theology" of Hildegard of Bingen, see Barbara Newman, *Sister of Wisdom: St. Hildegard's Theology of the Feminine* (Berkeley and Los Angeles: University of California Press, 1987), 42–88.

6. Torres's commentary on this passage reveals that for him the principal cause of the Fall was Eve's putting on airs: "Y nota mucho que si el siervo antiguo tentó antes a Eva, no solo fue porque la vio muger y más flaca que Adán, sino creo que tanbién le fue grandíssima ocasión verla tan melindrosa en aquellas huidas de Adán." Torres goes on to observe that Eve's *melindrosidad* has been passed on to many of her daughters: "Y no nos espantemos que sus hijas, las que son perversas, lo sean, pues lo fue su madre antes que del todo perdiese la primera inocentia. . . . Así que de las que no lo son nada, grande y varonil y más que varonil es su valor y diníssimas son de honra y de gloria, pues de cosa que les venía tan nascida, y a mi juicio no la menos mala y peligrosa, se escaparon. Y las que lo son poco demos infinitas gracias a Dios. Y de las que son mucho no ay cosa más insufrible ni peor, porque florece en ellas esta perniciosíssima y primera mala raíz de su engendradora a Eva. Y aunque les viene de tan lexos, les ase y se les arraiga como veciníssima, que es mucho de las tales huir y apartarse de sus esposos y maridos y de las personas que son obligadas amar y a las que más las aman y más sanamente y a quien más, según Dios, deven." In the passage that immediately follows, Torres continues to rail against these most perverse daughters of Eve: "Y por el mismo caso con melindres serpentinos se apartan, dándoles mil desacrimientos[?] y tormentos de garrocha y se llegan a otras personas que havían de huir cielo y tierra con mil inventiones, por mil vías. Aborrescen a sus maridos y nunca les ternán el rostro alegre y aman a sus rufianes y se pierden por ellos, haciéndoles mil charicias y atractiones, aunque sean negros asquerosos sin narices. Y dexan a sus maridos, aunque sean gentiles honbres y se pierdan por ellas, y quieren a sus mancebos, aunque les sean crueles verdugos y sayones. Y ya hallan para esto mil raçones y buscan diez mil ocasiones y tienen por bien empleadas las almas perdidas y las vidas en tal caso." Finally, Torres connects the behavior of these evil women to that of Eve: "Así que sin saver lo que se hacen, imitan a Eva, su primera madre en su primer pecado, el qual fue origen de todos los pecados y de la perditión de todo el género humano, no porque ella amase a otrie más que a su marido—que no avía otrie, que si le huviera, a Dios, que es el que solo lo puede saver, queda el juicio de lo que hiciera—mas porque a su marido hermoso más que el sol y amoroso sobre todos los hijos de los hombres y dio ella melindrosamente, que no sé qué otra cosa fuese que no melindre, en huir d'él sin para qué y darle pena. Y por esta ocasión el vafro[?] y astuto sierpe creo que la tentó primero, o porque la havía como oído y visto más defectuosa. Y Adán, desventurado, como era nimio en amarla y en achariciarla, qu[e]riéndola más que a Dios, por atraherla a sí y no contristarla . . . la primera cosa que le rogava comió la mançana." The commentary ends with a stern warning to the reader to beware of women who seek to imitate Eve's role in the Fall: "Guárdate de ellas y si no te responden bien a buen amor, mira lo que haces quando te provocan a deshonestidad y a las cosas que Dios vedó. Si en lo

concedido de Dios no te quieren, guárdate no te hagan hacer lo prohibido. Y avísote que no tomes la mançana vedada de sus manos, aunque te la ofrezcan con mil donaires y juegos, que la muerte de muerte eterna está en ella y el diablo, tu mortal enemigo y suyo, es que engaña y mata con ponçoñosa fruta a entramos" (*Conorte,* fol. 445v).

7. Torres was quite impressed by the allegory of the four pillars. In fact, he found it so clever that, since Juana herself would have been incapable of inventing it, he believed the passage constituted yet another proof of the divine origin of her words: "que bien parece que poca parte tenía la simple virgen en la esplicatión, no más verdaderamente de ser órgano divino de la voz de Dios, que ella ni imaginar ni soñar no pudo tales cosas, aunque huviera oído quatro años de theología. Son muchos los que los an oído que será harto entender bien el artificio d'estas palabras divinas" (*Conorte,* fol. 446v).

8. Scriptural exegetes who wished to attribute Adam's disobedience to his immaturity and innocence characterized him as a child. In chapter 11 of his *Exhortation to the Greeks,* Clement of Alexandria remarks: "The first man played in Paradise with childlike freedom, since he was a child of God" (*The Exhortation to the Greeks. The Rich Man's Salvation,* trans. G. W. Butterworth, The Loeb Classical Library [London: William Heinemann, and New York: G. P. Putnam's Sons, 1919], 237). Saint Irenaeus relates Adam's and Eve's lack of awareness of their nakedness to their child-like innocence: "And Adam and Eve . . . *were naked and were not ashamed,* for their thoughts were innocent and childlike, and they had no conception or imagination of the sort that is engendered in the soul by evil, through concupiscence, and by lust. . . . For this reason they *were not ashamed,* as they kissed each other and embraced with the innocence of childhood" (*Proof of the Apostolic Preaching,* trans. Joseph P. Smith, S.J. [Westminster: Newman Press, and London: Longmans, Green and Co., 1952], 56). Peter Comestor makes a similar observation: "Sic et pueri si videantur pudenda eorum non erubescunt, quia beneficio aetatis motam erubescibilem nondum senserunt" (*Historia Scholastica,* in Migne, *Patrologia Latina,* vol. 198, col. 1072).

9. This sort of ship imagery had become commonplace by the late fifteenth and early sixteenth centuries. Sebastian Brant's *Narrenschiff* and Gil Vicente's *Barcas* trilogy are obvious examples.

10. For a more detailed commentary on these matters, see Chapter 5.

11. Actually, Juana conflates Proverbs 6:20 and Proverbs 3:11–12 ("My son, reject not the correction of the Lord: and do not faint when you are chastised by him: For whom the Lord loveth, he chastiseth: and as a father in the son he pleaseth himself").

12. For a detailed commentary on the final pages of the *Conorte,* see Chapter 5.

13. For a brief study of several versions of the legend, see chapter 9 ("Woher stammt des Mannes Bart?") of Oskar Dähnhardt's *Natursagen,* 4 vols. (Leipzig and Berlin: Teubner, 1907), 1:228–235.

14. The text is edited in Reinhold Kontzi, *Aljamiado Texte,* 2 vols. (Wiesbaden: Steiner, 1974), 2:405. In Appendix B, I offer a modernized version of Kontzi's text as well as my own English translation.

15. The text is edited by Dähnhardt in his *Natursagen* 1:232–233. Appendix C

includes both a slightly modernized version of Dähnhardt's text and my own rough English translation.

16. For a study of literary and exegetical treatments of Genesis, see J. M. Evans, *"Paradise Lost" and the Genesis Tradition* (Oxford: Clarendon Press, 1968). For changing conceptions of the figure of Eve, see John A. Phillips, *Eve: The History of an Idea* (San Francisco: Harper and Row, 1984).

17. For the tradition of the apple as the fruit of the Tree of Knowledge, see Karl Heisig, "Woher stammt die Vorstellung vom Paradiesapfel?" *Zeitschrift für die neutestamentliche Wissenschaft und die Kunde der älteren Kirche,* 44 (1952–53) 111– 118, and Hans-Günter Leder, "Arbor Scientiae. Die Tradition vom paradiesischen Apfelbaum," *Zeitschrift für die neutestamentliche Wissenschaft und die Kunde der älteren Kirche,* 52 (1961) 156–189.

18. However, Jewish commentators, and following them certain of the church fathers, argued that before the Fall Adam and Eve had been arrayed in garments of light. See Louis Ginzberg, *The Legends of the Jews,* trans. Henrietta Szold, 7 vols. (1925; Philadelphia: The Jewish Publication Society of America, 1936–1942), 5:103–104.

19. Dähnhardt observes that Eve's rebelliousness in the beard legend appears to be a calque of the legend of Lilith (*Natursagen,* 229). For the theme of female subordination and its festive inversion in early modern Europe, see Natalie Zemon Davis, "Women on Top," in her *Society and Culture in Early Modern France* (1965; Stanford: Stanford University Press, 1975), 124–151.

20. This is, however, the inference in Juana's interpretation of the allegorical pageant, in which childish games clearly denote a state of innocence: "E las gentes pareçían todas como niños e niñas, a sinificar que quando El crió el primer honbre e la primera muger, estavan al prinçipio en tanta puridad e linpieza e inoçençia como están agora los niños quando enpieçan a saber jugar e gorgear, que no tienen de otra cosa cuidado sino de irse en pos de su padre e de su madre. De lo qual se gozan los padres quando los ven fazer aquellos juguezitos e quando veen cómo se están riendo" (*Conorte,* fol. 447r). Childhood is similarly associated with inno- cence in the sermon on the Flight into Egypt. When the Lord transforms the Holy Innocents into the age they would have been had they not been slain, the Innocents beg to become children again, for they prefer to remain innocent and completely free from sin: "Porque bien sabemos nosotros que no ay cosa con que tú más te huelgues que es con las ánimas inoçentes e linpias de pecado. Por tanto, Señor Dios Nuestro, tórnanos inoçentes e ayúntanos a ti que heres gloria de toda ánima que te ama e desea" (*Conorte,* fol. 70r).

21. In *Tirante el Blanco* the princess Carmesina says of her mother the em- press: "Aquella vieja de mi madre piadad tiene de sí misma, que también querría jugar, que huego de amor la quema y la fuerça de impaciencia" (*Tirante el Blanco. Versión castellana impresa en Valladolid en 1511 de la obra de Joanot Martorell y Martí Joan de Galba,* ed. Martín de Riquer, 5 vols. [Madrid: Espasa-Calpe, 1974], 3:25). In *Amadís de Gaula,* Book II, Chapter LXIV, when Oriana discovers that she is preg- nant, her companion Mabilia comments: "siempre me tuve por dicho que de tales juegos havríades tal ganancia" (Garci Rodríguez de Montalvo, *Amadís de Gaula,* ed. Juan Manuel Cacho Blecua, 2 vols. [Madrid: Cátedra, 1987], 1:920). For *jugar*

as a euphemism for sexual activity in Golden Age erotic poetry, see *Floresta de poesías eróticas del Siglo de Oro,* ed. Pierre Alzieu, Robert Jammes, and Yvan Lissorgues (Toulouse: France-Ibérie Recherche, 1975), poems 83, 84, and 141.

22. "la traía por fuerça algunas vezes e otras vezes la traía con halagos e con amor e la fazía llegar a él" (*Conorte,* fol. 445v).

23. "Why, then, did they [Adam and Eve] not have intercourse until they had left Paradise? The reason is that soon after the creation of the woman, before they had relations, they committed the sin because of which they were destined to die and because of which they went forth from the place of their blessedness" (St. Augustine, *The Literal Meaning of Genesis,* trans. John Hammond Taylor, S.J., 2 vols. [New York: Newman Press, 1982], Book IX, chapter 4, vol. 2:74).

24. The beard is an obvious symbol of masculinity, and that connotation was not unfamiliar to Christian exegetes. The *Paidagogos* of Clement of Alexandria establishes a clear relation between the beard as a sign of virility and man's dominance of woman: "God planned that woman be smooth-skinned, taking pride in her natural tresses, . . . But man He adorned like the lion, with a beard, and gave him a hairy chest as proof of his manhood and a sign of his strength and primacy. . . . His beard, then, is the badge of a man and shows him unmistakably to be a man. It is older than Eve and is the symbol of the stronger nature. By God's decree, hairiness is one of man's conspicuous qualities, and, at that, hairiness distributed over his whole body. Whatever smoothness or softness there was in him God took from him when He fashioned the delicate Eve from his side to be the receptacle of his seed, . . . What was left (remember, he had lost all traces of hairlessness) was manhood and reveals that manhood" (Clement of Alexandria, *Christ the Educator,* trans. Simon P. Wood [New York: Fathers of the Church, Inc., 1954], 214–215). For an overview of beards in the Middle Ages, see Giles Constable's introduction to *Apologiae duae: Gozechini Epistola ad Walcherum. Burchardi, ut videtur, Abbatis Bellevallis, Apologia de Barbis,* ed. R. B. C. Huygens (Turnhout: Brepols, 1985), 47–130). The connection between the beard and virility was commonplace in Golden Age Spain. Sebastián de Covarrubias notes: "La barba, cerca de los egypcios, era símbolo de la virilidad y de la fortaleza, y assí dezimos vulgarmente es hombre de barba, para sinificar tiene uno valor" (*Tesoro de la lengua castellana o española* [Madrid: Ediciones Turner, 1977], 192). Conversely, beardlessness was interpreted as a sign of the lack of male genitalia: "Ser lampiño era indicio inequívoco de carecer de órganos genitales" (M. Herrero García, "Los rasgos físicos y el carácter según los textos españoles del siglo XVII," *Revista de Filología Española,* 12 [1925] 163).

25. In Tertullian's *Liber de carne Christi* Christ is the new Adam, while if a woman (Eve) was responsible for the Fall of man, another woman (Mary) would be responsible for man's Redemption. The temptation of Eve prefigured the Annunciation; as Eve believed the serpent, so Mary believed the angel Gabriel: "Igitur si primus Adam de terra traditur, merito sequens, vel novissimus Adam, ut Apostolus dixit, proinde de terra, id est, carne nondum generationi resignata, in spiritum vivificantem a Deo est prolatus. . . . Sed et hic ratio defendit, quod Deus imaginem et similitudinem suam, a diabolo captam, aemula operatione recuperavit. In virginem enim adhuc Evam irrepserat verbum aedificatorium mortis; in vir-

ginem aeque introducendum erat Dei Verbum exstructorium vitae: ut quod per ejusmodi sexum abierat in perditionem, per eumdem sexum redigeretur in salutem. Crediderat Eva serpenti: credidit Maria Gabrieli" (Migne, *Patrologia Latina*, vol. 2, cols. 827–828). In an Easter poem by Juan del Encina, Eve's emergence from the side of Adam is seen as a *figura* of the emergence of the Church from the lance-wound in the side of the crucified Christ: "Primero se figuró / aquesta gran ecelencia / en estado de ynocencia / al tiempo que Adán durmió, / quando Cristo le sacó / la costilla del costado, / de la qual hizo y formó / la que por muger le dio / con que fuesse acompañado. // Bien assí, tan bien dormido, / Jesucristo, nuestra luz, / en el árbor de la Cruz / fue su costado rompido, / con una lança herido, / do fue su sangre sacada, / de donde nos ha salido / y manado y procedido / la santa Yglesia sagrada" (*Obras completas* 1 : 91–92).

26. The Trinitarian gloss, and more concretely, the concomitant association of Eve with Christ, is central to Mother Juana's rehabilitation of Eve. Although her Trinity simile does not appear to follow received interpretations of Genesis, the question of whether it is unique to Juana's writings is ultimately irrelevant. Interestingly, for Father Torres the gloss is not only in all probability unique but constitutes yet another proof of the divine inspiration of Juana's words: "Nota la esposición d'esta authoridad y, por docto y curioso que seas, mira si es ésta notable. Y atrévome a decirte que rebuelvas todos los libros juntos y apostarte, que si bien lo notas, que no halles otra mejor y que será dicha. Si la hallares tal, no ves dónde tan propríssimamente sacó el artículo de la sanctíssima Trinidad en el decir Hijo al Espíritu Sancto y en decir de tu padre al Padre y de tu madre al Hijo y guardando los atributos apropriados a las divinas personas tan casta y germanamente como todos los theólogos del mundo lo pudieran hacer. Mira cómo quiso la sanctíssima Trinidad ahora al remate dar a entender cómo ella morava y hablava en esta su sierva. Y no te maravilles menos de cómo las vírgines milagrosamente lo escr[iv]ieron tan ordenada y concertadamente y tan grave y eloquentemente como que de la virgen humilde lo pronunció. Y aprende a esplicar escriptura d'esta sancta, pues allí halló el artículo de la sanctíssima Trinidad donde nadie por ventura asta ella le havía hallado. Y de allí sacó cosas tan proprias y tan morales y tan provechosas que nadie más. Anda, que la sanctíssima Trinidad bivió y moró y habló en ella y no lo dubdes. Yo a lo menos no lo dubdo. Y así sea ella en mí y en todos. Amén" (*Conorte*, fol. 451v).

27. Caroline Walker Bynum, *Holy Feast and Holy Fast: The Religious Significance of Food to Medieval Women* (Berkeley and Los Angeles: University of California Press, 1987), 261–269.

28. Mother Juana's official interpretation is fraught with such ambiguities. By her own criteria God the Father is androgynous in His characterization because He partakes of the love and humility of the Son/woman. His alter ego, Adam, is characterized throughout the vision as an extremely (and perhaps exaggeratedly) loving person. Christ's patient suffering on the cross is viewed as a feminine trait, but that trait is demonstrated most cogently in the beard vision not by Eve, but by Adam, who suffers Eve's violence without striking back.

29. Father Torres fails to see the ironic results of Adam's love, for he views that love as yet another indication of Adam's superiority over Eve: "Queríala más él

a ella que ella a él. Y aun tanbién creo que Adán, que le tenía ventaja en todo—en saber y en fuerças y en prudentia y en sufrimiento—y así en aquel estado felicíssimo de inocencia el varón se aventajaba en amor y en todo a la muger así porque era esposo y marido como porque era padre y ella esposa y muger y hija engendrada de sus huesos. Y pues Dios eterno y omnipotente primero y más immediatamente crió Adán y puso los ojos en él y le hiço cabeça de Eva y principio de todo el género humano y depositó en él todo nuestro mal o todo nuestro bien y no en la muger Eva, raçón es que entendamos que tenía mejores partes y más patientia y prudentia y amor como por el Señor nos es sinificado en este divino sermón. Y aun creo que tenía más obedientia a Dios y más cuidado de guardar la unión y paz del matrimonio que Dios havía tan milagrosamente instituido y que con tanta bondad y charidad, tan poco havía, les havía encargado y encomendado y mandado. Y por esta su mayor obedientia después de su mayor sabiduría que en todo era muy más enseñado y en ninguna cosa fue engañado como Eva." Nonetheless, Torres believes that a reversal occurred after the Fall, for women became the more loving creatures: "En el estado de inocentia amava menos Eva, mas en el estado de pecado y de destierro, sacando a las malas, que las tales a Dios aborrecen y a sus próximos por diversas vías persiguen y matan, de las buenas pues digo commúnmente son mayores que sus maridos y los aman más y son más devotas y humildes y obedientes y pacíficas. Y entre otras cosas, ya como ellas son las que los engendran a los hombres y no salen ellas de sus huesos sino ellos de sus vientres y les costamos más dolor que no costó Eva [a] Adán, tiénennos ya en todo más amor. Y así ellas son en todo mejores. Y así ves aquí cómo el Señor aprueba lo que todos comúnmente sentimos de la mujer, que es más humilde, obediente, piadosa y mansa que el honbre, raçón es que pues el Hijo, Verbo encarnado, las honró tanto que las aventajó en estos apellidos tan honoríficos y tan virtuosos a los honbres. Y creo que lo hiço así por el amor que tuvo a su Madre y a ser hijo de muger. Y tal como la Virgen que le engendró y parió y crió y que ella lo mereció y quiso que fuesen figura y significasen la persona suya del mismo Hijo de Dios, Verbo encarnado, Hijo tanbién de muger, obediente asta muerte de cruz, manso y perdonador de sus enemigos y intercesor por ellos, así es raçón que lo hagan ellas. ¡Y ay de las que no lo hacen y faltan a tan alta obligatión y figura!" (*Conorte*, fol. 444rv).

30. For the development of the association between Eve, lust, and sin in rabbinic and apocryphal literature, see Bernard P. Prusak, "Woman: Seductive Siren and Source of Sin? Pseudepigraphal Myth and Christian Origins," in *Religion and Sexism: Images of Woman in the Jewish and Christian Traditions,* ed. Rosemary Radford Ruether (New York: Simon and Schuster, 1974), 89–116.

31. In a fourteenth-century Cornish Creation play, Eve blackmails Adam into eating the forbidden fruit: "Not to believe me is to lose me and my love. You'll never see me again as long as you live." To which Adam replies: "Oh, Eve! Rather than set you against me, I will do anything you want me to do. Give me the apple, I'll eat it" (*The Cornish Ordinalia: A Medieval Dramatic Trilogy,* trans. Markham Harris [Washington, D.C.: The Catholic University of America Press, 1969], 8–9). The notion that Adam was led to sin out of his affection for Eve is already insinuated in Saint Augustine: "After the woman had been seduced and had eaten of the forbidden fruit and had given Adam some to eat with her, he did not wish to make

her unhappy, fearing she would waste away without his support, alienated from his affections, and that this dissension would be her death" (*The Literal Meaning of Genesis,* Book XI, chapter 42, vol. 2:176). In the commentary on one of her visions, Hildegard of Bingen suggests that the devil approached Eve because he was aware of her power over Adam: "Quia sciebat mulieris mollitiem facilius uincendam quam uiri fortitudinem, uidens etiam quod Adam in caritate Euae tam fortiter ardebat ut si ipse diabolus Euam uicisset, quidquid illa Adae diceret, Adam idem perficeret" (*Scivias,* ed. Aldegundis Führkötter, OSB, and Angela Carlevaris, OSB [Turnhout: Brepols, 1978], 19). Likewise, Alonso de Madrigal observes that while Eve believed what the serpent told her, Adam "non credidit aliquid istorum, sed solum comedit ut mulierem non contristaret. Credidit enim quod, si non comederet de fructu, quem ei mulier presentabat, ipsa tedio moreretur" (*Super Genesim Commentaria* [Venice, 1507], fol. 39v).

32. For the contrast in the characterization of Adam and Eve, see Phyllis Trible, *God and the Rhetoric of Sexuality* (Philadelphia: Fortress Press, 1978), 113.

33. Traditionally, if Eve was to be redeemed, it was through her association with the Blessed Virgin. See Phillips, *Eve,* 131–135.

34. The love-and-power motif is also present in the allegorical pageant (God's ability to destroy the world is tempered by His love for humankind) and in the exegesis of Proverbs 6:20, which contrasts the castigating Father and the compassionate mother/Christ.

35. The motif is not infrequent in women's visions. In Hildegard of Bingen's *Scivias,* for example, a celestial voice orders her to write what she hears: "Dic ergo mirabilia haec et scribe ea hoc modo edocta et dic" (*Scivias,* 3).

36. "But I suffer not a woman to teach, nor to use authority over the man: but to be in silence. For Adam was first formed; then Eve. And Adam was not seduced; but the woman being seduced, was in the transgression" (I Timothy 2:12–14).

37. Ian Maclean, *The Renaissance Notion of Woman* (Cambridge: Cambridge University Press, 1980), 18.

38. Saint Augustine argued that sexual differences affect only the body, the soul having no sex: "Some have conjectured that at this point the interior man was created, but that his body was created afterwards where Scripture says, *And God formed man of the slime of the earth.* We should therefore take the expression, *God created man,* to refer to his spirit; whereas the statement, *God formed man,* would apply to his body. But they do not realize that there could have been no distinction of male and female except in relation to the body" (*The Literal Meaning of Genesis,* Book III, chapter 22, vol. 1:98).

39. Since both man and woman have a rational soul, Saint Augustine refers to woman as *homo,* that is to say, a human being: "By the same token, in the original creation of man, inasmuch as woman was a human being [*homo*], she certainly had a mind, and a rational mind, and therefore she also was made to the image of God" (*The Literal Meaning of Genesis,* Book III, chapter 22, vol. 1:99).

40. At the end of the Creation sermon, the Lord addresses the question of the reception of *El libro del conorte,* comparing the book to food: sinners whose sense of taste has been embittered through disbelief will find that these scriptures

taste bad, while those in a state of grace will find them sweeter than honeycomb (fols. 451v–452r). Although Juana attributes the words of the book to God Himself, it could be argued that she offers the book to her readers and listeners as Eve offered the apple to Adam. Just as (according to Juana) Adam ate the apple as a means of placating Eve and of demonstrating his love for her, the receivers of Juana's text are invited to taste it, and thereby to accept its divine inspiration, as a demonstration of their love of God and His words.

II. The Mother Hen

The motif of patient resignation in the face of bodily pain recurs through-out Mother Juana's life, for various illnesses kept her in a state of almost constant suffering. Her biographers relate her sicknesses and the concomi-tant pain explicitly to Christ's Passion. Thus, the *Vida* recounts how Christ appeared to her in a vision and said:

"Pues me escogistes a mí, el qual fui varón leproso e por tal tenido e reputado en el tiempo de la mi Passión, por esposo e marido, e hezistes casamiento comigo, dán-doosme toda sin me negar cosa de que yo quisiese haçer de vos, y he tenido tanta parte en vos quanta he querido, pues donde a havido tal comunicaçión çierto es que se os havía de pegar algo de mis enfermedades. Por eso quien bien ama a de sufrir a su amado qualquier cosa que por él se le recresca." (*Vida*, fol. 61r)

("Since you chose me, who was a leper and considered and deemed such at the time of my Passion,[1] as husband and spouse, and you were wedded to me, giving yourself to me, without denying me anything I might wish to do with you, and [since] I have shared in you as much as I have wished, then where there has been such intimacy, surely some part of my illnesses had to infect you. Therefore, who-ever loves well must suffer from the lover whatever [affliction] befalls him.")

Thus, it is Christ Himself who introduces the motif of the imitation of Christ, emphasizing the relationship between His "bride"'s sufferings and those He endured during His Passion. To imitate Christ is above all to suffer with Him and in Him the pains of the Passion. Bynum has pointed out the importance of the motif of suffering in the lives of medieval holy women: bodily pain provides a means of saving souls, because the suffer-ings of such women fuse with those of the crucified Christ and with those of the souls in Purgatory.[2] Offering their pain for the salvation of others, these women imitate Christ's redemptive role.

This chapter will concentrate on an episode (see Appendix D) that illustrates the intimate relationship between bodily suffering and the possi-bility of achieving the salvation of the souls in Purgatory. Studied in the light of a number of other pertinent visions, the episode reveals how Mother Juana uses a series of traditional images to enhance her role as co-redeemer. Although a woman, she appropriates certain "masculine" powers that later turn out to be "feminine," for another of her strategies consists of demonstrating the feminine aspects of masculine figures, in order to associate herself with them (as in the case of Christ) or to surpass them (as in the case of Saint Francis). In this way Juana makes possible and justifies the widening of her own sphere of action.

When Mother Juana is shown in a vision the punishments that the souls in Purgatory suffer for their sins, she asks permission to assume those punishments so that the souls can have a rest. Her wish is granted, and the *Vida* (fol. 99v) relates that she would often take upon herself the sufferings of those in Purgatory. Her official biography then tells how she discovered a secret regarding those souls. One of the results of her constant illnesses was that her limbs became chilled. It occurred to her that placing heated pebbles among the bedclothes would be an effective way of warming her hands and feet, so she asked her companions to bring her a stone. When they began to heat the stone in a brazier, Juana heard a moaning voice that said: "Is there any greater cruelty?" It seemed to her that the voice was that of a soul from Purgatory, and she ordered the stone removed from the fire. She begged the soul's forgiveness for harming it and asked how it had come to be in the stone. The soul answered that such was the will of God.

When Juana asks her guardian angel to explain the phenomenon, he answers that many souls suffer in that way and compares the stones to a sort of hospital. It is God's will, he says, that Juana herself become such a hospital and that stones containing souls from Purgatory be placed on her joints and limbs so that she can alleviate their suffering by taking it upon herself.

Juana orders her companions to bring to her cell all the stones they can find. Upon placing them in her bed, she can tell immediately whether or not they contain souls. Her *Vida* recounts that, thanks to the diligence of her companions, she always has "a supply of souls in the hospital of her charitable limbs."[3] The torments she assumes are immense:

Y como las ánimas viniesen tan llenas de penas y fuegos y fríos, todo muy ensufrible, e con otros muchos tormentos, luego las tomava ella e las juntava con sus dolorosos miembros, a cuya causa partiçipava en mucho grado de las penas que ellas traían, quedándole sus miembros con muy acreçentados y grandes dolores y con tan reçios fuegos que le pareçía estar ella metida en los mesmos fuegos de purgatorio, tanto que de neçessidad muchas vezes le hazían aire e otras le ponían paños mojados en agua fría sobre sus quebradas coyunturas. Y en tiempo de calores le heran tan rezios de sufrir estos dolores y fuegos que la hazían dar muy grandes gemidos y gritos, pidiendo ayuda a la magestad divina para poder llevar tan insufribles y reçios tormentos. Y en este travajo estava muchos días junto sin tener alivio día ni noche ni tomando cosa con que se pudiese substener. (*Vida*, fols. 101v–102r)

(And since the souls arrived so full of pain and extreme heat and cold, all quite unbearable, and with many other torments, she then took them and clasped them to her painful limbs, on account of which she shared in high degree the pains they were suffering. Her limbs were left with increased and extreme pains and with such severe heat that it seemed to her that she was in the very fires of Purgatory, and so much so that they would often fan her or place cloths soaked in cold water on her broken joints. And in hot weather these pains and fires were so hard to endure that she would moan and cry out in pain, asking His Divine Majesty's help to suffer such unbearable and harsh torments. And she would spend days in this travail without any sort of relief, day or night, nor did she eat anything nourishing.)

The nun endured not only intense heat comparable to that of Purgatory but also extremely painful cold:

E ansí como las ánimas traían pena de crueles fuegos, ansí otras vezes traían de frío muy insufrible y le davan tanta fatiga y travaxo de padesçerlo como en la pena del calor, porque ninguna cosa le dava calor ni descanso, aunque acaeszía tenerle puesto alrededor de su cuerpo tres o quatro cosas llenas de brasas muy ençendidas. Y con los demasiados fríos que las ánimas partiçipaban le creçían todos sus dolores en mucho grado y le causaron enfermedad en las hijadas y estómago de muy creçidos dolores y en toda la oquedad de su cuerpo. Y tanto hera el travajo y dolores que padeçía, que dava doloros[os] gritos e gemidos. Y estos travajos y tormentos acaesçía algunas vezes durarle un mes y otras vezes quinze días y más y menos, según hera la voluntad de Dios. (*Vida*, fol. 102v)

(And just as some souls brought the pain of cruel fires, so others brought unbearable cold. And enduring it gave her as much travail and hardship as did the pain of heat, for no remedy warmed her up or gave her relief, even though it often happened that three or four containers of hot embers would be placed around her body. And with the intense cold that the souls imparted to her, her pains increased to a considerable degree, and they caused affliction in her loins and stomach and in all her body cavity with still greater pain. And so great was the travail and pain she suffered that she gave out woeful cries and moans. And it happened that these pains and torments would last sometimes for a month and other times a fortnight and more or less, according to the will of God.)

New souls would replace those that had completed their purgation "through Our Lord's sacred Passion and the help of the holy mother Church . . . and through the merits of this blessed soul."[4] Thus, Juana's official biography is careful to underscore the motif of the co-redemption: the salvation of the souls from Purgatory is due not only to Christ's

Passion and to the prayers and good works offered by the Church but also to Juana's sufferings. The nun is encouraged to continue to suffer for the souls in Purgatory because when she experiences a mystical rapture, she can see the fruits of her travails in a vision of the souls that, released from Purgatory, have ascended to Heaven. Some of these souls have been suffering for 300 or 500 years, and "all of them were so lonely, for there was no longer anyone left to remember to offer prayers for them, save those offered by the holy mother Church for all the dead in general."[5] Juana plays a Christomimetic role when she assumes the sufferings of others to bring about their salvation. She suffers a passion analogous to that of Christ and achieves an analogous result: the salvation of souls. It is, then, no accident that Christ's Passion was read aloud to her to help her endure such bodily sufferings (*Vida*, fol. 102v).

The image of Mother Juana lying in a bed full of stones evokes another image, of a mother hen brooding her eggs, an association that is not arbitrary, for a later vision (see Appendix E) explicitly confirms the nun's role as a figurative mother hen. As will become apparent, the hen was traditionally associated with Christ and to a lesser degree with Saint Francis. Concretely, the symbolic hen was related to Christ's Passion and to His maternity. Thus, not only does Mother Juana appropriate Christ's redemptive role, but that appropriation underscores a significant relationship: as she identifies with the Redeemer, the latter, through the maternal image of the hen, is identified with women.

In the vision that relates the stones episode to the hen motif, Saint Francis appears to Mother Juana as she is lying in her bed full of stones. The saint observes that God has given her the bed "for a nest as to a bird or hen that is brooding its eggs so that live birds or chicks can be hatched from them."[6] Saint Francis then tosses three dozen eggs of various sizes into the bed. The saint's leave-taking recognizes that Juana has become a sort of co-redeemer, for he establishes an explicit relation between the symbolic hatching of the eggs and Christ's Passion. Juana kisses Saint Francis's feet and he kisses her on the head, saying, "I wish to kiss the sufferings of my Lord Jesus Christ in you, my daughter."[7] The gloss that follows underscores the co-redemption motif, explaining that the little birds and chicks that come out of the eggs are the souls that "through Our Lord God's Passion and through the pain that she suffered were succored and saved."[8] The eggs Saint Francis tossed into Juana's bed were the souls of those who had commended themselves to him, and that he in turn had brought to her so that she could help them. Thus, Saint Francis himself recognizes the identity between Juana's torments and Christ's Passion when he says that in kissing her, he kisses the sufferings of the Savior. The Seraphic Father further recognizes that, as a co-redeemer, Juana has been empowered to participate in Christ's saving role.

A curious inversion underlies the Saint Francis vision. The Seraphic Father abdicates his role as heavenly advocate for those devoted to him and begs Juana to intercede for them in his place. The lesson to be derived from the episode would appear to be that turning to Mother Juana for aid can be more effective than turning to a traditional advocate like Saint Francis. The reasoning leading to such a conclusion would be that, while in this instance a saint like Francis can but plead for those devoted to him, that is to say, serve as an intermediary between God and the faithful, Mother Juana can intervene more actively in the salvation of souls, for she herself assumes their sufferings. What was implicit in the stones episode becomes explicit in the Saint Francis vision: Juana's sufferings not only enable her to save souls but are also a calque of Christ's Passion. Appropriating the role that Saint Francis cedes to her, Juana surpasses and in a sense even discredits the saint at the same time that she enhances her own role as co-redeemer.

Mother Juana's effectiveness in saving souls from Purgatory is expressed in an image that is clearly feminine in its maternal connotations: Juana's "passion" is compared to a hen who broods her eggs. But the nun's suffering of torments equivalent to those of the Passion is not the only link between herself and Christ, for her *imitatio Christi* is further underscored by the fact that in the Bible Christ compares Himself to a mother hen. Specifically, Christ refers to Himself with the maternal and thereby "feminine" image of the symbolic hen in Matthew 23:37, when He addresses Jerusalem, exclaiming: "Jerusalem, Jerusalem, thou that killest the prophets, and stonest them that are sent unto thee, how often would I have gathered together thy children, as the hen doth gather her chickens under her wings, and thou wouldest not?"[9] Thus, the stones episode re-creates the image that Christ uses to refer to Himself: both Juana and Christ are symbolic hens that, like good mothers, seek to protect their offspring. The motif of the eggs, associated as it is with the stones in Juana's bed, recalls the stoning of the prophets. Thus, Mother Juana appropriates not only Christ's redemptive role but also a symbol closely associated with Him.[10] In turn, the delivery of souls from Purgatory, and thereby the very Passion of Christ, is revealed to be a "feminine" activity through its association with the mother hen.

Indeed, the motif of Christ's Passion as a maternal event is clearly manifested in Juana's Creation sermon when Christ explicates Proverbs 6:20, comparing the Crucifixion to a woman giving birth:

por quanto nos parió a todos con muy grandes dolores e tormentos en el tienpo de la su muy cruda e amarga Passión. E que como le costamos tan caros y el parto con que nos parió fue tan fuerte que gotas de sangre le fazía sudar, no puede fazer otra cosa sino rogar e abogar continuamente delante el Padre por nosotros como madre muy piadosa, deseando que nos salvemos e salgan a luz nuestras ánimas, por que sus dolores e tormentos no sean en vano padeçidos. (*Conorte,* fol. 451v)

(inasmuch as He gave birth to all of us with very great pains and torments at the time of His cruel and bitter Passion. And since we cost Him so dearly and the birthing through which He bore us was so arduous that it made Him sweat drops of blood, He can do naught but intercede before the Father for us like a very compassionate mother, desiring that we be saved and that our souls be born, so that His pains and torments will not have been suffered in vain.)

The insistence on Christ's feminine side is not new: the motif dates back to the Fathers of the Church.[11] Nonetheless, what is significant in the episode of the stones is that Juana establishes an implicit relation between herself, who gives birth to saved souls in her bed full of stones, and Christ, who gives birth to saved souls on the bed of the cross.[12] It is the image of the maternal hen that links the two cases: both Christ and Juana are mothers whose sufferings effect the salvation of their spiritual children.[13]

The brief mention of the stoning of the prophets in the biblical episode of Christ's address to Jerusalem could have sufficed to suggest to Mother Juana the stones motif. Nonetheless, at least worthy of consideration is the possible connection with the cycle of Gospel readings for the liturgical year. The biblical verse in which Christ compares Himself to a hen corresponds to the Gospel that was read for the Feast of Saint Stephen, the first martyr, who was, of course, stoned to death. Thus, the juxtaposition in the liturgy of the commemoration of the first Christian martyr with the biblical text that contains the image of Christ as a hen could have suggested to Mother Juana the connection between the stones and intense suffering: the stones are the instruments of Stephen's martyrdom, and their roundness recalls the eggs associated with the divine hen maternally concerned for her chicks. Yet another link between the nun and the first martyr is that both were vehicles for God's revelation: Juana, of course, received many visions; Stephen, at the moment of his martyrdom, had a vision of Christ at the right hand of God (Acts 7:55–56). Thus, both are visionaries who undergo suffering associated with stones.

Whatever the relationship between Mother Juana and Saint Stephen, it is the Christomimetic motif of the hen, and concretely, the association between the hen and Christ's Passion, that underscores the vital significance of the stones episode. The connection between the hen and suffering was enhanced by centuries of biblical exegesis of Matthew 23:37, the theme of the hen who becomes ill, suffers, and even dies for her chicks being particularly frequent in Saint Augustine. Here is a representative passage, taken from his commentary on Psalm 58:

Something else I am admonished to say in this place by the loftiness of our Head Himself: for He was made weak even unto death, and He took on Him the weakness of flesh, in order that the chickens of Jerusalem He might gather under His wings, like a hen shewing herself weak with her little ones.[14] For have we not observed this thing in some bird at some time or other, even in those which build nests before our eyes, as the house-sparrows, as swallows, so to speak, our annual guests, as storks, as various sorts of birds, which before our eyes build nests, and hatch eggs, feed chickens, as the very doves which daily we see; and some bird to become weak with her chickens, have we not known, have we not looked upon, have we not seen? In what way doth a hen experience this weakness? Surely a known fact I am speaking of, which in our sight is daily taking place. How her voice groweth hoarse, how her whole body is made languid? The wings droop, the feathers are loosened, and thou seest around the chickens some sick thing, and this is maternal love which is found as weakness. Why was it therefore, but for this reason, that the Lord willed to be a Hen, saying in the Holy Scriptures, "Jerusalem, Jerusalem, how often have I willed to gather thy sons, even as a hen her chickens under her wings, and thou hast not been willing."[15]

Saint Augustine thus relates the hen motif to suffering and concretely to the Passion as an example of Christ's maternal concern for chicks/sinners.[16] As Bynum has pointed out, the connection between Christ's maternity and His suffering humanity is not arbitrary: the dichotomy between His humanity and His divinity was seen as a reflection of the dichotomy between woman and man.[17] Indeed, the motif was widely disseminated in the late Middle Ages, especially among holy women, who identified with Christ's "feminine" humanity. Concretely, such women equated their sufferings with those of the Passion. So once again the hen image underscores the parallel between Mother Juana's sufferings and those of Christ, for both individuals take upon themselves with maternal affection the pain of their spiritual children. Saint Augustine depicts a maternal Christ who plays the role of self-sacrificing mother. When she assumes the sufferings of the souls in Purgatory, Mother Juana associates herself with Christ's more "feminine" side, His holy humanity, which was symbolized by the hen that suffers for her chicks.

The presence of Saint Francis in one of Mother Juana's visions is not surprising, inasmuch as she belonged to the Third Order of Saint Francis. But the saint's appearance in the stones episode has a more specific explanation: Saint Francis likewise compared himself to a hen. One of the primary Franciscan sources, the *Legend of the Three Companions,* recounts a vision that the Seraphic Father received when he was seeking a cardinal to attend to the spiritual direction of his nascent order:

Blessed Francis made this request because of a vision in which he had seen a small, black hen with hairy legs, and feet like those of a domestic pigeon; and this hen had so many chickens that she could not possibly shelter them under her wings and they ran about beyond her. When blessed Francis awoke and thought over this vision in the light of the Holy Spirit, he realized that he was the hen, and he said: "I am that hen, by nature small and black, whereas I should be simple as a dove, flying up to heaven on the wings of love and virtue. The Lord, in his mercy, gives and will give me many children whom I cannot protect by my own strength; therefore, I must put them under the care of our holy Mother the Church, and she will protect and nourish them under the shadow of her wings."[18]

Saint Francis's vision is recalled in *El libro del conorte* in the sermon for his feast day (see Appendix F).[19] When Christ sees that the Church militant is going to ruin, He begs the Father to turn over to Him a little brown hen (that is, Saint Francis) so that His Church can be restored. The Father agrees and Christ addresses Francis from a crucifix.[20] The Lord then explains why He calls the saint a little brown hen:

E declaró el Señor, diziendo que llama El a San Françisco la gallina morenita porque así como la gallina se trabaja por sacar los huevos que le echan, aunque no los a ella puesto e son de otras gallinas, y está por sacarlos en penitençia fasta que se para amarilla e muerta de hanbre, e quando los a sacado, dexa ella de comer por darlo a los pollos, así por semejante fizo el glorio[so] San Françisco, que estuvo en penitençia fasta que se paró muy amarillo y enfermo por traer muchas ánimas a Dios, aunque no heran sus fijos carnales. E por dar e ofreçer a Dios gran manada de ánimas, estava sienpre en lloro, e dexando de comer manjares corporales por darles a ellos enxenplo que lo fiziesen así e se fartasen e deleitasen más de los manjares espirituales que de los corporales. E por darles exenplo que continuamente deven llorar e lagrimar e trabajar por ofreçer a Dios muchas manadas de ánimas. E que por esto le llama El algunas vezes, aunque está en su santo reino muy triunfante e gozoso, la gallina morenita. (*Conorte,* fol. 370r)

(And Our Lord expounded, saying that He calls Saint Francis the little brown hen because just as the hen labors to brood the eggs that are given to her, even though she has not laid them and they belong to other hens, and in order to hatch them she does penance until she becomes jaundiced and half-dead from hunger, and when she has hatched them, she stops eating in order to feed the chicks, so likewise did the glorious Saint Francis, who did penance until he became quite jaundiced and ill in order to bring many souls to God, even though they were not his biological offspring. And in order to give and offer to God a great flock of souls, he wept constantly, and ceasing to take earthly sustenance in order to set an example that they should do likewise and be satisfied and delight more in spiritual foods than in earthly ones. And to set for them an example that they should constantly weep and cry and labor to offer God many flocks of souls. And for this reason He sometimes calls him, even though he is all triumphant and happy in His holy kingdom, the little brown hen.)

Saint Francis himself seems to recognize in Christ's use of the hen image the proof of the perfection of his imitation of the Redeemer, for the Seraphic Father quotes to Christ the biblical verse in which the Lord compares Himself to a hen:

"O Dios mío e Señor mío, a ti me conparas, que aun tú dizes, Señor: 'O Jerusalén, así te deseo meter debaxo de mis alas como la gallina faze a los pollos por guardarlos del vilano[21] tragador.'" (*Conorte*, fol. 370r)

("O my God and my Lord, you compare me to yourself, for even you say, O Lord: 'O Jerusalem, I wish thus to place you under my wings as does the hen her chicks in order to protect them from the gluttonous hawk.'")

In the episode that follows, the members of the Franciscan order stand out from the members of the other orders in the celestial processions. Saint Francis is accompanied by those devoted to him, to his order, or to his habit. Christ asks the Seraphic Father to bare his breast: "Come here, my seraphic friend and my standard-bearer. Show me your breasts." The saint answers: "My breasts, O Lord, here they are, for these [members of the Franciscan order and its supporters] that I bring with me were the breasts of my desires."[22] Then the Lord asks Saint Francis to show Him his mantle. When the angels spread out the mantle, it covers the whole earth, thus symbolizing how the Franciscan order "is scattered throughout the entire world."[23]

As will be seen later, the motifs of the breast and the mantle, together with that of the mother hen, form part of a conscious effort on the part of Mother Juana to depict a feminized Saint Francis.[24] She carries this strategy even further in her treatment of the episode of the saint's reception of the stigmata. Praising His standard-bearer, the Lord emphasizes that while other martyrs suffered at the hands of the infidels, Francis was martyred by God Himself when he was given the stigmata. Thereupon, Christ re-creates the scene of the imposition of the stigmata, asking Saint Francis if he wishes to become His wife and be united with Him. Francis answers that he will obey Him in every way, "as does the wife who is subject and obedient to her husband. . . . And thus He was so united with him in that moment that He impressed upon him His five wounds in the same way that He received them on the cross."[25]

The motif of the divine espousals reappears in the episode that follows, when Christ expresses His desire to become Saint Francis's son-in-law, betrothing Himself to all the friars, nuns, and tertiaries of his order. Francis asks three boons of Christ: he requests special rewards for those members of his order who distinguished themselves for their spiritual perfection; he seeks punishments for friars and nuns who offered a negative example; and he asks for curses upon the persecutors of his order. Christ answers that He will grant all three petitions.

Next, the *Conorte* recounts the episode of the special boon granted on the anniversary of Saint Francis's death. Two ladders appear, one red, the other white, that extend from Purgatory to Heaven.[26] Christ and Saint Francis descend the ladders, their wounds lighting up Purgatory and thus causing the demons to flee. The saint walks at Christ's side, asking the suffering souls who wear the Franciscan habit if they recognize him and his companion. If the souls say no, they may attempt to climb the ladders, but very few arrive at the top; the rest are cast down by angels. If the souls say yes, they are allowed to climb to the top of the ladders. Sometimes Christ permits Saint Francis to realize this mission alone. In such cases Francis leads the saved souls

todas alrededor de sí, así como la gallina quando lieva gran manada de pollos. E dixo el Señor que como le veen los demonios ir así tan çercado de ánimas, se levantan e van en pos d'él por se las arrebatar todas e despedaçarlas entre sus uñas con muy gran crueldad, así como faze el vilano quando lieva los pollos. Y el glorioso San Françisco toma todas las ánimas e las recoge y encubre [debaxo de su manto[27]], así como faze la gallina a los pollos, que los anpara debaxo de sus alas para los defender del vilano. (fol. 372v)

(all of them around him, as does the hen when she leads a great flock of chicks. And the Lord said that when the devils see him leaving thus surrounded by souls, they arise and chase after him to snatch them all away from him and to tear them to pieces most cruelly with their claws, as does the hawk when it carries off the chicks. And the glorious Saint Francis takes all the souls and gathers them together and covers them up [under his cloak], as does the hen to her chicks, for she shelters them under her wings to protect them from the hawk.)

But this provokes the anger of the demons, who engage Francis in combat until God intervenes to help the saint.[28]

Finally, the sermon uses the allegory of a convent to develop the motif of the friar or nun disobedient to his or her superiors. The convent is divided into good and evil nuns, and the latter manage to lure the former into sin. The efforts of the abbess and the chaplain to rectify the situation prove counterproductive. When they die, everyone—good nuns, bad nuns, the chaplain, and the abbess—ends up in Hell. The sad moral is that not only the friars, nuns, and superiors, but also the lay people of Juana's time, are like the sinful souls in her allegory.

The sermon for the Feast of Saint Francis constitutes a singular re-creation of the hen motif. According to Franciscan tradition (a tradition that would have been quite familiar to Mother Juana, given her status as a member of the Third Order), Francis's hen dream had a political thrust, for the saint himself interpreted it in terms of his concern for the spiritual direction of his nascent order. Mother Juana's sermon, on the other hand, associates the hen motif with the most celebrated episode in the life of the founder of her order, the imposition of the stigmata. That is to say, instead of having political overtones, the episode acquires theological overtones: Saint Francis is another Christ. His imitation of the Redeemer's life was so perfect that he was even privileged to bear His five wounds. For this reason Juana's sermon emphasizes the twin themes of redemption and salvation. The relation the sermon establishes between the stigmata/Passion and the hen image occurs likewise in Mother Juana's life in the stones episode. This helps to explain why Juana ignored the political implications the hen dream had in the *Legend of the Three Companions* and gave the hen motif theological overtones in her sermon. Both Saint Francis and Mother Juana are symbolic hens who imitate Christ: concretely, they imitate the Passion, thereby becoming co-redeemers.

At the beginning of the sermon for the Feast of Saint Francis, Christ observes that the Father often hides His secrets from the lettered and the learned while revealing them to the humble and lowly:

"Padre mío poderoso, graçias te fago porque ascondiste tus escondidos e altos secretos a los letrados e sabios e los revelaste a los sinples e despreçiados e humilldes." (*Conorte*, fol. 369v)

("My powerful Father, I give you thanks because you hid your secret and profound mysteries from the lettered and the wise and revealed them to the simple and despised and humble.")[29]

Although it is evident that the Lord refers to the case of Saint Francis, it is nonetheless to be understood that Mother Juana is yet another of these simple and humble souls. The same notion appears in the sermon devoted to the pains of Hell, in which the Lord says that sometimes the learned read the Scriptures without understanding them, only later to hear them explicated by an unlettered person, and then they understand:

E dixo su divina magestad que algunas vezes permite El que lean los letrados las Santas Escrituras e no las entiendan, e después las oigan dezir algunas personas sinples y entonçes las entienden mejor. E que por eso no deven despreçiar a ninguno que diga la palabra de Dios e la denunçie con caridad e amor de los próximos e deseo de su salvaçión. (*Conorte*, fol. 407v)

(And His Divine Majesty said that sometimes He allows the learned to read the Holy Scriptures and they do not understand them, and then [He lets] unlettered people hear them and then they [the learned] understand them [the Scriptures] better. And for this reason no one should look down on anyone who preaches the word of God and expounds it with charity and with love for his neighbors and with desire for their salvation.)

The passage suggests a relation between Mother Juana and those who preach the word of God for the benefit of their neighbors. In any case the sermon discredits book-learning and exalts the infused wisdom closely associated with the unlettered and particularly with women.[30] The lowly hen, although exalted by its association with Christ, symbolizes the humble creatures through which the Lord has chosen to reveal Himself.

Concurrently with its development of the hen image, the sermon for the Feast of Saint Francis re-creates another motif widely disseminated in the late Middle Ages, namely, the theme of the Madonna of the Cloak. This iconographic motif depicts the Virgin with a voluminous mantle that shelters a multitude of suppliants.[31] According to Emile Mâle, the image expresses "avec une clarté admirable, la confiance de tous les hommes en la puissance auxiliatrice de la Vierge."[32] The motif of the protective mantle was transferred to other saints, particularly to Saint Ursula, in order to express a similar confidence in their protective powers.[33] In the sermon for the Feast of Saint Francis the mantle motif is applied to the Seraphic Father himself, for his cloak covers the entire world. Thus, the maternal concern associated with the Virgin Mary is here transferred to Saint Francis. The association is not accidental, for it is suggested by the hen image: in the same way that the hen shelters her chicks under her wings, so the order protects its followers with the Franciscan habit.

The protective powers of the Franciscan habit are likewise highlighted in another section of the sermon for the Feast of Saint Francis. The Franciscan habit was invested with almost magical powers, for it was believed that to die in that habit ensured salvation.[34] The sermon introduces this belief when Christ explains that

por la horden de San Françisco se salvan muchas ánimas, así de honbres como de mugeres, por muchas maneras. Unos por tener devoçión con el ábito, por quanto es figura e semejança de la su cruz, e porque en persona que tenía tal ábito enprimió El las sus llagas. Esto fue en el glorioso San Françisco, el qual debaxo de aquel ábito las truxo por espaçio de dos años ascondidas, por lo qual tiene tantas indulgençias e perdones. E que otros se salvan porque tienen devoçión de morir en este santo ábito. (*Conorte,* fol. 370rv)

(many souls, of both men and women, are saved in many ways through the Franciscan order.[35] Some because of their devotion to the habit, inasmuch as it is a sign and likeness of His cross and because He impressed His wounds on a person who had such a habit. This was on the glorious Saint Francis, who bore them for two years hidden under that habit, for which reason it has so many indulgences and pardons. And others are saved because they adopt the pious practice of wearing this holy habit when they are dying.)

In the episode in which Saint Francis descends to Purgatory, those wearing his habit, as we have seen, are the only ones permitted to attempt to climb the ladders. Just as the hen protects her chicks under her wings, so Saint Francis protects his followers, sheltering them under his mantle or protecting them with his habit. In so doing Saint Francis plays a maternal, and thereby feminine role, for he appropriates the mantle associated with the Virgin Mary at the same time that he imitates the mother hen. If Saint Francis is both hen and mother because the pain of the stigmata is associated with the maternal and suffering humanity of Christ, in Juana's sermon it is Christ Himself who identifies the stigmata, a replication of the Passion, as the source of the protective powers of the Franciscan habit.

In effect, gender confusion is a persistent motif in the sermon for the Feast of Saint Francis. That androgyny is manifested first and foremost in the principal images that the sermon re-creates, namely, the hen and the mantle. As has been observed, the image of Christ as mother hen underscores His maternity, and therefore, His humanity, which is to say, Christ's feminine aspect. Similarly, the iconographic motif of the Madonna of the Cloak appears to have inspired the way in which the sermon treats the theme of the mantle/habit of Saint Francis: the saint protects those devoted to him as the Virgin does her followers, maternally sheltering them under her mantle. The section in which Christ asks His standard-bearer to bare his breast evokes a maternal Saint Francis, whose breasts are ever ready to nurture his followers.[36] But the feminization of Saint Francis culminates in the episode of his union with Christ, when the stigmata motif acquires conjugal overtones. At the moment of the impression of the stigmata Christ and Saint Francis are united as man and wife. It is obvious that here the motif of the soul as the bride of the Lord has been carried beyond a simple analogy. The metaphor has become literal, for Saint Francis appropriates the role of wife in order to be united in marriage to Christ. As Bynum observes, although cases of stigmatization are frequent in the lives of medieval holy women, they are scarce among male saints. In fact, Saint Francis was the only male saint to possess all five of Christ's wounds in visible stigmata.[37] It is perhaps no accident, then, that in Mother Juana's recreation of the stigmatization, Saint Francis is not a man but a "woman," since Christ has changed him into a figurative wife.

The connection between the hen image, Christ's Passion, and Saint Francis is manifested in yet another of Mother Juana's visions. Saint Dominic and Saint Francis appear to her and, smiling, the former says to the latter:

"Ya save Vuestra Sanctidad que esta hija que vos tanto amas en la caridad de Christo, la qual llamas vuestra gallinita, porque devajo de sus alas cría y ampara muchas ánimas de vuestra orden y aun también de la mía, parézeme, señor, a mí que es mi fija por derecho y no vuestra, pues fue primero llamada a mi orden y desseada de mis monjas y aun también de mis frailes y buscada con arto cuidado. E quando ella fue a tomar el ábito a vuestra bendita orden, si la mía estuviera tan çerca como la vuestra, señor, le tomara en la mía porque tenía notiçia d'ella y por esto deve ser mi hija." (*Vida*, fol. 76v)

("Your Holiness already knows that this daughter whom you love so much in Christ's love, the one whom you call your little hen because under her wings she nurtures and protects many souls of your order and even of mine too, it seems to me, my lord, that by right she is my daughter and not yours, for she was first called to my order and coveted by my nuns and even by my friars as well and sought out with extreme diligence.[38] And when she went to receive the habit in your blessed order, if mine had been as close by as yours, my lord, she would have received it in mine because she knew of it, and for that reason she should be considered my daughter.")

In the episode that follows, an episode that can be considered a moment of self-exaltation on Juana's part, the two friars dispute the spiritual paternity of the visionary. They finally agree that she should be allowed to choose between the two habits that they show her: Saint Dominic's white habit (which symbolizes the blessedness and purity of the Virgin Mary) or the bloody Franciscan habit (which symbolizes the Passion and the wounds of Christ). Juana answers that she prefers the habit stained with the blood of Christ's Passion (*Vida,* fol. 77r). In renouncing the white Dominican habit, associated with the Virgin Mary, Juana rejects the opportunity to identify with a strictly feminine figure. Instead, she chooses the habit associated with a more complex and ambiguous sexual identity: Saint Francis and Christ are biologically men, but Mother Juana's consistent strategy has been to emphasize the feminine features of such male figures. Moreover, in asserting her adherence to the Franciscan order, Juana also asserts her identification with Christ's suffering humanity, for through the stigmata Saint Francis is another Christ.

Until now this chapter has dealt with the series of redeeming figures—Christ, Mother Juana, Saint Francis—who suffer for the sake of the souls in Purgatory. But attention must also be paid to the recipients of these spiritual benefits, that is, to the souls themselves. The fate of the soul after death was an obsession for the faithful. There was nothing more terrible than sudden death, for dying while in mortal sin meant eternal damnation. Gaining Heaven was almost a secondary goal, because it was assumed that only the most holy would go directly to Paradise. Nearly all the saved would spend time in Purgatory, the length to be determined by the gravity of their sins. Naturally, the time spent in Purgatory could be shortened by means of certain earthly endeavors, for it was believed that the living had the power to help the dead. In order to complement the suffrages that the Church offered up for the sake of all the dead, it was important to have masses said, to pray, and to fast for the benefit of the deceased members of one's family.[39]

In view of the certainty that nearly everyone would end up in Purgatory, it is not surprising that the theme of Purgatory occupies so prominent a place in Mother Juana's visions. The nun's power to act directly for the benefit of the souls in Purgatory through the assumption of their sufferings would have been a boon to her contemporaries, concerned not only for their relatives' salvation but also for their own. This explains the poignancy of certain souls mentioned in the stones episode. Their great-great-grandchildren had forgotten all about them, and thus no living family members were offering suffrages to help shorten the purgation process. Those souls had already been in Purgatory for 300 or 500 years,[40] and it thus appears that the suffrages that the Church offered for all the dead were a rather slow means of succor. This underscores the importance of extraordinary redeeming figures like Mother Juana, who, with the maternal concern of the hen who looks after her chicks, could help such "orphan" souls to be released from Purgatory. This also explains the lesson to be drawn from the sermon for the Feast of Saint Francis: dying in the Franciscan habit is effective not only because of the habit's powers but also because that devotional practice could provide the opportunity to be rescued from Purgatory by the saint himself, when he descended to release those devoted to him.

Such extraordinary means of redemption aside, the quantitative aspect of salvation must have been a constant preoccupation for Juana's contemporaries. How many masses, how many prayers, how many alms were necessary to release a soul from Purgatory? This explains the importance of another power that Mother Juana possessed, namely, the ability, at least in certain cases, to discover the fate of the souls of the departed.[41] In this way the relatives of the deceased could find out whether the latter needed more suffrages. Thus, as a channel of divine grace, Mother Juana, although not canonized, offered one advantage that traditional saintly advocates lacked: she walked among the living, providing a sort of peephole into the next world. As a visionary, that is, a locus of spiritual power, Juana participated in two worlds, the terrestrial and the celestial. So it was that those faithful who wanted to know of events in the other world could deal directly with a person of flesh and blood, who was also endowed with exceptional spiritual powers.

There is, nonetheless, an episode that seems to demonstrate the limits imposed on the ability of holy women to save souls. Mother Juana's *Vida* (fol. 105rv) relates an episode much like Saint Francis's raids on Purgatory. Her guardian angel enjoyed the privilege of descending to Purgatory on Wednesdays, Fridays, and Saturdays. In a vision Juana accompanies him in order to watch over the "fish" he catches in the lake of Purgatory. The angel tosses a hook into the lake and, after praying to the Lord and to the Virgin Mary, pulls out several souls, which he turns over to Juana. The *Vida* explains that God has allowed him to rescue the souls most devoted to the Passion, souls that had performed some good work on Friday. It must be noted that only men—Saint Francis and Juana's guardian angel[42]—are permitted to carry out these raids on Purgatory. Women are allowed to assume the sufferings of such souls, but they may not play the more active role of descending to rescue them, unless it be in an auxiliary capacity. Nonetheless, this limitation on the role of women in the physical rescuing of souls from Purgatory is compensated for by their appropriation of the Christomimetic role of suffering for the release of the souls of the dead. Thus, in the long run the relative passivity of women turns out to be as effective as the activity of men.

Two events in Mother Juana's *Vida* (the stones episode and the Saint Francis vision) and the sermon for the Feast of Saint Francis share the image of the mother hen that looks after the well-being of her chicks. But the hidden link that joins the three episodes is Christ Himself, or more specifically, the imitation of Christ as Redeemer. Juana is another Christ because she takes upon herself the sufferings of the souls in Purgatory in order to effect their salvation. Even as Christ addressed Jerusalem before His Passion, comparing Himself to a hen, the redemptive role that Juana appropriates is actualized in the stones/eggs episode, which in her vision Saint Francis will relate explicitly to the hen image. For his part, Saint Francis, the second Christ, the only man whom Christ deemed worthy of receiving the stigmata, is the little brown hen who strives to help those devoted to him. When he descends to Purgatory, assuming the role of savior, the Seraphic Father likewise appropriates the role of figurative hen.

Sixteenth- and seventeenth-century readings of Juana's writings reveal not only what readers saw in her but also the preoccupations of their own times. Brother Antonio Daza devotes the greater part of chapter XVII of the first version of his biography of Mother Juana to the stones episode (Daza 1610, fols. 77r–83r). However, when Daza rewrites the book under Inquisitorial pressure, that chapter is suppressed. Evidently, the subject was considered too polemical in Counter-Reformation Spain. In effect, it appears that the question of Purgatory was to be handled with supreme delicacy. Daza's first version of his biography begins the chapter on Purgatory with the following warning:

Entramos en un piélago tan profundo de cosas que Dios reveló a santa Juana acerca de las ánimas y penas de Purgatorio, que por hallar particular dificultad en algunas, aunque todas llenas de suavidad y de dotrina muy provechosa para las almas, me hallo obligado en este capítulo, y en el que se sigue, ha hazer, no solo el oficio de historiador, sino también de parafrastre, y particulares escolios en las márgenes, declarando en ellos lo más dificultoso d'estas revelaciones. (Daza 1610, fol. 71rv)

(We enter so deep an ocean of things that God revealed to holy Juana concerning the souls and punishments of Purgatory, that because some of them are particularly knotty, although all are replete with sweetness and useful doctrine for souls, in this chapter and in the one that follows,[43] I find myself obliged to perform not only the task of biographer, but also that of exegete, and [to add] special annotations in the margins, to explain in them the most obscure aspects of these relevations.)

As has been pointed out, the second version of Daza's biography of Mother Juana omits, among other things, the stones episode. Daza justifies the suppression of certain revelations relating to Purgatory as follows:

Mas ha parecido convenir dexar de referir muchas d'ellas, porque aunque son muy conformes a la dotrina de los Santos, y a gran multitud de exemplos que en sus libros se hallan, no están escritos en la lengua vulgar, ni para que anden en manos de todos sin especial declaración. La que en rigor tienen semejantes casos, se explica propiamente por términos más adoptados para las escuelas, que para usar d'ellas en un libro como éste, que se escrive para que ande en las manos de todos; de los quales muchos hallarían piedra de escándalo en lo que bien y piadosamente entendido, es de mucha edificación. (Daza 1613, fol. 81r)

(But it has seemed suitable to omit many of them [such revelations], because although they are in accord with the doctrine of the saints and with a great many cases found in their writings, these are not written in the vulgar tongue nor should they be in everyone's hands without special commentaries. Those [commentaries] which are in fact usual in such cases are most properly couched in a language more appropriate to scholarly institutions than for use in a book like this that is written for everyone to read; many would find a source of scandal in that which, properly and piously understood, is of extreme edification.)

Later, when Brother Pedro Navarro wrote his own biography of Mother Juana, he included the stones episode, but he added to it certain annotations that seek to defend, among other things, the fact that souls can be punished in places other than Purgatory itself (Navarro, 518–521, 531–534).

The stones episode merited a similarly ambiguous fate during Juana's beatification process; it was one of the passages censured by Cardinal Bona in the course of his examination of Juana's *Vida*. Brother Coppons's defense, after rectifying several textual details, underscores that the episode in question is not a vision but the description of an actual experience.[44] He then quotes a series of authorities to prove that souls can be punished in places other than Purgatory (*Reparos,* fol. 37r).

The anonymous censor of the Escorial manuscript of *El libro del conorte* found nothing blameworthy in the sermon for the Feast of Saint Francis until the very end, in the passage that develops the allegory of the convent of nuns. He crossed out the offending passages, probably because he considered indecorous such a negative characterization of the religious life. Father Francisco de Torres in turn censured the censor in his marginal annotations (1567–1568) to the *Conorte*. For Torres the convent allegory "is a very worthy parable of our times and someone who knows them well composed it," for "we are mingled together in such a way, the good and the evil, superiors and subjects, that we do harm to one another." He goes on to lament that "there is so much of this in the religious orders" and that there is "desire for wealth, delights of the flesh, and points of honor among nobles and soldiers." [45] Finally, he prays that God will enlighten the heads of the religious orders, who are the candelabra of the Church.

Torres's desire to defend the *Conorte* leads him to comment even upon passages that escaped the censoring pen of his predecessor. For example, in the episode that precedes the convent allegory the Lord describes the punishment deserved by the friar (or nun) disobedient to his superior: he should walk with a stick in his mouth and a noose around his neck, dragging himself along the ground like a toad. Meanwhile, his companions should recite certain psalms for his benefit (*Conorte*, fol. 373rv). For Torres, the punishment is both just and exemplary and should be adopted by the Franciscan province of Castile. Nonetheless, in the twenty-three years he has been a friar, he has witnessed but a single case of obstinate disobedience (*Conorte*, fol. 373v).

The passage in the Saint Francis sermon in which the members of the Franciscan order appear in Heaven with clothing more resplendent than that worn by the other religious orders evokes a sort of prayer in which Torres praises the strictness of the Franciscan rule, asking the Lord's help in complying with such rigorous precepts (*Conorte*, fol. 370r). Apropos of the passage describing the salvation of some souls because their devotion to Saint Francis is greater than to any other saint, Torres observes that God does not mind if the faithful commend themselves to lesser saints than Saint Francis. The friar goes on to avow his own devotion to Saint Joseph and Saint John and, continuing with the personal note, remarks that it was twenty-three years ago to the day that he received the Franciscan habit in the very same monastery of San Juan de los Reyes in which he is recording these annotations. The commentary ends with a prayer in which Torres asks for the protection of Saint John (*Conorte*, fols. 370v–371r).

Father Torres's observations on the scene of the stigmatization of Saint Francis begin with an exhortation to future readers of the *Conorte*: "Note this with as worthy consideration as it deserves. And if this is not possible, do what you can." [46] God, observes Torres, has worked through Saint Francis so marvelous a miracle that it could not be duly extolled on all the paper in the world. He then goes on to develop the writing image, comparing the stigmatization to God's signature on the body of the saint: "not on dead paper but on living and virginal parchment did God seal and sign with living blood, and not with ink, that issued from His feet and hands and from within His pierced heart through His fortunate and blessed side."[47] Thus, Christ turned Saint Francis into "a living portrait of Himself and another He and a second Christ."[48] Finally, Torres expresses his full approval of the way in which the sermon re-creates the hen image: "How well explicated the hen simile!"[49]

In his evaluation of *El libro del conorte* during Juana's beatification process, Father Esparza criticizes the preeminent place that the Franciscan order occupies in the heavenly processions, the exaggerated devotion to the Franciscan habit, the relation the sermon establishes between the habit and the cross, Saint Francis's raid on Purgatory, and the convent allegory. Father Coppons's defense reiterates the argument that Juana's visions are a manifestation of the Lord's mercy and divine providence (*Reparos*, fols. 47v–50v).

It would be unfair to reduce the criticisms of the official examiners of Mother Juana's life and works to a question of quarrels among religious orders. The censors did not criticize the belief in the miraculous powers of the Franciscan habit because it was a Franciscan devotion, but because by the mid-seventeenth century such beliefs were considered superstitious and could no longer be tolerated. More significantly for the focus of this chapter, the censors never questioned the redemptive role that Mother Juana appropriated, nor did they criticize her appropriation of the hen image, closely associated with Saint Francis and with Christ Himself, to symbolize that role.

Notes

1. Isaiah 53:4 ("Surely he hath borne our infirmities, and carried our sorrows, and we have thought him as it were a leper, and as one struck by God and afflicted") was traditionally interpreted as a prophecy referring to Christ. See Saul Nathaniel Brody, *The Disease of the Soul: Leprosy in Medieval Literature* (Ithaca and London: Cornell University Press, 1974), 103–104.

2. Caroline Walker Bynum, *Holy Feast and Holy Fast: The Religious Significance of Food to Medieval Women* (Berkeley and Los Angeles: University of California Press, 1987), 171.

3. "en el hospital de sus caridosos miembros bastamiento de ánimas" (fol. 101r).

4. "mediante la Sancta Passión de Nuestro Señor e ayuda de la sancta madre iglesia . . . y por los méritos de esta bienabenturada" (*Vida*, fol. 101v).

5. "todas heran tan solas, que no havía quien d'ellas se acordase para les hazer bien sino el que la sancta madre iglesia haze en general por todos los difuntos" (*Vida,* fol. 103r).

6. "por nido como a páxaro o gallina que está empollando sus huebos por que d'ellos nazcan páxaros vivos o pollitos" (*Vida,* fol. 107r).

7. "Quiero yo besar los dolores del mi Señor Jesuchristo en ti, filia mea" (*Vida,* fol. 107r).

8. "mediante la Passión de Nuestro Señor Dios y los dolores que ella padesçía heran ayudadas y remediadas" (*Vida,* fol. 107r).

9. Cf. Luke 13:34. The image reappears in *El libro del conorte* in the sermon inspired by the Gospel in which Christ weeps over Jerusalem. Christ addresses the city, saying: "A ti digo, Gerusalén, que tienes los edifiçios muy altos e fuertes e todos tus fijos metidos debaxo de ti como la gallina los pollos" (fol. 306v). In a gloss the Lord explains that "quando El fizo este llanto sobre Gerusalén, no solamente llorava El por los que le avían de cruçificar e por los de aquella çibdad sola, mas llorava con grande conpasión e dolor sobre todas las ánimas que se avían de perder e condenar por sus propias culpas e maldades, así entonçes como agora" (fol. 307r).

10. The Gospel passage also raises the question of the prophet, whether of the Old Testament or Christ Himself, whose message was not accepted by the people. Did Juana identify with Christ in this way as well? That is to say, did she believe that the revelations she made known were misunderstood or unwelcome?

11. For the motif of Christ as mother, see André Cabassut, OSB, "Une dévotion médiévale peu connue. La dévotion à 'Jésus notre mère,'" *Revue d'Ascétique et de Mystique,* 25 (1949) 234–245; Eleanor McLaughlin, "'Christ My Mother': Feminine Naming and Metaphor in Medieval Spirituality," *Nashotah Quarterly Review,* 15 (1975) 228–248; and chapter 4, "Jesus as Mother and Abbot as Mother: Some Themes in Twelfth-Century Cistercian Writing," in Caroline Walker Bynum, *Jesus as Mother: Studies in the Spirituality of the High Middle Ages* (Berkeley and Los Angeles: University of California Press, 1982), 110–169.

12. Cf. the *Pagina meditationum* of Marguerite d'Oingt: "Ha! Domine dulcis Ihesu Christe, quis vidit unquam ullam matrem sic partu laborare! Sed cum venit hora partus tu fuisti positus in duro lecto crucis unde non poteras te movere aut vertere aut membra exagitare sicut solet facere homo qui patitur magnum dolorem" (*Les oeuvres de Marguerite d'Oingt,* ed. Antonin Duraffour, Pierre Gardette, and Paulette Durdilly [Paris: Les Belles Lettres, 1965], 78). Likewise, Julian of Norwich writes: "We know that our own mother's bearing of us was a bearing to pain and death, but what does Jesus, our true Mother, do? Why, he, All-love, bears us to joy and eternal life! Blessings on him! Thus he carries us within himself in love. And he is in labour until the time has fully come for him to suffer the sharpest pangs and most appalling pain possible—and in the end he dies" (*Revelations of Divine Love,* trans. Clifton Wolters [Baltimore: Penguin, 1966], 169).

13. The motifs of Christ as mother hen and of the Passion as a birthing are juxtaposed in Saint Anselm's "Prayer to Saint Paul": "And you, Jesus, are you not also a mother? / Are you not the mother who, like a hen, / gathers her chickens under her wings? / Truly, Lord, you are a mother; / for both they who are in labour / and they who are brought forth / are accepted by you. / You have died more than

they, that they may labour to bear. / It is by your death that they have been born, / for if you had not been in labour, / you could not have borne death; / and if you had not died, you would not have brought forth" (*The Prayers and Meditations of Saint Anselm*, trans. Sister Benedicta Ward [Harmondsworth: Penguin, 1973], 153).

14. With regard to the weakness motif, Saint Augustine seems to be recalling I Corinthians 9 : 22, in which Saint Paul says: "To the weak I became weak, that I might gain the weak. I became all things to all men, that I might save all." In like manner, Mother Juana, upon assuming the sufferings of the souls in Purgatory, becomes ill along with the spiritually ill.

15. Saint Augustine, *Expositions on the Book of Psalms*, trans. by members of the English Church, 6 vols. [Oxford: John Henry Parker, 1847–1857], 3 : 136. In his commentary on Psalm 90, Augustine says: "For the comparison of the hen to the very Wisdom of God is not without ground; for Christ Himself, our Lord and Saviour, speaks of Himself as likened to a hen; *O Jerusalem, Jerusalem, how often would I have gathered thy children together, even as a hen gathereth her chickens, and ye would not.* . . . There is nothing offensive in the name of the hen: for if you consider other birds, brethren, you will find many that hatch their eggs, and keep their young warm: but none that weakens herself in sympathy with her chickens, as the hen does. We see swallows, sparrows, and storks outside their nests, without being able to decide whether they have young or no: but we know the hen to be a mother by the weakness of her voice, and the loosening of her feathers: she changes altogether from love for her chickens: she weakens herself because they are weak. Thus since we were weak, the Wisdom of God made Itself weak, when the Word was made flesh, and dwelt in us, that we might hope under His wings" (*Expositions on the Book of Psalms* 4 : 286–287). By the late fifteenth century, the motif was widely disseminated in spiritual writings. In the *Vita Christi* of Ludolph of Saxony, for example, one reads: "Pone aquí Christo exemplo de la gallina para mostrar ser muy grande el amor que El tiene a su pueblo, porque la gallina parece tener entre todas las otras aves mayor afección e diligencia para criar e conservar sus pollos. Ca tan grande es el amor que les tiene que en la hora que los vehe enfermos, luego ella enferma e, defendiéndolos con sus alas, pelea contra el milano. E bien ansí la sabiduría de Dios, enferma por el recebimiento de la carne humana, nos ampara e defiende del enemigo e nos sostiene e conserva con su gracia" (*Segunda parte de la vida de Nuestro Señor Jesuchristo*, trans. Fray Ambrosio Montesino [Alcalá, 1503], fols. 249v–250r).

16. Saint Anthony of Lisbon comments upon Matthew 23 : 37 in a sermon for the Feast of Saint Stephen: "A galinha com pintainhos doentes põe-se doente. Ao chamá-los para comer, tanto clama que enrouquece. Ao protegê-los com as asas guarda-os do milhafre eriçado. Assim Cristo, sabedoria do Pai, adoeceu para acudir à nossa doença." Saint Anthony goes on to compare Christ's arms stretched out on the cross to the protective wings of the hen: "De igual modo, para nos proteger, estendeu na cruz os seus braços, como se foram asas, e, eriçado de espinhos, guardou-nos do diabo, que maquinava raptar-nos" (Santo António de Lisboa, *Obras completas*, trans. Henrique Pinto Rema, OFM, 3 vols. [Lisbon: Editorial Restauração, 1970], 3 : 195–196).

17. *Holy Feast*, 263.

18. *Legend of the Three Companions,* trans. Nesta de Robeck, in St. Francis of Assisi, *Writings and Early Biographies,* ed. Marion A. Habig (Chicago: Franciscan Herald Press, 1983), 948–949. The vision is also recounted in the *Floreto de Sant Francisco* (Seville, 1492), chapter 10, sig. B 2r. The *Floreto* was known to Mother Juana; her *Vida* (fol. 15r) mentions that the book had been read to her.

19. The Vatican manuscript combines into a single sermon (fols. 601v–617r) what are two contiguous sermons in the Escorial manuscript: that devoted to the exaltation of the Blessed Virgin, Saint Michael, and the other angels, and that devoted to Saint Francis.

20. The episode corresponds to Saint Francis's conversion. While the future saint was praying in the ruined church of Saint Damian in Assisi, Christ's voice addressed him from a crucifix, telling him to repair His church. Mother Juana transforms the ruined church of Saint Damian into a symbol of the entire Church, thus magnifying Saint Francis's role. For the conversion episode, see Thomas of Celano's *Second Life,* Book I, chapter VI, trans. Placid Hermann, OFM, in Saint Francis of Assisi, *Writings,* 370–371.

21. Mother Juana consistently uses the dialectal form *vilano* instead of the more usual *milano.* For example, in her sermon for the Feast of Saint Anne, the chicks (the sinners) take refuge under the fragrant squash plant (the Virgin Mary) so that the *vilano* (Satan) will not carry them away (*Conorte,* fol. 287rv). The motif of the kite or hawk that carries off the hen's chicks or eggs is frequent in biblical exegesis. For example, in his commentary on Psalm 90, Saint Augustine asks: "But in what manner does God defend thee? *He shall defend thee between His shoulders;* that is, He will place thee before His breast, that He may defend thee under His wings: if thou acknowledge thy weakness, in order that as a weak chicken thou mayest fly beneath the wings of thy mother, lest thou be seized by the kite; for the powers of the air, the devil and his angels, are kites, and their wish is to seize upon our weakness" (*Expositions on the Book of Psalms* 4:298–299). Saint Bonaventure's commentary on Luke 13:34 reads: "Comparatur autem *gallinae* in *conversatione,* quia gallina sua pietate et vigilantia movetur ad pullos et eos congregat et eos alis defendit contra rapacitatem milvi" (*Opera omnia,* 10 vols. [Quaracchi: Typographia Collegii S. Bonaventurae, 1882–1902], 7:357).

22. "Ven acá, mi amigo seráfico y alférez mío. Muéstrame tus tetas. . . . Mis tetas, Señor, helas aquí, que éstos que aquí traigo comigo fueron las tetas de mis deseos" (*Conorte,* fol. 370v). In the sermon for the Nativity of the Virgin Mary, the breasts of Our Lady represent her good wishes: "E naçerle tetas desde chiquita fue sinificaçión que dende que ella nasçió del vientre de su madre, tuvo tetas de buenos deseos e de muy grande amor con su Dios e Criador" (*Conorte,* fol. 337r).

23. "está desparzida por todo el mundo" (*Conorte,* fol. 370v).

24. The motif of Francis as mother appears in the saint's earliest biographies. Thomas of Celano relates how Brother Pacifico called the saint "dearest Mother"; in another passage Saint Francis refers to himself as mother: "I wish that my brothers would show themselves to be children of the same mother" (*Second Life,* Book II, chapters XCIX and CXXXVI, in Saint Francis, *Writings,* 473, 506). Saint Bonaventure observes that Francis "seemed to have a mother's tenderness in caring for the sufferings of those in misery" and that seeing a soul in sin caused him to weep

"so compassionately that he seemed to be in travail over them continually, like a mother in Christ" (*Minor Life*, trans. Benen Fahy, OFM, in Saint Francis, *Writings*, 809). Finally, the Acts of the Process of Canonization (1253) of Saint Clare relate a vision in which Saint Francis nursed Clare: "When she reached Saint Francis, the saint bared his breast and said to the Lady Clare: 'Come, take and drink.' After she had sucked from it, the saint admonished her to imbibe once again. After she did so what she had tasted was so sweet and delightful she in no way could describe it" (Clare of Assisi, *Early Documents*, trans. Regis J. Armstrong, OFM Cap. [New York: Paulist Press, 1988], 144). Marco Bartoli interprets Clare's vision as the expression of the saint's dependence on Francis, as when the child becomes psychologically one with the mother. See his "Analisi storica e interpretazione psicanalitica di una visione di S. Chiara d'Assisi," *Archivum Franciscanum Historicum*, 73 (1980) 457.

25. "así como faze la muger que está sugeta e obediente a su marido. . . . E que así fue tan ayuntado con el en aquella hora que le inprimió las sus çinco llagas de la manera que las resçibió en la cruz" (*Conorte*, fols. 370v–371r).

26. A gloss explains that the color red symbolizes the Passion, the color white the Virgin Mary.

27. *Vat.*, fol. 608v. The Vatican manuscript thus makes explicit the symbolic equivalence between the hen's wings and Saint Francis's cloak.

28. In this passage, Mother Juana reworks a tradition regarding the privilege that Christ granted Saint Francis when He gave him the stigmata: "I have given you the Stigmata which are the emblems of My Passion, so that you may be My standard-bearer. And as I descended into Limbo on the day when I died and took from there by virtue of these Stigmata of Mine all the souls that I found there, so I grant to you that every year on the day of your death you may go to Purgatory and by virtue of your Stigmata you may take from there and lead to Paradise all the souls of your Three Orders, that is, the Friars Minor, the Sisters, and the Continent, and also others who have been very devoted to you, whom you may find there, so that you may be conformed to Me in death as you are in life" (*Little Flowers of Saint Francis*, trans. Raphael Brown, in Saint Francis, *Writings*, 1450).

29. Christ's words are a paraphrase of Matthew 11:25 ("I confess to thee, O Father, Lord of heaven and earth, because thou hast hid these things from the wise and prudent, and hast revealed them to little ones") and of Luke 10:21.

30. The opposition between the book-learning of the scholar and the infused knowledge associated with the visionary experience of women also appears in the prologue of the *Libro de la oración* of Juana's contemporary Sister María de Santo Domingo: "Sus palabras de doctrina tan alta y tan provechosa, siendo mujer sin letras y aldeana, es gran confusión para los hombres y mucha mayor para los letrados, los quales contra ellos pueden mejor dezir por ella lo que Sant Augustín contra sí por Sant Antón: 'Levántanse los indoctos y arrebatan el cielo y nosotros con nuestra sciencia çapuzámonos en el infierno.' Digo, señor, indoctos por sciencia acquisita, porque de la sciencia infusa el Spíritu Sancto le dio tanta a esta su sierva quanta a otra." See the facsimile edition with an introductory study by José Manuel Blecua (Madrid: Hauser y Menet, 1948), sig. A 2r.

31. For the development of the iconographic motif of the Madonna of the Cloak, see Paul Perdrizet, *La Vierge de Miséricorde: Etude d'un thème iconographique* (Paris: A. Fontemoing, 1908). In Juana's Assumption sermon the Virgin appears

wearing a great mantle decorated with pearls and precious jewels. The mantle protects a large crowd of blessed souls, and the Lord explains that "el manto de su
gloriosa e sagrada madre hera tan grande que cabían debaxo d'él más de quinientos
mill millares de los que subieron a la postre. E tiniéndolos ella así a todos debaxo de
sus alas e manto, estava mayor que todo el mundo" (*Conorte*, fol. 318r). For the re-
creation of iconographic motifs in the visions of female mystics of the Middle
Ages, see C. Frugoni, "Le mistiche, le visioni e l'iconografia: rapporti ed influssi,"
in *Temi e problemi nella mistica femminile trecentesca* (Rimini: Maggioli Editore,
1983), 137–179.

   32. Emile Mâle, *L'Art religieux de la fin du Moyen Age en France*, 3d ed. (Paris:
Armand Colin, 1925), 201.

   33. Perdrizet, *La Vierge de Miséricorde*, 220–222.

   34. For the practice of donning a religious habit *in articulo mortis*, see Louis
Gougaud, *Dévotions et pratiques ascétiques du Moyen Age* (Paris: Desclée de Brouwer
and P. Lethielleux, 1925), 129–142.

   35. A fifteenth-century Castilian manuscript enumerates the privileges and indulgences granted to those devoted to the Franciscan order. See Atanasio López,
OFM, and Lucio María Núñez, OFM, "Descriptio codicum franciscalium biblio-
thecae ecclesiae primatialis toletanae," *Archivo Iberoamericano*, 1 (1914) 548–549.

   36. The sermon highlights the symbolic equivalence between the maternal
images of the mantle and the breasts through the verbal parallelism between the
two divine commands: "Muéstrame tus tetas" and "Muéstrame tu manto" (*Conorte*,
fol. 370v).

   37. Bynum, *Holy Feast*, 200.

   38. The *Vida* (fol. 6r) recounts how one of Juana's aunts, a Dominican nun,
had asked her father and relatives to allow her to enter the Dominican convent.
Her family refused, for God had reserved her for another order.

   39. For an overview of the suffrages that the living offered for the dead as
expounded by Saint Thomas Aquinas and his disciples, see Jacques Le Goff, *La
naissance du Purgatoire* (Paris: Gallimard, 1981), 367–370.

   40. In Juana's sermon "The Preeminences of Friday" angels plead for the release of souls who owe thousands of years in Purgatory (*Conorte*, fol. 239r).

   41. *Vida*, fols. 52r–53r, 75r–76r, 107r–108r.

   42. Although angels are theoretically sexless, it is obvious that Juana and her
companions consider her guardian angel to be a masculine being.

   43. Brother Daza refers to the stones episode.

   44. "Advertendo in primis, quod haec, de quibus mentio sit in praesenti, non
sunt imaginariae representationes, sicut fere omnia supra dicta, sed sunt verae, et
reales rerum manifestationes, vel ad earum modum narratae in textu" (*Reparos*, fol.
36v).

   45. "es muy dina parábola de nuestros tiempos y quien los conoce bien la
dixo . . . de tal manera estamos mezclados malos y buenos, perlados y súbditos,
que los unos y los otros nos dañamos . . . en las religiones ay tanto d'esto . . . codi-
cia de hacienda, deleites de la carne y puntos de honra entre cavalleros y soldados"
(*Conorte*, fol. 373v).

   46. "Esto nota con tan dina consideratión como merece. Y si esto no te es
possible, haz lo que pudieres" (*Conorte*, fol. 371r).

47. "Dios no en papel muerto sino en pergamino vivo y virginal selló y firmó con sangre viva, y no con tinta, que salía de sus pies y manos y de dentro de su coraçón partido por su dichoso y bienaventurado costado" (*Conorte*, fol. 371r). Torres applies to Saint Francis the commonplace comparison between the body of the crucified Christ and a manuscript. For example, Jordan of Saxony writes: "This law undefiled, since it cleanses defilement, is charity, which you will find beautifully written, when you look on Jesus our Saviour, stretched out on the Cross as a parchment, written in purple, illuminated with his holy blood. Where, dearest, I ask you, can the lesson (*lectio*) of charity be so well learnt?" (quoted in Beryl Smalley, *The Study of the Bible in the Middle Ages* [1952; Notre Dame: University of Notre Dame Press, 1964], 283). The application of the manuscript simile to Saint Francis appears as early as a poem of 1226 on the stigmatization. See John V. Fleming, *From Bonaventure to Bellini: An Essay in Franciscan Exegesis* (Princeton: Princeton University Press, 1982), 13.

48. "un retrato suyo bivo y otro El y segundo Christo" (*Conorte*, fol. 371r).

49. "¡Qué bien esplicada la conparatión de la gallina!" (*Conorte*, fol. 370r).

III. The Guitar of God

The image of the visionary as a musical instrument is traditional in the Fathers of the Church; it most often appears with reference to the Old Testament prophets. Athenagoras, writing in about 177, refers to "the Spirit of God who moves the lips of the Prophets as if they were musical instruments." The prophets spoke out, "the Spirit making use of them as a flautist might play upon his flute."[1] Such imagery involves necessarily the equally traditional motif of God as a musician. Similarly, Hippolytus, in his *Treatise on Christ and Antichrist* (ca. 200), compares the prophets to musical instruments and Christ to a plectrum that causes them to speak: "For these fathers were furnished with the Spirit, and largely honoured by the Word Himself; and just as it is with instruments of music, so had they the Word always, like the plectrum, in union with them, and when moved by Him the prophets announced what God willed."[2]

In the Middle Ages such musical images were taken up by female mystics when they too wished to portray themselves as passive instruments of God's revelation. At the end of her *Liber vitae meritorum* (1163), Hildegard of Bingen warns her readers not to tamper in any way with what she has written, for her words are divinely inspired. Hildegard has been but God's instrument, for such miraculous phenomena are not wrought by her own power but by that of God, as when a string is touched by a harpist, it does not of itself produce the sound but does so through the touch of the player.[3] In a letter to another female mystic, Saint Elizabeth of Schönau, Hildegard ponders the nature of divine inspiration, comparing the recipient of such miraculous favors to a trumpet "that merely produces sounds but does not cause them; someone else blows into it, so that it will produce the sound."[4]

Mother Juana de la Cruz uses such musical images to describe her humble role in the reception of her visions: she is but the passive instrument of the divine will.[5] Significantly, such moments of personal self-referentiality coincide with moments of textual self-referentiality in the revelations, that is, those passages in which Juana from within the text of her sermons asserts and defends their divine inspiration, for God is the ultimate source of her authority. The beginning of the sermon for the Feast of the Invention of the Holy Cross explains why such revelations have been manifested in the first place. God, says Juana, has noted that the need for His manifestation is great, for faith and charity have become lost on earth, and the Eucharist is treated with irreverence.

viendo El cómo se perdía Dios en la tierra e se perdía la fe y el amor y caridad con El e con los próximos, e viendo quán sin reverençia es tratado en el sacramento, e viendo las grandes eregías e abominaçiones, demandó liçençia al Padre çelestial para venir a fablar en esta boz. En la qual boz no venía tan encubierto que no cono-çiesen claramente que hera El, Dios verdadero, por quanto traía boz formada, como faze el tañedor quando tañe, que no suena su boz mas la de la flauta o tron-peta con el resollo que le da. Assí, El dando el soplo de su boca, fablava ella en la su graçia e virtud. E por semejante fablava El mesmo en esta boz como faze el que fabla por la zebretana, que suenan las palabras claras. (*Conorte*, fols. 278v–279r)

(seeing how God was being lost on earth and faith and love and charity toward Him and toward one's neighbors were being lost, and seeing how He was being treated so irreverently in the Eucharist, and seeing the great heresies and abomina-tions, He asked the heavenly Father's permission to come to speak in this voice. In which voice He did not come so concealed that they would not clearly recognize that it was He, the true God, inasmuch as He spoke in an audible voice, as when the musician plays, it is not his own voice that sounds, but the voice of the flute or trumpet by means of the breath that he blows through it. Thus, with Him supply-ing the breath of His mouth, she spoke through His grace and power. And like-wise He spoke in this voice as does he who speaks through an ear-trumpet,[6] for the words come through clearly.)

God's speaking through Juana's voice is thus explicitly compared to a mu-sician playing upon his instrument. Therefore, when the Lord underscores the divine inspiration of the sermons by simply asserting that they are His very words, Juana abdicates any authorial role by emphasizing her func-tion as the passive instrument of God's revelation.

In the sermon for the Feast of the Transfiguration the musical image reappears in a similar context, namely, the explanation of God's decision to reveal Himself at that time and in that way. The Lord has come to speak through Juana because of His desire that all be saved. He has also come to invite everyone to the spiritual nuptials and to warn that all must do pen-ance, for the kingdom of God is near. The elucidation of the major themes of His message again makes use of the flute image:

E tanbién venía a tañer con esta boz como faze el tañedor que tañe la flauta e la faze sonar con el resollo que le da, por quanto El es el gran tañedor que sabe fazer muchos sones. Porque quando El fablava de su sagrada Passión, conbidava a llanto. E quando fabla[va] de las penas del infierno e de purgatorio, conbidava a temor e a contriçión. E quando fablava de su gran misericordia, conbidava a esperança. E quando fablava del reino de los çielos e de los grandes bienes e consolaçiones que en él ay, convidava a gozo e alegría. (*Conorte*, fol. 301r)

(And He also came to sound forth with this voice as does the musician who plays the flute and makes it sound with the breath that he supplies, for He is the great musician who is able to make many sounds. Because when He spoke of His sacred Passion, He invited mourning. And when He spoke of the pains of Hell and Purgatory, He invited fear and contrition. And when He spoke of His great mercy, He invited hope. And when He spoke of the kingdom of Heaven and of the great riches and comforts it contains, He invited joy and happiness.)

This amplification of the analogy between the visionary and a musical instrument necessarily involves as well the traditional motif of God as musician.

The musical image returns in a similar context of self-referentiality at the end of the sermon for Saint Luke's Day. The Lord notes that it is out of goodness and charity that He has chosen to perform such marvels as His speaking through Juana's mouth:

E dixo el Señor que como agora en este tienpo amostrase El en la tierra por sola su bondad e caridad tan grandes maravillas e benefiçios, assí como hera en tener El por bien de desçender a fablar por la boca d'esta bienaventurada sierva suya, así como en boz de tronpeta muy sonante e provechossa para los que de buena voluntad e con fe e amor lo oían. (*Conorte*, fol. 384v)

(And the Lord said that since in these times He was manifesting such great marvels and favors on earth only out of His goodness and charity, as in His consenting to come down to speak through the mouth of His blessed servant, as with the voice of a trumpet resounding and beneficial for those who heard it with good will and with faith and love.)

The musical image is introduced to emphasize both the salubrious nature of the message and Juana's passive role in the determination of that message. The trumpet recurs in the sermon "Concerning Heavenly Symbols":

Fablando el Señor, declarando e diziendo las cosas e figuras siguientes, primeramente dixo que es tan grande el amor que El tiene a los pecadores que no solamente viene en el sacramento cada vez que es llamado con las palabras de la consagración, mas que tanbién venía en esta boz quando hera su voluntad, así como en boz de tronpeta, amonestando e alunbrando y enseñando todo lo que convenía para salvaçión e provecho de las ánimas. (*Conorte*, fols. 348v–349r)

(When the Lord was speaking, uttering and expounding upon the following matters and symbols, He said first of all that His love for sinners is so great that not only does He come in the Eucharist every time He is called by the words of the consecration, but that He also came in this voice when it was His will, as with the voice of a trumpet, warning and enlightening and teaching all that was necessary for salvation and the benefit of the souls.[7])

The trumpet appears as a traditional symbol of preaching in medieval dictionaries of commonplace scriptural allegories.[8] Such a connection is particularly relevant to Mother Juana because thus far the references to herself as a trumpet have occurred within the context of what people referred to as her sermons. Preaching was, needless to say, a male prerogative, but Juana's mystical experience provided an acceptable justification for her taking on simultaneously the sanctioned female role of visionary and the canonically male role of preacher.[9] Despite her lack of priestly status, Juana was thus authorized to perform an ecclesiastical function otherwise denied to women. The association between the visionary experience, the delivery of sermons, and the traditional image of the trumpet provided further validation of her usurpation of the male prerogative of preaching.

In the passages quoted thus far, the musical images have occurred in moments of self-consciousness in which Juana seeks to underscore her passive role in the revelation of her sermons and simultaneously to defend their divine inspiration. Specifically, Juana has been compared to a wind instrument, namely, a flute or trumpet. A significant variant of such musical images informs the vision that will constitute the nucleus of this chapter (see Appendix G) because Juana becomes not a wind instrument, but a stringed instrument.

The vision begins as Juana is conversing with her guardian angel, Saint Laruel, who is conveniently absent from treatises on angelology.[10] Male authority figures are rare in Juana's biography, which, significantly, was composed by a female companion.[11] The confessor, usually omnipresent in the lives of such holy women—he often serves as amanuensis and biographer as well—is scarcely mentioned.[12] Otherwise, men appear only when absolutely necessary, and then in a radically polarized fashion: they either function as straw men, that is to say, doubters or scoffers who exemplarily come to recognize Juana's holiness, or they appear as beneficent helper figures. At first glance, as the ostensible explicator of the visions recounted in the *Vida* and despite his technically androgynous status, the angel Saint Laruel functions as a male authority figure; however, since only Juana can see and hear him, she herself becomes the ultimate authority for his interventions.[13] The discreet presence of her guardian angel in the *Vida* visions avoids a completely unmediated contact with the divine and simultaneously allows Juana to exercise a degree of control over that mediating figure, for it is she who reports the words of Saint Laruel.[14]

The revelation proper beings with a coup de theatre that is typical of the morphology of Juana's visions: the usually resplendent clothing of her angel suddenly changes into that of a poor, mendicant pilgrim. When she asks what has caused this metamorphosis, Saint Laruel explains that God has sentenced Juana to numerous trials and tribulations and that he has donned that outfit to beg the Virgin Mary and the saints to offer their prayers as alms for Juana. As a test of Juana's patience in the face of adversity, it is God's will to break that organ or trumpet through which He is wont to speak and to reduce it to a sickly and painful state:

le plaçía y hera su voluntad de quebrar aquel órgano o trompeta en qu'El hablava e le quería mudar e trasmudar en otro estado que pareçiese muy menospreçiado y enfermo y muy lastimado e doloroso e quexoso, que casi no pareçiese el que solía. E hablava con la mesma, diziendo: "Juanica, tú heres este órgano que digo, que quiero que seas despreçiada e abilitada e gravemente atormentada por probar tu paçiençia." (*Vida,* fol. 59r)

(it pleased Him and was His will to break that organ or trumpet through which He spoke and He wished to change and transform it into another state so that it would appear quite scorned and sickly and very pitiful and doleful and plaintive, in such a way that it would no longer seem its former self. And He spoke to her, saying: "Juanica, you are this organ of which I speak, for I wish you to be scorned and disgraced and gravely tormented in order to test your patience.")

A few days later Juana's body becomes completely paralyzed, her joints painfully twisted; others must feed her. When she asks her guardian angel the reason for this, he reminds her that when God caused stigmata-like marks to appear on her hands and feet, she begged Him to take them away because she felt herself unworthy.[15] Now He has determined to impress upon her the pain and suffering of His Passion.

This prophecy is realized on Friday, June 21, the vigil of the Feast of Saint Achatius and his Ten Thousand Companions. In a vision Juana sees a field in which the companions of Saint Achatius are being crucified while the crucified Christ comforts them, saying that since He suffered such a death for their sake, it is only right that they should suffer similarly for Him. Juana is terrified, and when she asks her guardian angel to explain the vision, he replies that she is to share the same fate. Christ Himself suddenly appears before her and asks if she wishes to taste that fruit. She responds that she will do whatever He wills. Christ then embraces her, placing His feet, His knees, the palms of His hands, His head, and finally His entire body against hers. Juana experiences the sensation of a multitude of sharp, burning nails piercing her body, and she hears a terrible hammering sound, similar to that heard in the performance of Passion plays. She becomes filled with Christ's presence and the taste and sweetness of His love:

Entonçes miróme el Señor y dixo: "¿Quieres tú gustar de esta fruta?" Yo respondí: "Señor, quiera vuestra sancta voluntad e no más ni menos." Entonçes abrazóme el Señor y puso sus pies en mis pies y sus rodillas en mis rodillas—todo las alimpió— e sus palmas en las mías e su caveza e cuerpo todo junto con el mío. Y quando esto hizo, fue tanto lo que sentí que me parezía entravan en mí muchedumbre de clavos muy agudos e ardientes. E sonava estruendo enrededor a manera de quando hazen la remembranza de Nuestro Señor, dando martilladas. Inchávase con la presencia suya e con el gusto y dulçor de su amor. (*Vida*, fol. 60r)

(Then the Lord looked at me and said: "Do you wish to taste this fruit?" I answered: "Lord, as you desire and neither more nor less." Then the Lord embraced me and placed His feet on my feet and His knees on my knees—He purified them completely—and His palms on mine and His head and body against mine. And when He did this, what I felt was so intense that it seemed that there was a multitude of very sharp, burning nails piercing me. And there sounded a din all around as when they perform a Passion play, striking blows with a hammer. It [my body] was filled with His presence and with the taste and sweetness of His love.)

The pain is intense, but still greater is the pain she experiences upon recovering her bodily senses. She feels as if the limbs, veins, and joints of her body have become like the pegs and strings on a guitar and that Christ is playing upon that instrument and making harmonious music:

Parézeme veo todos los miembros e benas e coyunturas de mi cuerpo hechas como a manera de cuerdas e teclas o clavijas de vihuela e a Nuestro Señor tocarlas con sus sacratíssimas manos, atañer con ellas a manera de instrumento o vihuela e azer muy dulçe e suave son de armonía. (*Vida*, fol. 60r)

(I seem to see all the limbs and veins and joints of my body transformed into the strings and keys or pegs of a guitar and Our Lord playing on them with His most holy hands, playing on them as upon an instrument or guitar and making a very sweet and gentle harmonious sound.)

When the pitch rises, the pain increases, while the low notes lessen the pain. As He plays, Christ sings words of great consolation.

The vision is a striking variant of the traditional image of the body as a musical instrument. It is all the more remarkable because the musical image is interwoven with a series of other traditional motifs that are in perfect harmony with the context of the vision. The component motifs include: the visionary as musical instrument, God as musician, the body and/or soul as musical instrument, suffering as music, Christ's Passion as a musical event, the embracing of Christ, the tasting of Christ, and illness as a context for the mystical experience. It is precisely these analogues and resonances that will be explored in the rest of this chapter.

Christ's embrace literally impresses upon Juana the experience of the Passion. In point of fact, the touching of God or the mystical experience as physical contact with Him are frequent motifs in devotional texts. An embrace similar to that in Juana's vision was experienced by Angela of Foligno, who on Holy Saturday of 1294 had a vision in which she imagined herself embracing Christ in the sepulcher:

first she kissed Christ's breast . . . and then she kissed His mouth, from which (she said) she received a marvelous and ineffably delectable odor, which she breathed from His mouth. . . . And then she rested her cheek against Christ's cheek, and Christ placed His hand on her other cheek and drew her toward Him. And this faithful servant of Christ heard Him say these words: "Before I was laid in this sepulcher I held you tightly so."[16]

Angela's and Juana's visions share not only the detailed physiological description of the divine embrace, but also the connection between the embrace and the Passion of Christ.

The experience of physical contact with God is found in the writings of both male and female mystics. Nonetheless, Bynum sees such sensual encounters as one of the ways in which holy women identified with Christ's suffering humanity. *Imitatio Christi* for such women meant "union—fusion—with that ultimate body which is the body of Christ. The goal of religious women was thus to realize the *opportunity* of physicality. They strove not to eradicate body but to merge their own humiliating and painful flesh with that flesh whose agony, espoused by choice, was salvation. Luxuriating in Christ's physicality, they found there the lifting up—the redemption—of their own."[17] Thus, while Juana shares with other late-medieval holy women the desire to suffer and thereby to redeem, her *imitatio Christi* goes beyond merely offering her suffering for the sake of the souls in Purgatory: she will actually undergo a passion like Christ's, thus more fully realizing her identification with Him.

The mystical experience as the tasting of God is but suggested in Juana's vision when Christ invites her to taste the fruits of the Passion. Nonetheless, such food motifs are central to feminine spirituality of the

Middle Ages. Bynum has commented upon the curious reversal that takes place in the case of the tasting of God: woman, whose social role it was to prepare and serve food, becomes the recipient, while Christ assumes the "feminine" role of nurturing provider of food.[18] Indeed, the motif of a nurturing Christ is frequent in Juana's other visions.[19] In the Epiphany sermon, for example, the metaphor found in Ezechiel 34:14 ("I will feed them in the most fruitful pastures") is dramatized in Juana's typically literal fashion. As Christ repeats the words of the gospel, wine flows from the wound in His side while water flows from His right hand. Another precious fluid issues from His left hand, exquisite foods come out of the wounds on His feet, and loaves of bread and pastries emerge from the wounds and scourge-marks on His body. Christ addresses the blessed with great love, inviting them to eat and drink, for it is written that He is the living bread (John 6:51) and the true vine (John 15:1):

El Señor les respondió, diziendo: "Agora, mis amigos, yo os hartaré e os recrearé, que escrito es que en mí son hallados pastos de holgança e deleite e abastamiento." E diziendo estas palabras, a desora se le abrió la llaga de su sagrado costado e le manava d'él un caño de vino muy eçelente e oloroso e suave. E caía en todos los cálices e taças e henchíalo todo. E de la mano diestra le salía un caño de agua muy clara e olorosa, e por semejante caía en todos los cálices e taças e aguava el vino e tenplávalo. E de la mano siniestra le manava otro licor muy preçioso e oloroso e de las llagas de los pies le salían muchedunbre de manjares. E luego voló en alto e púsose sobre las mesas, e a desora salieron de todas las llagas e açotes que padeçió en su sagrado cuerpo muchedunbre de panes e roscas muy rezientes e dulçes e sabrosos. E hablávalos El muy amorosa e beninamente, diziendo: "Tomad, mis amigos, e comed y enbriagaos de las dulçedunbres e manjares de mí mesmo, que escrito es de mí que yo soy pan e vino muy dulçe e manjar muy sabroso de los que me saben gustar. E tanbién es escrito que yo soy pan vivo que desçendí del çielo e yo soy verdadera vid e vosotros los sarmientos." (*Conorte,* fol. 50v)

(The Lord answered them, saying: "Now, my friends, I will satisfy you fully and refresh you, for it is written that in me are found pastures of pleasure and delight and abundance." And as He said these words, suddenly the wound in His sacred side opened and there came forth a flow of very excellent and fragrant and sweet wine. And it flowed into the chalices and cups and filled them all up. And from His right hand there came forth a flow of clear and fragrant water, and likewise it fell into all the chalices and cups and watered and tempered the wine. And from His left hand there issued another very precious and fragrant liquid and from the wounds on His feet came a multitude of viands. And then He flew up on high and placed Himself above the tables, and suddenly from all the wounds and scourge-marks that He suffered on His entire body came forth a multitude of freshly baked and sweet and delectable loaves of bread and pastries. And He spoke to them very lovingly and kindly, saying: "Take, my friends, and eat and become drunk with the sweetness and food of myself, for it is written of me that I am bread and very sweet wine and a very savory food for those who know how to taste of me. And it is also written that I am the living bread that descended from Heaven and I am the true vine and you the branches.")

Christ's body and blood have literally become the bread and wine of the Eucharist. The faithful literally eat the bread of His flesh and drink the wine of His blood. As Bynum observes, to eat God meant "to become suffering flesh with his suffering flesh; it was to imitate the cross."[20] Thus, in the guitar vision when Juana accepts the invitation to taste the fruit of the Passion, her flesh becomes Christ's suffering flesh, her body the cross.

Medieval Christianity adopted the Pythagorean notion of the harmony of the spheres, and the theme of God as a musician who plays the world lute became a frequent metaphor for the concord of the universe.[21] The final image of Juana's vision is of Christ as musician, who plays upon the nun's body and sings to her. Juana assigns to Christ the attributes of the secular lovers of her time: Christ the musician-lover is assimilated to the serenading cavalier of the sixteenth century. Juana combines here the traditional images of God the musician, Christ the lover-knight,[22] and the nun as bride of Christ,[23] a constellation of images that reappears in a brief vision preserved in a volume of miscellaneous revelations and traditions from the convent where the visionary lived. As proof of how much the Lord loves the convent, Juana reminds her companions that she has often seen the Lord Bridegroom, dressed in courtly finery, strolling through the cloister, playing upon a golden guitar, and singing most sweetly:

> Esta casa, Padre,
> es de mi santa madre.
> Esta casa y este lugar,
> no le entiendo olvidar. (*Casa*, fol. 17r)

> (This house, O Father,
> belongs to my holy mother.
> I do not intend to forget
> this house and this place.)

Although the verses are infelicitous, they do nonetheless evoke the image of Christ as serenading lover. As is typical in the revelations of Mother Juana, a traditional religious metaphor is made literal as Christ is cast in the role of a sixteenth-century lover who comes courting with guitar in hand.[24]

Just as God "tuned" the universe, so He could "tune" the individual soul so that it would harmonize with His divine will. Music and its effect on both body and soul thus furnished a set of ready-made religious metaphors: harmony was associated with a state of grace, while disharmony denoted a state of sin. The body or soul as a musical instrument that must be tuned, that is to say, harmonized with God's will, is a frequent motif. Thus, in the guitar vision Juana speaks of the purifying effect of Christ's embrace on the body that will become a musical instrument (*Vida,* fol. 60r).

A similar reference to the cleansing and harmonizing effect of Christ's Passion on the soul can be found in the writings of Juana's contemporary Sister María de Santo Domingo, who experienced a mystical rapture upon hearing a clavichord or harpsichord played. Her companions heard her exclaim:

O sweet and good Jesus! Who but He who as He created them was able to tune and play them can recognize souls out of tune? What sin untuned, your blood tuned. . . . O good Jesus, when I heard that music playing, my heart was hardened and my soul was saddened, as I saw that I was not in tune so that you might play sweetly upon me. The instrument of my soul was not in concord so that you might touch it with the gentle hand of your love, of your will, for I had not come unto you so that the strings of its virtues might be cleansed with your most holy blood.[25]

Here, the soul is clearly viewed as a musical instrument that must be tuned so that Christ can play upon it.[26] More specifically, as in Juana's guitar vision, it is Christ's Passion that accomplishes that cleansing/tuning effect.

It is not unusual to find the Passion itself described in musical terms. In his commentary on Psalm 56:9, Saint Augustine evokes the Passion as taking place to a musical accompaniment:

The flesh therefore working things divine, is the psaltery: the flesh suffering things human is the harp. Let the psaltery sound, let the blind be enlightened, let the deaf hear, let the paralytics be braced to strength, the lame walk, the sick rise up, the dead rise again; this is the sound of the Psaltery. Let there sound also the harp, let Him hunger, thirst, sleep, be held, scourged, derided, crucified, buried.[27]

For Saint Bonaventure, Christ, the living vine stretched out on the cross, becomes a harp: "Your Spouse has become a Harp, the wood of the cross being the frame and His body, extended on the wood, representing the chords."[28] In the revelation of Sister María de Santo Domingo to which I have previously referred, Christ's wounds are music to the sinner,[29] while the blood that flows from the crucified Christ is a sweet melody:

so later at the moment of your death another four, your most sacred hands and feet, torn open for us,[30] emitted compassionate and loving cries to sinners that we should clasp you, take courage, and rejoice in you. Your most holy blood is the gentle song of these four that invites us with a sweet melody to harmonize our souls with you so that you may tune us with it and so that you may play upon us and dwell within us.[31]

The association between music and the Passion was developed along rather different lines by such authors as Clement of Alexandria, who saw Christ as an Orpheus figure, the singer of the New Song of Christianity,[32] a connection further developed by Christian interpreters of pagan myths in the *Ovide moralisé* tradition, who viewed Orpheus as Christ, Eurydice as the human soul, the serpent as Satan, and Orpheus's lyre as the cross.[33] Thus, in the allegorized myths appended to Martín de Reyna's Castilian translation of Jacobus de Cessolis's *De ludo scachorum*, Orpheus is Christ and his lyre is the cross:

What is the melody of Orpheus's voice but the sermons that Christ delivered and His marvelous teachings? What is the harp He played but the mysteries of the Passion He received on the cross, which was the true harp, whose strings were the sinews, bones, and flesh of Our Redeemer, stretched out like the strings on a guitar on the tree of the cross?[34]

F. P. Pickering observes that the identification of the cross with a harp became commonplace.[35] In Spain, the cross is usually identified with the guitar or vihuela. Mendicant preaching was doubtlessly crucial in the dissemination of the motif, as is evinced in a sermon by the Dominican friar Juan López de Salamanca (d. 1479), who combines the notion of the cross as a musical instrument with the notion of David as a prefiguration of Christ: "For just as David, by playing his guitar, cured Saul who was possessed, so Our Lord, playing upon the guitar of the Cross with sharp cries, was to heal the world that was all twisted."[36] In a sermon by Saint Vincent Ferrer (d. 1419), David's guitar is similarly associated with Christ's Passion: "Saul was possessed, and sometimes the devil seized him and so greatly disturbed him that he [the devil] drove him completely mad. And David, when he saw that, would go and take up his guitar and play it for him. . . . Now, where did that power come from? Not from the guitar but from the sign of that which the guitar signified, and it signified the Passion of Jesus Christ."[37]

Reminiscences of the Passion are to be found throughout Juana's guitar vision. It was experienced on a Friday, the day of the Passion, which was also the vigil of the Feast of Saint Achatius and his Ten Thousand Companions, who suffered death by crucifixion. Such artists as Dürer depicted the martyrdom of the Ten Thousand as a calque of the Passion.[38] Christ's embrace feels to Juana as if the nails of the Passion were being driven into her body. The loud noise she hears reminds her of the hammering sounds that accompanied the episode of the Crucifixion in Passion plays. Although the canonical Gospels do not refer explicitly to such a din, the connection between musical instruments and the Passion is established in Juana's Holy Thursday sermon, which contains a novelesque account of Jesus' betrayal in which the Roman soldiers arrive at the Garden of Gethsemane with horns, trumpets, and clanking armor (*Conorte*, fol. 151v).[39] Ultimately, in the guitar vision Juana becomes the cross that Christ played to redeem humankind, and yet, she is simultaneously identified with Christ Himself as her own body relives the Passion.

The guitar vision is but the climax of the identification between Mother Juana and the suffering humanity of Christ that she and other holy women sought throughout their lives. Bynum has pointed out that the reception of the stigmata and analogous religious experiences are a distinguishing feature of late-medieval women's spirituality, for among males only Saint Francis was believed to possess all five of Christ's wounds in visible stigmata.[40] Such women seek a literal *imitatio Christi:* their bodies become God's suffering body. In Juana's case her identification with the suffering and therefore redeeming humanity of Christ was seen to go back to even before her conception, for her official biography opens, not with her birth, but with the founding of the convent whose abbess she would later become. In 1449 the Virgin Mary appeared several times to a peasant girl named Inés and commanded that a church, called Santa María de la Cruz, be built on the site. After the ecclesiastical authorities had carried out an official investigation of the apparitions, the church was built just as the Virgin had ordered, and soon a group of holy women, among them Inés, built a house nearby. This was the origin of the convent that would eventually adopt the rule of the Third Order of Saint Francis and whose first abbess would be Inés.[41]

One day the Devil appeared to Inés, threatening to destroy the convent, and in time he managed to lure the unfortunate abbess into sin. The Virgin Mary bewailed the perdition of her house and begged her Son to restore the honor and virtue of her convent by creating a creature more perfect than the first, a child to be named Juana. Christ answered that at that moment He had begun to create a male child, but that out of love for

His mother, He would change it into a female. This He did, but He allowed the infant Juana to be born with an Adam's apple as a sign of the prenatal miracle (*Vida,* fols. 1v–3r).

In 1497 Juana professed in the convent of Santa María de la Cruz, where she distinguished herself for her virtues, asceticism, and mystical experiences. In 1509 she was elected abbess, thereby completing the cycle that had begun with the fall of the first abbess. Many years later, in a vision the Virgin Mary reminds Juana of her role as second foundress of the convent. Our Lady observes that she replaced Inés with Juana just as the Holy Spirit replaced Judas with Saint Mathias and Lucifer with Saint Michael:

Y por tanto, hija, como a segunda fundadora de mi casa y en lugar de la primera, te estableçí como hiço el Spíritu Sancto a Sancto Mathía en lugar de Judas, y como Sant Michael en lugar de Luçifer. (*Vida,* fol. 111v)

(And therefore, my daughter, I established you as second foundress of my house and in place of the first, as did the Holy Spirit to Saint Mathias in place of Judas and to Saint Michael in place of Lucifer.)

The Christomimetic pattern is evident: the story of the foundation, fall, and restoration of the convent is a calque of the creation, fall, and redemption of humankind. Inés is cast as an Adam figure, while Juana becomes a redeeming Christ figure who is brought into the world to remedy the original sin of Inés.

The linking of the foundation episode to Juana's birth shows how her contemporaries read her life: the mold in which her biography is cast follows the redemptive pattern that links Juana's life to that of Christ. Indeed, the imitation of Christ's redemptive role is a frequent motif in Juana's life, for variations of the Christomimetic pattern occur obsessively in the mystic's official biography. As mentioned earlier in the Introduction, when certain ecclesiastics tried to take a benefice away from her convent, Juana secured a papal bull to confirm the convent's right to the benefice. A companion denounced her for acting without official permission and for spending too much money in obtaining the bull. As a result Juana was forced to step down, and the nun who had falsely accused her became the new abbess. Juana's biography creates a frame for this event in which Juana's "passion" re-creates mimetically certain elements of Christ's Passion. Juana's future removal from office is revealed to her in a vision that she experiences while praying before an image of the Agony in the Garden. The image addresses Juana, saying that just as in the garden He had begged the heavenly Father to revoke the sentence of death placed upon Him, so He had prayed in vain that Juana be spared these tribulations:

salió de la imagen del Señor del Huerto una voz que pareçía a manera de lloro, diziendo: "Mançilla tengo de ti, viendo las sentençias que sobre ti están dadas por el mi Padre çelestial. E assí como no fue . . . revocada la mía en el tienpo de mi Passión, aunque yo lo rogué y lloré, no quiere la divina clemençia no revocar ni dexar de executar tus penas." (*Vida,* fol. 79r)

(from the image of the Agony in the Garden came forth a voice as of lamentation, saying: "I pity you, seeing the sentences my celestial Father has passed on you. And as my [sentence] was not . . . commuted at the time of my Passion, even though I begged for it and wept, the divine clemency does not wish to repeal or fail to carry out your punishment.")

Bynum has pointed out the significance of suffering in the lives of medieval holy women. Bodily pain is seen as a means of saving souls, for the sufferings of such women are viewed as merging with those of Christ on the cross and with those of the souls in Purgatory.[42] Offering their suffering for the salvation of others, such women imitate the redemptive role of Christ. Thus, when Christ speaks to Juana through the image of the Agony in the Garden, He says that Juana should be consoled, since the suffering she will endure will benefit not only her but also those souls that have commended themselves to her:

las quales [penas] no pasarán por ti sola, pues muchas ánimas se te an encomendado, de cuyos peccados las penas todas de ese mundo son pequeñas para satisfazerse. (*Vida,* fol. 79r)

(which sufferings will not happen only for your sake, for many souls have commended themselves to you, whose sins all the sufferings in this world scarcely suffice to satisfy.)

The fact that Juana's paralyzing and painful illness provides the context for the guitar vision has several important ramifications. The association between music and bodily suffering, especially that undertaken as penance, is traditional. The nun who composed the early fourteenth-century *Vitae sororum* of Unterlinden said that the sound of the nuns flagellating themselves was more delightful to the ears of the Lord than any music.[43] Saint Vincent Ferrer (d. 1419) compared penance to a guitar because of its effect on the body: "Let us now see why penance is called a guitar. Good people, you know well that a guitar is [made of] dry wood that is hollow inside; similarly, a person becomes dry and hollow through penance. That is to say, such a person always goes around drained and dry and empty inside; that is to say, in his heart there is neither malice nor evil desires."[44]

There is also a significant connection between illness and the visionary experience, for sickness is often seen as a preparatory purgation for the contemplative life.[45] Statistically, illnesses are very frequent in the lives of female saints, whereas they are largely absent from those of their male counterparts. Similarly, visions and other supernatural phenomena occur more often among female than among male saints.[46] Thus, the combination of illness and the reception of visions is not peculiar to Mother Juana's mystical experience, but replicates a pattern frequent in the lives of medieval holy women.

The guitar vision has a circular trajectory, for it begins and ends with the image of the body as a musical instrument. Yet, there is a dynamic of transformation here, because not only are the instruments different in the two parts of the revelation but their function changes as well. The vision begins as God announces His desire to break the trumpet or organ through which He is wont to speak. The figurative use of the musical instrument to refer to the visionary harks back to the self-referential passages in the revelations previously commented upon: the visionary or prophet is but the passive instrument through which God speaks. By the end of the vision Juana has become a guitar played by Christ. At first glance it appears that there has been no movement save the substitution of one musical instrument for another. Juana seems to be the same passive instrument she was at the beginning of the vision. But such is not the case, for Juana has become the instrument of the Passion, the cross. Her striving to achieve an ever more perfect *imitatio Christi* has culminated in her actually reliving the Passion. In the course of the vision the term *passive* has acquired the force of its etymological meaning, for the intimate connection between music and Christ's Passion and between the cross and the harp or guitar indicates that the instrument Juana has become is of quite a different order from the trumpet associated with the Old Testament prophets. Just as her body has been transformed by the reliving of the Passion, so God has broken the visionary trumpet and transformed it into the guitar of His Passion.[47]

Juana's vision may seem surprising and even shocking to our modern sensibilities. If that is the case, such a reaction is not unique to our times: generations of readers chronologically closer to Juana were similarly troubled by her extravagant imagery. The author of Juana's first printed biography, Father Antonio Daza, was forced by Inquisitorial pressure to issue a revised version. The 1610 edition reproduces in its essential details the account of the vision found in Juana's official biography, including both the initial image of Juana as the organ that God wishes to close off and the final apotheosis of the body as a guitar played upon by Christ (fols. 83v–85r). The 1613 edition juxtaposes the vision in question with a previous one in which Juana received stigmata-like marks, which she later asked be taken away. This revised version merely states that Christ embraced Juana, leaving her with the pains of His sacred Passion (fols. 78v–79r). Omitted are the detailed limb-by-limb description of the embrace and the motif of the body as a guitar.

Tirso de Molina's dramatic trilogy, *La Santa Juana* (1613–1614), seems to be based on the first version of Daza's biography.[48] At the end of the third act of the second play, Tirso juxtaposes a vision of Saint Francis displaying the stigmata with a vision of the crucified Christ, who embraces Juana, thereby impressing upon her the stigmata.[49] Tirso thus appears to conflate two episodes in Juana's life, the embrace found in the guitar vision and the earlier episode that left her with stigmata-like marks. It is not surprising that Tirso saw the dramatic possibilities of the embrace in all its plasticity. Nonetheless, although he was familiar with the episode of Christ's playing upon Juana's body as if it were a musical instrument, the playwright presumably felt it unsuitable for dramatic representation.

Father Pedro Navarro's voluminous 1622 biography offers a severely truncated account of the vision, ending with the episode of painful paralysis (pp. 734–739). The Crucifixion-like embrace and the guitar episode are absent.[50] Furthermore, Navarro radically transforms the initial musical image by which God expressed His desire to break the organ or trumpet through which He had revealed Himself. Instead, God refers to Juana as a clay vessel, announcing His plan to break that fragile object and to form a new and different vessel.[51]

In the middle of the seventeenth century Juana's writings and biography were submitted to official Roman censors as part of her beatification process. Cardinal Giovanni Bona, who was charged with the task of examining the *Vida*, assimilated the guitar vision to the reception of the stigmata. He censured the hands-against-hands, feet-against-feet, body-against-body embrace, perhaps because it seemed inappropriately sensuous: he used the term *corpus corpori copulante*. Bona linked the embrace to another objectionable vision in which angels were seen kissing and embracing nuns, concluding: "These things are similarly indecorous and taste of the flesh."[52] Father Joseph Coppons's defense of the passages censured by Cardinal Bona insists on the detail that the embrace occurred during one of Juana's mystical raptures. Kissing and embracing, he says, are not to be understood as indecorous actions, but rather assimilated to the holy kiss mentioned in I Corinthians 16:20 and other biblical and patristic texts (*Reparos*, fols. 18v–19v). As an epilogue, let it be remembered that the questionable orthodoxy of some of Juana's visions was the principal reason for the negative outcome of her beatification process.[53]

The varying reactions of Juana's close contemporaries reveal that even, for them there was something disconcerting in her extravagant imagery. Yet, there is nothing in the guitar vision that is without precedent in the writings of the church fathers or in the experience of other mystics and devotional writers. The necessary division of the vision into its component elements has done little justice to Juana's capacity to synthesize traditional themes, a synthesis that is intimately connected with her own lived experience. The musical image that forms the nucleus of the vision is central to Mother Juana's mysticism, for it is the point of intersection of the most significant aspects of her perception of the divine: the theme of illness as the preparatory stage for the encounter with the sacred, the mystical experience as a physical contact with God, the notion of the visionary as a musical instrument played by God, and the *imitatio Christi* that culminates in the participation in the Passion. What Juana has done is to give a new configuration to a series of traditional motifs and images, a configuration that epitomizes the essential traits of her experience of the divine.

Notes

1. Robert A. Skeris, *CHROMA THEOU. On the Origins and Theological Interpretation of the Musical Imagery Used by the Ecclesiastical Writers of the First Three Centuries, with Special Reference to the Image of Orpheus* (Altötting: Verlag Alfred Coppenrath, 1976), 30.

2. Skeris, *CHROMA THEOU*, 102.

3. "ac miracula Dei non per se, sed per illa tacta profert, quemadmodum chorda per citharoedam tacta, sonum non per se, sed per tactum illius reddit" (*Analecta Sanctae Hildegardis*, ed. Joannes Baptista Card. Pitra [Monte Cassino, 1882], 244). In Book II of her *Causae et curae*, Hildegard compares the airy and permeable body of a woman to the frame of a lyre pierced with holes for the strings: "ipsae apertae sunt ut lignum, in quo chordae ad citharizandum positae sunt, et quia etiam fenestrales et ventosae [sunt]" (ed. Paul Kaiser [Leipzig: Teubner, 1903], 105).

4. "sicut tuba, quae solummodo sonos dat, nec operatur; sed in quam alius spirat, ut sonum reddat" (Epistola XLV, in Migne, *Patrologia Latina*, vol. 197, col. 217).

5. According to the visionary Mother Isabel de Jesús (1586–1648), Christ called her his trumpet and his carillon ("También me llamó trompeta, y campana"). See Electa Arenal, "The Convent as Catalyst for Autonomy: Two Hispanic Nuns of the Seventeenth Century," in *Women in Hispanic Literature: Icons and Fallen Idols,* ed. Beth Miller (Berkeley and Los Angeles: University of California Press, 1983), 164.

6. The same image is used in the *Vida* (fol. 28r) to refer to the way in which the Lord speaks through Juana's mouth: "quando ella llamava al Señor Dios todopoderoso o quando su divina magestad le dava el resuello de su spíritu se oye la voz por la persona d'ella como se oye por una zerbatana quando una persona habla a otra."

7. For remarks on the equivalence between God's revelation through Juana and His manifestation in the Eucharist, see Chapter 5.

8. In the *Liber in distinctionibus dictionum theologicalium* of Alan of Lille the trumpet symbolizes "manifesta praedicatio" and "praedicator qui varia tribulatione productus est in amplitudinem charitatis" (Migne, *Patrologia Latina,* vol. 210, col. 981). Likewise, the trumpet is the "sonus praedicationis" in the *Allegoriae in universam Sacram Scripturam* once attributed to Rabanus Maurus (Migne, *Patrologia Latina,* 112, col. 1069). In a sermon by Saint Vincent Ferrer, the trumpet is compared to preaching: "E aquests són los preÿcadors qui preÿquen la paraula de Déu, car la preÿcació és quasi com una trompa, car axí com en una trompa ha molts canons, axí la preÿcació ha moltes parts" (Sant Vicent Ferrer, *Sermons,* vol. 5, ed. Gret Schib [Barcelona: Barcino, 1984], 205).

9. Other women who engaged in preaching include Saint Umiltà, Saint Hildegard, Blessed Angela of Foligno, and Saint Catherine of Siena. See *Medieval Women's Visionary Literature*, ed. Elizabeth Alvilda Petroff (New York and Oxford: Oxford University Press, 1986), 21, notes 60–61.

10. The personalized angel Laruel is reminiscent of Sapiel and Emanuel, who guarded Saint Umiltà (d. 1310). See Elizabeth Petroff, *Consolation of the Blessed* (New York: Alta Gaia Society, 1979), 139–140. Similarly, the angel Splenditello appeared to Benedetta Carlini in seventeenth-century Italy. See Judith C. Brown, *Immodest Acts: The Life of a Lesbian Nun in Renaissance Italy* (New York and Oxford: Oxford University Press, 1986), 64–66.

11. Other cases in which the life and/or revelations of a woman were written down by one or more female companions include Mechthild of Hackeborn (d. 1298 or 1299) and Gertrude of Helfta (d. 1301 or 1302). Nonetheless, such female biographers are hardly the rule, especially in the late Middle Ages. A notable exception is the *vita* of Eustochia of Messina (d. 1485), which was written by several of the nun's companions.

12. Catherine of Siena's life, for example, was written by her confessor, Raymond of Capua; John of Marienwerder was both spiritual director and biographer of Dorothy of Montau (d. 1394).

13. Saint Laruel does not appear in the *Conorte,* in which Christ Himself explicates the visions.

14. Likewise, an angel serves to interpret from within the visions of Saint Elizabeth of Schönau (1129–1165).

15. The episode is recounted in *Vida*, fol. 38v.

16. "Et dixit quod osculata fuit primo pectus Christi . . . et postea osculata est os eius; ex quo ore dicebat quod admirabilem et inenarrabiliter delectabilem odorem acceperat, qui respirabat ex ore eius; . . . Et postea posuit maxillam suam super maxillam Christi, et Christus posuit manum suam super aliam maxillam et strinxit eam ad se, et ista fidelis Christi audivit sibi dici ista verba: Antequam iacerem in sepulcro tenui te ita astrictam" (Ludger Thier, OFM, and Abele Calufetti, OFM, *Il libro della Beata Angela da Foligno (Edizione critica),* 2d edition [Grottaferrata: Collegium S. Bonaventurae ad Claras Aquas, 1985], 296).

17. Caroline Walker Bynum, *Holy Feast and Holy Fast: The Religious Significance of Food to Medieval Women* (Berkeley and Los Angeles: University of California Press, 1987), 246.

18. Bynum, *Holy Feast,* 285, 288–289.

19. Other cases include the sermons for Epiphany (*Conorte,* fol. 50v), for the Feast of Saint Nathaniel (*Conorte,* fol. 333r), and for the Feast of Saint Major (*Conorte,* fol. 355v), as well as the sermon devoted to the parable of the good shepherd (*Conorte,* fol. 178r).

20. Bynum, *Holy Feast,* 54.

21. See Leo Spitzer, *Classical and Christian Ideas of World Harmony,* ed. Anna Granville Hatcher (Baltimore: The Johns Hopkins Press, 1963), 7–20.

22. For the theme of Christ as courtly lover in medieval literature, see Sister Marie de Lourdes Le May, *The Allegory of the Christ-Knight in English Literature* (Washington, D.C.: The Catholic University of America, 1932), 1–29.

23. For the motif of the nun as bride of Christ, see John Bugge, *Virginitas: An Essay in the History of a Medieval Ideal* (The Hague: Martinus Nijhoff, 1975), 59–67.

24. For the theme of Christ as courting lover in Golden Age Spain, see Cristóbal Cuevas, "El tema sacro de 'La ronda del galán' (¿Fray Luis fuente de Lope?)," *Fray Luis de León: Actas de la I Academia Literaria Renacentista,* ed. Víctor García de la Concha (Salamanca: Universidad de Salamanca, 1981), 147–169.

25. "¡O dulce y buen Jesú! ¿E quién sabrá conoscer el destemple de las almas sino el mesmo que criándolas las supo templar y las sabe tañer? Lo que destempló el pecado templólo tu sangre. . . . O buen Jesú, que oyendo tañer aquello, endurecióse mi coraçón y entristecióse mi alma, mirando que no estava yo templada para que tú dulcemente en mí tañesses. No estava concertado el instrumento de mi alma para que pusiesses tú la mano suave en él del amor tuyo, de la voluntad tuya, con que la tañes, por no me haver yo llegado a ti para que las cuerdas de las virtudes d'ella fuessen con tu sacratíssima sangre polidas" (*Libro de la oración de Sor María de Santo Domingo,* with an introductory study by José Manuel Blecua [Madrid: Hauser y Menet, 1948], sig. C 6r). One of the engravings in Father Juan de Rojas's *Representaciones de la verdad vestida sobre las siete Moradas de Santa Teresa de Jesús* (1677) uses the guitar to symbolize the *timor Dei* that should characterize the Séptimas Moradas. Miguel Herrero García comments: "Una cítara o guitarra, templada secretamente por impulsos del Cielo, significa cómo el alma es gobernada por Dios cuando ha llegado a este estado; pero se ve también una mano infernal que intenta desconectar el instrumento haciendo saltar las cuerdas" (Miguel Herrero

García, "El grabado al servicio de la mística," *Revista de Ideas Estéticas,* 3 [1945] 348–349). In an anonymous seventeenth-century(?) Mexican painting the Christ-Child is seen surrounded by the instruments of the Passion and playing upon the cross as if it were a guitar. See Santiago Sebastián, "La imagen de la cruz como instrumento musical," *Traza y Baza,* 6 (1976) 120–121.

26. In *The Flowing Light of the Godhead* of Mechthild of Magdeburg (1210–1297), God says to the human soul: "du bist ein lire vor minen oren" (*Offenbarungen der Schwester Mechthild von Magdeburg oder Das fliessende Licht der Gottheit,* ed. P. Gall Morel [1869; Darmstadt: Wissenschaftliche Buchgesellschaft, 1963], 62). In a later passage, the soul expresses in musical terms its desire for union with God ("Du weist wol wie du rüren kanst / Die seiten in der sele min. / Eya, des beginne alzehant, / De du jemer selig müsist sin" [142]), and God replies that for the moment He can only partially reveal Himself: "Und mine seiten sont dir süsse klingen / Nach der truwen koste diner langen minne. / Jedoch wil ich vor beginnen / Und temperen in diner sele mine himmelschen seiten" (143).

27. Saint Augustine, *Expositions on the Book of Psalms,* trans. by members of the English Church, 6 vols. (Oxford: John Henry Parker, 1847–1857), 3:94–95. In his commentary on the Apocalypse, Saint Augustine compares the crucified Christ to a harp: "Cithara enim, id est, chorda in ligno extensa, significat carnem Christi passioni conjunctam" (*Homilia IV, In B. Joannis Apocalypsim Expositio,* in *Sancti Aurelii Augustini Hipponensis Episcopi Opera Omnia,* 11 vols. [Paris: Gaume Fratres, 1836–1838], 3:2, col. 3118). For an overview of musical imagery in Saint Augustine, see Henri Ronde, S.J., "Notes d'exégèse augustinienne: 'Psalterium et cithara,'" *Recherches de Science Religieuse,* 46 (1958) 408–415.

28. *The Mystical Vine,* in *The Works of Bonaventure,* trans. José de Vinck, *I. Mystical Opuscula* (Paterson, N.J.: St. Anthony Guild Press, 1960), 171.

29. "¡Quán dulce música es al pecador tus piadosas llagas!" (sig. D IV).

30. There is a play on words here: *rasgar* can mean both to rip or tear and to strum a stringed instrument.

31. "assí después en tu muerte otros quatro, tus sacratíssimas manos y pies, por nosotros rasgados, davan bozes piadosas y amorosas a los pecadores que nos abracemos a ti, nos esforcemos y alegremos en ti. Es el canto suave d'estos quatro tu sacratíssima sangre que con melodía suave nos conbida a que concertemos nuestras almas contigo para que nos temples con ella y puedas tañer y morar en nosotros" (*Libro de la oración,* sig. D IV).

32. Skeris, *CHROMA THEOU,* 56–57.

33. John Block Friedman, *Orpheus in the Middle Ages* (Cambridge: Harvard University Press, 1970), 124–128.

34. "La melodía de la voz de Orpheo, ¿qué otra cosa es sino los sermones que Jesuchristo hazía, y su maravillosa doctrina? La harpa que tañía, ¿qué otra cosa es sino los misterios de su Passión que recibió en la cruz, que hera la verdadera harpa, las cuerdas de la qual heran los nervios, huesos y carnes de Nuestro Redemptor, estirados como cuerdas en la vihuela, en el árbol de la cruz?" (*Dechado de la vida humana,* trans. Martín de Reyna [Valladolid, 1549; facsimile ed. Valencia: Castalia, 1952], fol. 56v).

35. F. P. Pickering, *Literature and Art in the Middle Ages* (London: Macmillan, 1970), 285–301. See also Jacques Fontaine, "Les symbolismes de la cithare

dans la poésie de Paulin de Nole," in *Romanitas et Christianitas: Studia Iano Hen-rico Waszink A.D. VI Kal. Nov. A. MCMLXXIII XIII lustra complenti oblata*, ed. W. den Boer et al. (Amsterdam and London: North-Holland Publishing Company, 1973), 129–130.

36. "que ansi como David taniendo la guitarra sanava a Saúl, que era demo-niado, assí Nuestro Señor, tocando la guitarra de la cruz con agudas bozes, avia a sanar al mundo, que era todo atorcijado" (*Libro de los evangelios moralizados* [Za-mora, 1490], sig. N 5v).

37. "Saül ere endemoniat, e algunes de vegades lo prenie lo dimoni e·l contur-bave axi fortment, que tot lo regrave. E David, quan vehie açò, anave e prenie la guitarra e sonave-li davant. . . . Ara, d'on exie aquella virtut? No de la guitarra, mas de la figura de allò que la guitarra significave, e significave la Passio de Jesu-christ" (Sant Vicent Ferrer, *Sermons*, vol. 5, 174–175). The figural connection be-tween David's harp and Christ's cross is common. Thus, in the *Liber Allegoriarum Veteris Testamenti* of the Pseudo-Hugh of Saint Victor the cithara is a *figura* of the cross: "David adhuc puer in cithara suaviter, imo fortiter canens, malignum spi-ritum qui exagitabat Saulem compescebat; non quod ejus cithara tantam virtutem haberet, sed figura crucis Christi, per lignum et chordarum extensionem mysticæ gerebat, quae jam tunc daemones effigabat" (Migne, *Patrologia Latina*, vol. 175, col. 692). And in the Castilian translation of the *Viola animae*: "Mucho me agrada el exemplo que pusiste porque el instrumento musical de David con el qual alançava el Demonio del cuerpo de Saúl da muy claramente a entender la cruz del Salvador. Porque assí como las cuerdas estendidas en la harpa tañen y suenan con mucha suavidad, assí el Señor cantó en la cruz una muy dulce melodía" (*Coloquio spiritual de la Passión de Nuestro Señor Jesuchristo* [Sevilla, 1529], fol. 32rv).

38. Dürer's painting the *Martyrdom of the Ten Thousand* (1508) establishes a connection between the Passion of Christ and the martyrdom of Saint Achatius and his companions. Erwin Panofsky observes how "in the painting two of the martyrs are crucified, quite like the Thieves, on rough-hewn crosses while a regular cross, still on the ground between them, awaits a Christ-like victim patiently stand-ing in the second plane" (*The Life and Art of Albrecht Dürer* [1955; Princeton: Princeton University Press, 1971], 121).

39. James H. Marrow points out that the association of musical instruments with the Passion was derived from Old Testament references to music accompany-ing the sacrifice of animals. At least in northern Europe, however, the musical motif was very rarely related to the seizure of Christ, the most common association being to the bearing of the cross. See Marrow's *Passion Iconography in Northern European Art of the Late Middle Ages and Early Renaissance: A Study of the Transfor-mation of Sacred Metaphor into Descriptive Narrative* (Kortrijk: Van Ghemmert, 1979), 153–161. In a mid-fifteenth-century Via Dolorosa by the so-called Perea Mas-ter (or one of his followers) a trumpet player accompanies Christ as He carries the cross. See Chandler Rathfon Post, *A History of Spanish Painting*, 8 vols. in 12 (Cam-bridge: Harvard University Press, 1930–1958), 6/1:287. Similarly, a soldier plays a horn in a Via Dolorosa of ca. 1500 by the so-called Master of Burgos (Post, 4/1:203). In a Crucifixion from the second half of the fifteenth century by a member of the school of Nicolás Francés, one of the tormenters blows a trumpet, which he aims directly at Christ as if it were a weapon. Simultaneously, another soldier pierces the

Savior's side with a sword (Post, 3:292). In Jorge de Montemayor's Passion poem (printed 1554) Christ was the instrument that played at the Last Supper. The twelve strings He played were the twelve Apostles, but one of them (Judas) was out of tune: "Música allí no faltaba, / que Christo era el instrumento, / y las cuerdas do tocaba / doze, y de tal fundamento, / que en sí mismo las templaba. / Y una dellas que ganancia / de dineros pretendía, / de destemplada en constancia, / con las otras no hazía / cláusula ni consonancia" (Jorge de Montemayor, Cancionero, ed. Ángel González Palencia [Madrid: Sociedad de Bibliófilos Españoles, 1932], 142).

40. Bynum, Holy Feast, 200.

41. For an analysis of the morphology and function of such apparitions, see William A. Christian, Jr., Apparitions in Late Medieval and Renaissance Spain (Princeton: Princeton University Press, 1981). The apparitions that led to the foundation of the convent of Nuestra Señora de la Cruz are analyzed on pp. 57–87.

42. Bynum, Holy Feast, 171.

43. "In aduentu Domini et per omne tempus quadragessime universe sorores post matutinas in capitulum diuertentes, siue ad loca alia oportuna diuersis flagellorum generibus corpus suum usque ad sanguinis effusionem lacerantes crudelissime et hostiliter ceciderunt, ita quod sonitus uerberancium se ubique per omne monasterium resonaret, ascendens in aures Domini Sabaoth suauior omni melodia" (Jeanne Ancelet-Hustache, "Les Vitae sororum d'Unterlinden: Edition critique du Manuscrit 508 de la Bibliothèque de Colmar," Archives d'Histoire Doctrinale et Littéraire du Moyen Age, 5 [1930] 340).

44. "Agora veamos por qué a la penitencia llama guitarra. Buena gent; bien sabedes que guitarra es madero seco e vano de dentro; así la persona torna seca e vacía por penitencia; esto es, que la tal persona siempre anda desmayada e seca e vacía de dentro, esto es, que en el su corazón non está malicia nin mal deseo" ("Sermones de San Vicente Ferrer: Sermón incompleto de San Vicente Ferrer: De vera sapientia,'" La Cruz [1873:2] 405). Saint Vincent Ferrer uses a similar image in his exegesis of Isaiah 23:16 ("Take a harp, go about the city, thou harlot that hast been forgotten; sing well, sing many a song, that thou mayest be remembered"). The harlot is the "ánima peccadora que está en peccat mortal" who should take up the guitar of penance: "Pren la guitarra, que és penitència. Veus per qué la appelle guitarra: bona gent; sabeu que guitarra és fust sech, e vana dintre; axí la persona torna sequa e esmayada ab la penitència, e vana de dintre, que's barya lo cor de tota malícia" ("Sermo unius confessoris et septem arcium spiritualium," in Sant Vicent Ferrer, Sermons, vol. 2, ed. Josep Sanchis Sivera [Barcelona: Barcino, 1934], 231–232). Cf. Sermons, vol. 3, ed. Gret Schib (Barcelona: Barcino, 1975), 86.

45. Ernst Benz, Die Vision: Erfahrungsformen und Bilderwelt (Stuttgart: Ernst Klett, 1969), chapter 1 ("Vision und Krankheit").

46. Donald Weinstein and Rudolph M. Bell, Saints and Society: The Two Worlds of Western Christendom, 1000–1700 (Chicago and London: University of Chicago Press, 1982), 228–232, 234–235.

47. Friedman observes that late-classical musical theorists viewed stringed instruments as belonging to a higher order than wind instruments: "The lyre, however, was often contrasted with the flute, or with wind instruments in general, in an allegorical fashion. Whereas stringed instruments were thought to appeal to and

have power over the rational part of the soul, wind instruments—like the martial trumpet or lascivious flute—were characterized by their power over the irascible and concupiscent passions, which held the soul to the earth when the lyre would draw it to the heavens" (*Orpheus in the Middle Ages*, 81).

48. Serge Maurel, *L'Univers dramatique de Tirso de Molina* (Poitiers: Université de Poitiers, 1971), 67.

49. Tirso de Molina, *La Santa Juana: Segunda parte,* ed. Xavier A. Fernández (Kassel: Edition Reichenberger, 1988), 150–153.

50. A foot-to-foot and hand-to-hand embrace does occur, however, in the earlier episode in which Juana receives the stigmata-like marks (p. 397). The vision of Saint Achatius and his companions is moved to an entirely different context (pp. 411–412).

51. Cf. Jeremiah 18 : 4 ("And the vessel was broken which he was making of clay with his hands; and turning he made another vessel, as it seemed good in his eyes to make it").

52. "Haec autem indecora sunt et carnem sapiunt" (*Reparos,* fol. iv).

53. *Toletana beatificationis et canonizationis Ven. Servae Dei Joannae de Cruce . . . Positio super dubio an stante non reperitione assertorum opusculorum originalium possit ad ulteriora in causa procedi. Relatio Reverendissimi Fidei Promotoris super statu causae* (Rome: Typis Reverendae Camerae Apostolicae, 1731), 7.

IV. The Chosen Vessels

The sermon for the Feast of Saint Clare exalts the saint by highlighting the theme of her virginity. Thus, it treats implicitly the motif of the nun as bride of Christ, for, as copatron of the Franciscan order, Saint Clare is an obvious role model for nuns. Nonetheless, the sermon goes considerably beyond the praise of virginity to contrast the power and authority available to female saints and those enjoyed by their male counterparts. This contrast is most evident in the implicit opposition between the sphere of action reserved for Saint Clare and that reserved for Saint Francis, the other copatron of the order.

The sermon (see Appendix H) can be divided into two parts, one devoted to the exaltation of Saint Clare, the other to the question of the souls in Purgatory. At the beginning of the sermon God summons all the celestial virgins, telling them to offer Him their vessels. The virgins assemble, and the Lord puts His hand into each one of the vessels, drawing forth fragrant liquids and flowers, which He smells and then offers to the other blessed souls for them to smell (*Conorte,* fol. 308r). Placed on tables in front of the Lord's nuptial bed, the vessels emit a radiance and a fragrance that ascend to the throne of the Holy Trinity.

The Lord greets Saint Clare, playfully punning on her name: "Come over here, my friend Clare, for you will understand me well when I say to you that, although there are others in my holy kingdom that are called 'clear,' they are few and not so remarkable as you."[1] Just as Saint Clare is about to offer her vessel to the Lord, He disappears so that the saint will have to search for Him with diligence and holy fervor.[2] Clare goes looking for the Lord, and, paraphrasing the Song of Songs, she asks her companions if they have seen Him: "Tell me, my lords and ladies, have you seen Him whom my soul loves?"[3] A gloss explains that Saint Clare's search and ardent desire for God is a sort of prayer.[4]

Suddenly, a great shining conch shell appears among Saint Clare's skirts. The shell opens, revealing Christ Himself, all handsome and resplendent. Saint Clare swoons, enraptured with love, kissing and embracing the Lord.[5] Christ orders her to rise and to show Him her vessel.[6] He embraces Saint Clare, and suddenly le salió de los pechos un caño como de órgano muy resplandeçiente, e le tañía El con su preçiosa boca e con sus manos tañía en el vaso que estava de la otra parte. E fazía muy dulçes e suaves e deleitosos sones e melodías. (*Conorte,* fol. 308v)

(there emerged from her chest a shining pipe as of an organ, and He played upon it with His precious mouth and with His hands He played upon the vessel which was on the other side. And He made very sweet and gentle and pleasing sounds and melodies.)

Saint Clare nearly faints from such divine gifts and pleasures. Nonetheless, while she is grateful to the Lord for these celestial favors, she also considers herself unworthy to be thus united with Him.

A gloss on the final folio of the sermon purports to explicate the conch shell episode, declaring that Saint Clare and the other holy virgins found Christ

ençerrado y escondido por fe e por graçia e amor en la concha de la mar de las tribulaçiones e angustias e trabajos e persecuçiones e martirios. Porque así como la margarita preçiosa se busca e se falla en las aguas muy fondas de la mar con grandes trabajos e peligros, que así por semejante le fallaron las gloriosas vírgenes en la mar d'este mundo, guardando su virginidad e linpieza e padeçiendo grandes persecu-çiones e trabajos. (*Conorte,* fol. 309v)

(enclosed and hidden, by means of their faith and grace and love, in the conch shell in the sea of tribulations and torments and travails and persecutions and sufferings. Because just as the precious pearl is sought and found with considerable efforts and dangers in the deepest waters of the sea, so likewise the glorious virgins found Him in the sea of this world, preserving their virginity and purity and suffering great persecutions and travails.[7])

The anonymous censor of the Escorial manuscript of the *Conorte* crossed out the passage that speaks of the golden organ pipe. Nonetheless, it was not that deletion that provoked a response from Father Torres but rather the passage at the end of the sermon when the Lord Himself explains the symbolism of the conch shell. Although that gloss was not at all censored, it seems clear that, upon finishing his reading of the sermon, Torres wished to vent his anger at what he no doubt considered a wrong interpretation of the text by his predecessor:

El no dar otra raya a la declaratión que el Señor hiço de la concha tan provechosa y tan conforme a fe es darnos a entender que con tan buena glosa hera bueno el testo y la parábola. Y que si no fuera tan apresurado en testar los testos sino que se esfor-[ç]ara un poco asta ver los sentidos de ellos, pues son casi todos los que en este libro están parabólicos, que aun el mismo que los rayó, con ser tan amigo de hecharles rayos [*sic*], escusara la furia de muchos, lo qual es fácil de ver todas aquellas veces que no borra las declarationes. (*Conorte*, fol. 309v)

(His not crossing out the very useful and doctrinally sound explanation the Lord gave of the conch shell leads us to believe that, if the gloss was good, then the text and parable are likewise good. And if he were not in such a hurry to censor the texts but made an effort to see the various levels of meaning, for nearly all those in this book are allegorical, then even he who crossed them out—despite his being so enamoured of censoring—would spare many his rage, which is easy to see whenever he fails to cross out the glosses.)

Thus, Torres not only criticizes his predecessor's censoring frenzy but also proposes a guideline for future readers: the allegorical passages must be read concurrently with their glosses.

The second part of the sermon begins with the arrival of angels who accompany souls from Purgatory. The souls have not completed the purgation of their sins, but at the request of Saint Clare they have been allowed to enjoy a brief respite from their suffering. The heavenly elect beg the Lord to free the souls completely from Purgatory, but He answers that it would not be just, since He has already favored them by not condemning them to Hell, as they deserved for their grievous sins. The souls themselves kneel before the Lord, reminding Him that during their earthly existence they had bought indulgences, gone on pilgrimages, and visited churches. But God asks them if they satisfied all the stipulated conditions when they purchased the indulgences.[8] Profoundly embarrassed, the souls dare not reiterate their petition. The angels and the heavenly elect try to intercede for them, saying that, although the souls did not satisfy completely the conditions of the indulgences, God's mercy suffices to save them. The Lord answers that the good works that the souls performed are not sufficient for salvation, and He orders the souls to return to Purgatory, promising that He will forgive a part of what they have left to pay. Finally, Christ welcomes a number of blessed souls recently released from Purgatory and presents them to the Father.

The anonymous censor of the *Conorte* crossed out only two passages in the sermon for the Feast of Saint Clare: the episode of the golden organ pipe previously discussed and the passage that deals with the conditions stipulated for the indulgences. The censoring of the latter passage provokes a strong reaction from Father Torres, who hastens to emphasize the orthodoxy of Mother Juana's words: "The conditions stipulated for the indulgences . . . are [sound] doctrine of all the holy doctors and scholastics."[9] Furthermore, what Juana says concerning indulgences and the remission of sins in exchange for good works "should be written in golden letters in these wretched times," when the Lutherans question the merit of such practices.[10] Luther himself, he adds, the source of this poison, denied the value of indulgences and Purgatory and even good works, thus ending up completely evil.[11] And so Mother Juana's champion, in his defense of the *Conorte,* not only reflects the most orthodox Church doctrine but also responds to an urgent contemporary need. At a historical moment when the doctrine of indulgences is being called into question, Mother Juana's words seem to constitute a defense of the traditional teachings of the Church.

The first part of the sermon for the Feast of Saint Clare revolves around the symbol of the vessel, which is of biblical origin, and that of the conch shell, which is derived from the bestiary. The episode in which Christ embraces Saint Clare, playing upon both the golden pipe and the vessel, evokes the guitar vision (see Chapter 3), for both visions juxtapose the traditional images of the virgin/nun as the bride of Christ, of the human body as a musical instrument, and of God as a musician. Indeed, the word *vaso* (vessel), in addition to its primary meaning of "container," has musical connotations. Isaiah 22:24 ("And they shall hang upon him all the glory of his father's house, divers kinds of vessels, every little vessel, from the vessels of cups even to every instrument of music [Vulgate: *omne vas musicorum*]") identifies the vessel as a kind of musical instrument. In a similar vein, Psalm 70:22 reads: "For I will also confess to thee thy truth with the instruments of psaltery [Vulgate: *in vasis psalmi*]; O God I will sing to thee with the harp, thou Holy One of Israel." Thus, music supplies the context for Saint Clare's celestial ecstasy, for both the golden organ pipe and the vessel have musical associations. The guitar vision, through the traditional connection between Christ's Passion and the lyre/guitar, underscored the relationship between music and suffering. Likewise, the sermon for Saint Clare's Day associates the saint's exemplary virginal state with both music and Christ's Passion. Indeed, the Fathers of the Church saw in the heroic preservation of one's virginity a kind of martyrdom.[12] Thus, the gloss that explicates the conch shell episode emphasizes the travails and sufferings that accompany the preservation of one's virginity and relates them by association to the martyrdom par excellence, the Passion.

Both the guitar vision and the Saint Clare vision are expressed in powerful sexual imagery. The juxtaposition of traditional masculine and feminine symbols results in tensions that blur the differences between sex-

ual roles and, furthermore, call into question the differences of power associated with differences in gender. In the guitar vision Juana underwent a
sort of "passion," becoming a feminine Christ. The Saint Clare vision reveals an analogous superimposition of sexual identities. Saint Clare's status
as biological female is underscored in the episode in which the conch shell
appears among her skirts and opens up to reveal Christ. This is a symbolic
birthing through which the saint seems to give birth to Christ Himself.
Saint Clare's status as female also comes to the fore in the golden pipe episode, for the location of the pipe on the saint's chest underscores her
maternity: she appears to nurse Christ as a mother would her child. This
stereotypically feminine image is juxtaposed with an undeniably masculine
one, for the golden pipe is also an obvious phallic symbol. Thus, the scene
in which Christ embraces Saint Clare juxtaposes the vaginal vessel with the
phallic organ pipe. In this way Saint Clare becomes a sort of hermaphro-
ditic figure embraced by a consequently androgynous Christ.

In this respect, Bynum observes that male authors, even when they
use feminine images (for example, Christ's maternity), are wont to emphasize the dichotomy between the sexes. In contrast, holy women use feminine images either to refer to themselves, thus underscoring their own
status as women, or to transcend such images, blurring the differences between the sexes to arrive at a sort of androgyny.[13] Similarly, despite what
appears to be a proliferation of often contradictory sexual symbols in the
Saint Clare sermon, the ambiguity of those symbols is eventually resolved
in the transcendence of sexual roles. As will become apparent, in Mother
Juana's visionary world the differences between such roles are the point of
departure for a series of observations on the power and authority appropriated by women in the face of the power and authority enjoyed by men.

Vaginal symbolism is associated not only with the vessel but also with
the conch shell. In the first place, the conch is a universal symbol of the
female sexual organ.[14] But even more important for the purposes of this
chapter is the religious symbolism of the conch established by medieval
bestiaries, which interpret the shell as the Virgin Mary and the pearl it
produces as Christ:

The pearl that is born from the dew and engendered in the stone [the oyster] signifies the uniqueness of Jesus; the stone from which it is born, Holy Mary; the
pearl that is born from the dew signifies grace incarnate. It was by means of grace
that the Son of God was presented to the Virgin; by grace He reaped salvation and
by grace He was conceived. As the stone opens without breaking and closes without [leaving] a crack, and as the stone transforms the dew, so the Virgin was

rendered holy, so the Virgin who bore Jesus conceived and gave birth. She conceived as a virgin, gave birth as a virgin, remained and will remain a virgin.[15]

Significantly, the gloss that Mother Juana juxtaposes with her revelation interprets Saint Clare's search for Christ as the virgins' search for the pearl (that is, Christ Himself) in the waters of the sea of earthly tribulations.[16] Thus, the relationship she establishes between the conch that produces the pearl and the holy virgins who give birth to Christ is founded on the implicit comparison with the Virgin Mother of God.[17] Like Mary, Saint Clare and the other virgins give birth while preserving their virginity. They are at once mothers and virgins.

The musical connotations of the word *vessel* in the Bible have already been pointed out. But the term also appears in other contexts pertinent to the Saint Clare sermon. In I Thessalonians 4:3–5 ("For this is the will of God, your sanctification: that you should abstain from fornication. That every one of you should know how to possess his vessel in sanctification and honour: Not in the passion of lust, like the gentiles that know not God") a connection is established between sexual abstinence and the human body as a vessel. Likewise, in the sermon for the Feast of Saint Clare, when the celestial virgins offer their vessels to the Lord, a gloss underscores the motif of the clean vessel as a symbol of the pure and virginal body and soul:

las santas vírgines nunca ensuziaron los vasos de sus cuerpos ni de sus ánimas con ningún amor ni deleite carnal ni terrenal, mas sienpre fueron puestos sus pensamientos e deseos e amor con solo Dios. E que por eso subían los olores de sus buenas obras delante de la Santísima Trinidad, así como fumo de ençienso e de perfumes muy olientes. (*Conorte,* fol. 308r)

(the holy virgins never sullied the vessels of their bodies or of their souls with any love or pleasure, either carnal or earthly, but always kept their thoughts and desires and love on God alone. And for that reason the fragrance of their good works rose to the throne of the most Holy Trinity like the smoke of incense and most aromatic perfumes.)

The connection between the vessel and virginity is also manifested in another biblical passage, namely, the parable of the ten virgins (Matthew 25:1–13). The virgins of the Gospel parable who await the bridegroom are analogous to Saint Clare and the other heavenly virgins who go to meet the divine Bridegroom.[18] The wise virgins take care to fill their vessels with oil; Saint Clare and her companions bear vessels filled with precious liquids and fragrant flowers. Traditional biblical exegesis gave positive connotations to the oil that the wise virgins bear in their vessels. For example, in the dictionary of biblical allegories formerly attributed to Rabanus Maurus, the oil has a whole gamut of meanings: interior grace, charity, devotion, and so on.[19] More concretely, in the traditional exegesis of the parable of the ten virgins, the oil is interpreted as good works. Thus, in his commentary on that parable, Saint Hilary interprets the vessels as the human body that conceals the treasure of the good conscience, while the oil represents the fruit of the good work.[20] It is therefore no accident that, as we have seen, in Mother Juana's Saint Clare vision a gloss explains that the aromas that rise from the vessels represent the virgins' good works (*Conorte*, fol. 308r).

Given the relevance of the theme of virginity to a community of nuns, it is not surprising that the parable of the ten virgins should be the topic of another of Mother Juana's sermons, a sermon dealing with some of the same symbols, namely, the vessels and the oil. In that sermon the wise virgins represent the virtuous; the foolish virgins, those who offend God.[21] A gloss, in accordance with a more or less standardized tradition of biblical exegesis, explains that the lamps symbolize the vessels of our bodies; the wicks, our souls; the oil, charity and good works; and the light, the Holy Spirit (*Conorte*, fol. 385v).

Later on in the sermon of the ten virgins, the heavenly elect perform an allegorical pageant inspired by the parable in which the metaphors of Christ as the living bread (John 6:51) and the living water (John 4:10) are literalized:

"Que escrito es que yo soy pan bivo que deçendí del çielo. E los que avéis sed veníos en pos de mí, que soy agua biva. E veníos para mí todos los que me amáis e deseáis, que yo os fartaré de los méritos de mi sagrada Passión e de las dulçedunbres de mi preçiosa humanidad." E dixo el Señor que así como El acabó de dezir estas palabras, a desora fueron todos los bienaventurados çercados d'El. E que El les tornó a dezir: "Tomad, mis amigos, cada uno de vosotros una de mis llagas." E así como acabó de dezir estas palabras, a desora fue abierta la llaga de su sagrado costado e le manava d'él agua biva e muy saludable e vino muy adobado. E de las llagas de sus sagrados pies e manos e de su preçiosa cabeça e de todas las otras llagas de su sagrado cuerpo le manavan infinitos manjares e dulçedunbres e licores muy preçiosos e suaves e deleitosos. (*Conorte*, fol. 387v)

("For it is written that I am the living bread that descended from Heaven. And those who thirst, come unto me, for I am the living water. And come unto me those who love and desire me, for I will fill you with the merits of my sacred Passion and with the sweetness of my precious Humanity." And the Lord said that as soon as He finished saying these words, all the blessed were suddenly surrounded by Him. And that He again spoke to them: "My friends, take, each one of you, one of my wounds." And as soon as He finished saying these words, the wound in His sacred side was opened and living and very salutary water and very well flavored wine issued from it. And from the wounds on His sacred feet and hands and from His precious head and from all the other wounds on His sacred body streamed forth infinite and most precious and sweet and delectable foods and sweetness and liquids.)

Christ then tells the blessed souls to choose one of His wounds and eat and drink of His divine sweetness and sustenance. The blessed apply their mouths to Christ's wounds and

manavan dulçedunbres e manjares e beveres e licores d'ellas en tanta manera que todos comían e se fartavan con tan gran dulçedunbre e deleite como los niños quando están mamando e les viene a sus madres muy abundosamente la leche, en tanto que los niños no paladean mas abren las bocas e tragan la leche muy suavemente en tanto que sus madres no sienten si maman ni si no. (*Conorte*, fol. 388r)

(sweetness and foods and beverages and liquids issued from them in such wise that all ate and sated themselves with great sweetness and delectation such as do children when they are nursing and the milk has come to their mothers in great abundance, so that the children do not take sips but rather do they open their mouths and swallow the milk very gently so that their mothers do not feel whether they are sucking or not.)

These images recall the golden pipe episode in the sermon for the Feast of Saint Clare. In both visions the blessed state of the elect, the worthy reward for their virtuous lives, is expressed through the image of a mother who nurses her children.[22] It matters little that in one case it is Christ who plays the maternal role and in the other case it is Saint Clare who resembles a mother, for in Mother Juana's visionary world the differences between the sexes are blurred. In this case the essential element is the maternal metaphor that the visionary uses to express the beatitude of the elect. Nonetheless, as is so often the case in Mother Juana's visions, the metaphor is made almost literal: Christ actualizes the image of the nursing mother. Through that appropriation of a stereotypically female role, Christ reveals His feminine aspect, His humanity that suffered the Passion.

The androgyny motif is also present in other parts of the Saint Clare and the ten-virgins sermons. I have already pointed out that in the sermon for Saint Clare's Day the metaphor of the virgin as the Lord's bride is made literal in the episode of the saint's heavenly ecstasy: through the divine embrace, Saint Clare is united (*ayuntada*) with the Lord (*Conorte*, fol. 308v). The verb *ayuntar,* in addition to its primary meaning of "to unite," can also mean "to have sexual intercourse." Thus, the sexual semantic charge of the verb connects it to the series of ambiguous sexual images that characterizes the sermons we are considering. In the ten-virgins sermon the wise virgins are the brides of the Bridegroom par excellence, and therefore represent all the blessed, be they men or women:

E que las ánimas que no se durmieron mientras bivieron en este mundo mas sienpre estuvieron en vela, tiniendo las lánparas de sus buenas obras ençendidas, esperando quándo avía de venir el Esposo, conviene a saber, quándo las llamaría Dios para que saliesen d'esta vida, dixo el Señor que las que así falla El tan aparejadas e aperçebidas para le resçebir entra con ellas a las bodas, por quanto es El el verdadero Esposo de todas las ánimas que El crió e redimió, llevándolas al reino de los çielos, cunpliéndolas de muchas joyas e gualardones, e dándoles a sí mesmo para que le gozen e posean muy llena e cunplidamente para sienpre. E que estas tales ánimas pueden ser dichas vírgines prudentes porque tuvieron prudençia para saberse salvar. (*Conorte*, fol. 385r)

(And that the souls of those who did not fall asleep while they lived in this world but were ever vigilant, keeping the lamps of their good works lit and waiting for the Bridegroom to come, that is, for God to summon them to leave this life, the Lord said that He enters into the nuptials with the souls that He finds so ready and waiting to receive Him, inasmuch as He is the true Bridegroom of all the souls that He created and redeemed, bringing them to the kingdom of Heaven, bestowing upon them many jewels and rewards, and giving them Himself so that they may enjoy and possess Him fully and perfectly forever. And that such souls can be said to be wise virgins because they had the prudence to know how to save themselves.)

Later, when an allegorical pageant is performed in Heaven, Christ insists on the fact that He is everything for all men (and for all women as well):

"E los que quisiéredes amor, en mí lo fallares, que yo soy verdadero amor e muy perfeto e puro e linpio e casto. E soy amor sin ruga e sin tacha e sin asco. E todos los que me quisiéredes en padre, en padre me fallares. E los que me quisiéredes en madre, en madre me fallares. E los que me quisieren en esposo, en esposo me fallarán. E los que me quisieren en esposa, en esposa me fallarán. E los que me quisieren en hermano o en amigo o en próximo o en conpañero, por semejante me fallarán para todo lo que quisieren, por quanto en mí es verdadero amor e deleite e fermosura de mirar." (*Conorte*, fols. 387v–388r)

("And those who seek love, you will find it in me, for I am true and most perfect and pure and undefiled and chaste love. I am love without wrinkle and without flaw and without filth. And all those who seek in me a father will find in me a father. And those who seek in me a husband, will find in me a husband. And those who seek in me a bride, will find in me a bride. And those who seek in me a brother or a friend or a neighbor or a companion, likewise will find in me everything they desire, inasmuch as in me is true love and delight and loveliness of countenance.")

Once again, Christ is cast as an androgynous figure, for the passage insists on the irrelevance of sexual roles for Him. The Lord is at once father and mother, bridegroom and bride.

In fact, at the end of the sermon the theme of Christ's androgyny re-appears in the context of the exegesis of the parable of the ten virgins:

E a esta sinificaçión (dixo el Señor) estavan en aquellos tálamos tan preçiosos que avía por todas las calles e cantones del reino de los çielos asentados en cada uno d'ellos solas dos personas, la una d'ellas hera El mesmo e la otra hera un santo o santa, a sinificar que muchos e sin conparaçión an de ser el número de los escogidos e bienaventurados, mas que solos dos an de ser los ayuntados en una fe e amor, conviene a saber, Dios y el ánima, que es Esposo verdadero de todas las vírgines prudentes, conviene a saber, de todas las ánimas bienaventuradas que le aman e sirven con todas sus fuerças e deseos e con linpieza de coraçón e de ánima e de cuerpo. (*Conorte,* fol. 388v)

(And in this respect—said the Lord—just two persons were seated on each one of those loveliest of marriage beds that were along all the streets and corners of the kingdom of Heaven: one of them was He Himself and the other was a male or female saint, which is to say that the number of the elect and the blessed will be many and incomparable, but that only two are to be united in one faith and love, namely, God and the soul, for He is the true Bridegroom of all the wise virgins, that is to say, all the blessed souls who love and serve Him with all their strength and desire and with a pure heart, soul, and body.)

Tálamos are marriage beds, and their presence in Heaven emphasizes once again the literal manner in which Mother Juana treats the topic of the soul as bride of the Lord.[23] Also reiterated is the identification of the wise virgins with the elect, whose "wisdom" has earned them Paradise. Further-more, the sexual connotations of the verb *ayuntar* once again round out the picture of a beatitude expressed in terms of a literalized nuptial meta-phor. Finally, the sermon brings out the theme of Christ's androgyny, for the Lord is seated on the marriage beds of all the blessed, be they male or female.

The parable of the ten virgins bears an implicit relation to the second part of the sermon for the Feast of Saint Clare, namely, the episode of the souls from Purgatory. These souls, although they purchased indulgences and went on pilgrimages, did not comply with all the conditions stipulated for the performance of such pious works, whence their implicit association with the foolish virgins of the Gospel parable. The perfect works of Saint Clare and the other heavenly virgins, that is to say, the wise virgins whose perfect works earned them salvation, are contrasted with the imperfect works of the souls from Purgatory, that is to say, the foolish virgins. The souls from Purgatory, thanks to their devotion to Saint Clare and the good works they did perform, were spared eternal damnation, but the imperfection of their works resulted in their consignment to Purgatory.

The interpretation of the second part of the sermon for Saint Clare's Day in the light of the parable of the ten virgins is supported by the patristic exegesis of the parable. A sermon by Saint Gregory the Great points out the intention with which the wise and foolish virgins carried out their good works:

Indeed, it must be noted that all of them have lamps, but not all have oil, for both the elect and the condemned display works good in and of themselves; but only those who seek inside the glory of that which they performed outside come to the Bridegroom with oil. . . . Then all the virgins arise, for both the elect and the condemned are awakened from the sleep of death. They trim their lamps, for they number the works for which they hope to receive eternal beatitude. But the lamps of the foolish virgins burn out, for their works, which on the exterior seemed shining in the eyes of men, turn dark inside at the coming of the Judge. And they do not obtain their due from God, because they already received from men the praises that they desired.[24]

It is unlikely that Mother Juana had a firsthand acquaintance with Saint Gregory's sermon. Nonetheless, she may at least have been familiar with similar texts that summarized traditional modes of interpreting the Gospel parable.[25] More than a sharp dichotomy between the elect and the damned, Saint Gregory's sermon (and other analogous texts[26]) establishes two levels of perfection. All the virgins have lamps, but not all have provided themselves with sufficient oil. All have performed works good in and of themselves, but the foolish virgins sought the praise of their neighbors, thus diminishing the value of their works. Hence, the parallel with the sermon for the Feast of Saint Clare, which establishes an analogous contrast between the elect and souls of lesser virtue.[27]

The exegesis of the parable of the ten virgins also raises the question of the "economics" of salvation,[28] for Saint Gregory interprets the trimming of the lamps as the enumeration of works in preparation for the encounter with the Bridegroom/Judge. The notion of salvation as something that could be purchased was widely accepted by the end of the Middle

Ages.[29] The faithful had masses said, performed good works, and said prayers in exchange for admission to Paradise. A good example of the economics of salvation is provided by one of Mother Juana's visions, which tells of the various fruits produced by the tree of life according to the day of the week. On Wednesdays, flowers, fruits, and banners bearing the name of Jesus sprout forth from the tree. Angels gather the standards and raise them up in honor of the Apostles, shouting like so many peddlers:

¿Ay quien venga a comprar el sancto reino de los çielos? ¡Ea! Vengan todos los que quisieren venir de su grado, que nosotros no hazemos a ninguno venir por fuerça. Empero, pregonamos e aconsejamos la fee muy çierta y verdadera, la carrera de vida y de salud. Enseñamos el camino del paraíso. Vengan los que sin dinero son redimidos sino por el gran preçio de la sangre del cordero. No teman de venir los pobres neçessitados, que por muy buen barato les venderemos el reino de los çielos. Que por el sancto baptismo y la fee de Jesuchristo, por guardar los mandamientos de Dios y hazer algunas buenas obras, por confisión y contriçión si cayeron en peccados, por satisfaçión e comunión e por los otros sacramentos de la Iglesia que ordenó el Spíritu Sancto, les venderemos el reino de los çielos a todos los que le quisieren comprar. (*Vida,* fol. 71r)

(Who will come and buy the holy kingdom of Heaven? Come on! Come all ye who wish to come of your own free will, for we do not force anyone to come. However, we peddle and preach the most certain and true faith, the path of life and salvation. We point out the road to Paradise. Come all those who, lacking money, are redeemed only through the high price of the blood of the Lamb. Let not the poor and needy fear to come, for we will sell them the kingdom of Heaven at a bargain. For in exchange for holy Baptism and the faith of Jesus Christ, for keeping God's commandments and performing some good works, for confession and contrition if they have fallen into sin, for penance and communion and for the other sacraments of the Church that the Holy Spirit ordained, we will sell the kingdom of Heaven to all those whosoever wish to purchase it.)

Thereupon, the angels bear the fruits of the tree of life to Purgatory in order to lessen the pain of the suffering souls. The marketplace vocabulary of the quoted passage is obvious: *comprar* ("buy"), *pregonar* ("hawk" or "peddle"), *dinero* ("money"), *preçio* ("price"), *por muy buen barato* ("at a bargain"), and *vender* ("sell"). The kingdom of Heaven is offered for sale in exchange for the money of good works, but if that is lacking, Paradise can be obtained even more reasonably through Christ's Passion.

Likewise, when in the sermon for the Feast of Saint Clare the angels plead for the liberation of the souls from Purgatory, emphasizing the good works the souls performed, the Lord tells them to do the appropriate calculations:

"Juzgaldo vosotros e contad: por tal bula quitaldes tantos años e por tal romería o estaçión quitaldes tanbién tantos, e por tal oraçión rezada a mi Pasión o a mi madre Santa María quitaldes por semejante tantos. E veréis vosotros cómo con todo esto no acaban aún de pagar ni cunplir." (*Conorte*, fol. 309r)

("You judge and calculate: for such and such an indulgence, subtract so many years and for such and such a pilgrimage or visit to a church subtract also so many, and for such and such a prayer said to my Passion or to my Mother Holy Mary subtract likewise so many. And you will see how with all that they do not even begin to pay or to fulfill their obligations.")

The passage is replete with terms borrowed from the language of commerce: the angels should *contar* ("count" or "calculate") and *quitar* ("subtract") so many years of Purgatory for such and such a good work. Nonetheless, when the accounts are settled, the angels will see that such works are not sufficient to *pagar* ("pay") what the souls owe.

In a similar vein, when in the ten-virgins sermon the foolish virgins seek the help of the wise virgins, that is, when they ask for some of the oil of their good works, the wise virgins reply that the foolish ones should go purchase the oil: "And if you do not have the oil of good works, go to Him who sells it, who is God, who created and redeemed you and has merits and boons to give you." [30] Thus, the sermon ends up questioning the very concept of the intercession of the saints, for the wise virgins (that is, the saints) answer that they can do nothing for the foolish virgins, since God is the source of all mercy and all good works. The notion of the good works of the saints as something "borrowed" is stressed later on in an allegorical pageant in which the blessed insist that the roses of their torments and penances, the lilies of their virginity, the treasures of their love and their asceticism, and the bread and pastries of their works of charity are not gifts that come from them but divine gifts: "O Lord, Our God, it is true that we offered you all those things, but you gave them to us, for none of them belongs to us." [31]

Other sermons go even further in dealing with the question of the insignificance of human works compared to the Redemption. In the sermon "Of Holy Doctrines" Christ insists that one does not enter Heaven through one's own merits but through the Passion:

"Aora bien, mis amigos, por que vean e conozcan todos cómo sólo en mí está el poder e la virtud e la graçia e que por mi Passión son todas salvas e perdonadas e no por sus mereçimientos sino por sola mi bondad, por lo qual en la mi virtud y en el mi poderío sean agora abiertas las puertas y entrado[s] vosotros. E meted esas áni-

mas que traés e sean bienaventuradas para sienpre e vean e conozcan cómo, por
mucho que an padesçido, mucho más padesçí yo por amor d'ellas." (*Conorte,* fol. 93r)

("Now then, my friends, in order for all to see and know how the power and the
virtue and the grace are in me alone, and how it is that through my Passion are all
saved and forgiven and not through their merits but through my goodness alone,
by virtue of my ability and my power let the gates now be opened and you be
admitted. And allow in the souls you bring and let them be blessed forever and let
them see and know how, no matter how much they have suffered, I suffered much
more out of love for them.")

Likewise, in the sermon devoted to the Temptation in the Desert a pageant is performed in which the Lord summons the heavenly elect and asks
if any one of them has ever been tempted. It turns out that not a single one
has never been tempted. Christ concludes that no one deserves to enter
Paradise, for one's own merits are not sufficient:

"assí es verdad que ninguno no es meresçedor de entrar en el vergel de las flores,
que es figura del santo paraíso e reino de Dios, aunque sean buenos e fieles, porque
sus propios meresçimientos no son bastantes. Enpero, ¡ea!, mis amigos, que yo soy
bastante para si estuvieren las personas que yo crié en el infierno sacarlas de allí y
traerlas al paraíso, conviene a saber, si estuvieren en pecado mortal o en tentaçiones
sacarlos d'ellas e traerlos a estado de graçia. . . . Por tanto tornad aora vosotros e
llamad por todo el çielo con las tronpetas e dezid que vengan todos los bienaventurados y entren en la figura que está hecha del infierno. Esto a sinificar que
ninguno de quantos honbres e mugeres ay en el çielo ni biven en la tierra no es
dino ni dina de entrar en este mi santo reino de los çielos por sus meresçimientos,
por muchos ni grandes que sean, mas antes son dinos todos del infierno. E por sola
mi misericordia se salvan los que se salvan." (*Conorte,* fol. 118r)

(thus it is true that no one deserves to enter the flower garden, which is a symbol of
holy Paradise and the kingdom of God, even though they be virtuous and faithful,
because their own merits are not enough. But, come now, my friends, for if the
persons I created are in Hell, I suffice to rescue them and to bring them to Paradise,
that is, if they are in mortal sin or facing temptations, to release them from them
and to bring them into a state of grace. . . . Therefore, return and with trumpets
summon all the blessed throughout Heaven and tell them to come enter the sym-
bolical representation of Hell. This means that not a single one of all the men and
women in Heaven or on the earth is worthy, neither man nor woman, to enter my
holy heavenly kingdom through his or her own merits, no matter how great they
may be, but rather they are all deserving of damnation. And through my mercy
alone are saved those who are saved.")

The passages just quoted can also be related to the question of sexual
roles and to the contrast between the spheres of action belonging to men

and women. If power is a divine gift, that is to say, something borrowed, then the power enjoyed by male saints is merely borrowed, if not factitious. On the other hand, the power conceded to women, however limited it may be, can be considered legitimate and even superior, for it is associated with the suffering humanity of Christ Himself. Thus, the power given to women is much more than something borrowed: it arises from the identification between Christ and the female sex. Likewise, if it is only through the Passion and through God's mercy that those who are saved are saved, then salvation is achieved through Christ's most "feminine" attribute, His suffering humanity. For example, when the Creation sermon attempts to rehabilitate Eve by associating with women the humility, the compassion, and the meekness of the Son—and more particularly, the patience with which Christ suffered the Passion (*Conorte*, fol. 444v)—it underscores the notion that Christ's saving mercy is a typically "feminine" quality.

In the Saint Clare sermon the episode of the souls from Purgatory raises the question of the effectiveness of the saint's intercessory powers at the same time that it addresses the theme of the relative value of activity and passivity. In effect, the sermon establishes an implicit contrast between Saint Clare and other heavenly advocates, highlighting the relative effectiveness of the intercession of advocates of one sex or the other. The sermon for the Feast of Saint Francis shows the Seraphic Father descending to Purgatory to liberate the souls of those devoted to him (see Chapter 2). When Mother Juana accompanies her guardian angel during his raids on Purgatory, she is not allowed to take an active role in liberating the souls, unless it be in a purely auxiliary capacity. In contrast, Saint Clare is not even permitted to fulfill an analogous auxiliary role. A dichotomy is thus established between activity and passivity. Only males are permitted to play an active role in the salvation of the souls in Purgatory; women can play but a passive role. Nonetheless, in Mother Juana's case that passivity turns out to be quite effective, for when in the stones episode she takes upon herself the sufferings of those in Purgatory (see Chapter 2), she undergoes a "passion" parallel to that of Christ, which results in the souls' release. On the other hand, Saint Clare ends up with the relatively passive role of pleading for the sake of the souls devoted to her, a role that turns out to be of limited effectiveness: the souls are given a momentary respite from their sufferings but are not completely released from them.

The fact is, in the sermon for the Feast of Saint Clare, the "masculine" attribute of God's divine justice predominates over the "feminine" attribute of His divine mercy. In the face of a God who requires a literal and almost legalistic compliance with His laws, the imperfect works of the souls in Purgatory turn out to be of little value. If other visions offer many examples of divine mercy, of the wide variety of means for salvation, and of the great number and power of heavenly advocates, the Saint Clare vision demonstrates the limits of such blind confidence. Indeed, the image of a severe God who constantly threatens to destroy the world, while not dominant in Mother Juana's visions, occurs with a certain frequency. Thus, in the sermon for the Feast of the Invention of the Cross, an allegorical pageant contrasts the Father's anger with the Son's mercy. The Father's anger against the world is so great that He would like to destroy it in a brief moment (*Conorte,* fol. 180v). In contrast, the Son, kneeling before the Father, offers Him the wounds and torments of His Passion, begging the Father to have mercy on sinners and to give them an opportunity to repent (*Conorte,* fols. 180v–181r). The passage emphasizes the delicate equilibrium between God's paternal and maternal tendencies, a balance that, as one is led to believe, could be upset at any time. But Christ pleads before the Father that the world not be destroyed, just as Saint Clare pleaded for the souls in Purgatory devoted to her. The fact that the saint achieved but a brief respite for the souls is offset by her association with the role of the merciful Christ. Thus, the limits of God's mercy, that is to say, of His "feminine" side, are related to the limits imposed on the actions of holy women. When Mother Juana contrasts the relative effectiveness of male and female advocates, she is simultaneously dealing with the contrast between God's justice and His mercy, that is, between His castigating paternity and His compassionate maternity.

But the relation of sexual roles to the Father/Son dichotomy raises a problem that Mother Juana resolves with characteristic ambiguity. If from an earthly perspective the intercession of male saints is more effective than that of female saints, a hierarchy is suggested: the advocacy of males is more valuable (more perfect?) than that of females. Nonetheless, this dichotomy does not prevail when viewed from God's point of view. If the compassion of women is related to Christ's humanity, and if the justice of men is related to that of the Father, it would be wrong to conclude that the Father's sphere of activity is superior to the Son's. Therefore, Mother Juana seems to be saying that in the same way that the activities of the three persons of the Holy Trinity are of equal value, from God's perspective the value of the good works of women is equal to that of the good works of men. This also explains why Juana insists on Christ's androgyny and on the concomitant irrelevance of the differences between the sexes.

Women cannot lose through their association with Christ; on the contrary, they gain in both power and authority. Moreover, when Juana extols feminine attributes (including her feminizing of Christ with the accompanying emphasis on the "Christ as mother" motif), she enables women to appropriate some of Christ's power, for if He is at once man and woman, then women acquire by association a prestige that allows them to transcend the limitations imposed upon their earthly sphere of action.

At first glance it appears that the roles allotted to the copatrons of the Franciscan order are clear-cut: Saint Francis is called upon to play an active and efficacious role, stereotypically masculine, while Saint Clare plays a passive role, of limited effectiveness, and thereby stereotypically feminine. Thus, the power and authority of men appear to be greater than the power and authority of women. But in Mother Juana's visionary world sexual differences become blurred, which constitutes a first step toward the collapse of such sexual stereotypes. Saint Clare is at once female and male, for she possesses both the vaginal vessel and the phallic organ pipe. Likewise, Christ is both male and female, for He is father and mother, bridegroom and bride. The ambiguous nature of these sexual roles and symbols blurs the differences between the power allotted to men and that allotted to women. In addition, the differences between the respective spheres of action of men and women turn out to be odious, for they reflect a point of view that is earthly, and therefore imperfect. In exalting Saint Clare, Mother Juana exalts all women, for she glorifies a series of attributes and activities closely associated with the female gender: virginity, giving birth, and nursing. But these activities also pertain to Christ: the Lord suckles the blessed souls and suffers the Passion like a mother giving birth.[32] Mother Juana, as if sensitized by the example of Saint Clare to women's limited resources for direct action, feminizes Christ and thereby empowers women by association. Through their identification with Christ, holy women are enabled to acquire a power and an authority often denied them in their daily life.

Notes

1. "Sal tú acá, amiga mía Clara, que bien me entenderás que digo a ti, que aunque aya otras en mi santo reino que se llaman claras, pocas son e no tan señaladas como tú" (*Conorte*, fols. 308rv). Puns on Saint Clare's name date back to the earliest biographical sources. According to a pious tradition, her mother gave her the name Clare because a heavenly voice told her that her daughter was to light up the world: "Ne paveas, mulier, quia quoddam lumen salva parturies, quod ipsum

mundum clarius illustrabit" (Michael Bihl, OFM, "Tres Legendae minores Sanctae Clarae Assisiensis [saec. XIII]," *Archivum Franciscanum Historicum*, 7 [1914] 39–40). The episode came to form part of the office for the Feast of Saint Clare. See, for example, the *Breviarium secundum morem romane curie* (Venice: 1481), n.p. In the life of Saint Clare attributed to Thomas of Celano, Saint Clare is "clear alike in name and in deed" (*The Life of Saint Clare Ascribed to Fr. Thomas of Celano,* trans. Paschal Robinson [Philadelphia: Dolphin Press, 1910], 6).

2. Which one is the shy maiden here? Christ seems to appropriate the role of the *doncella esquiva.* The motif of God's playful hiding also appears in the sermons for the Feast of Saint Lawrence (*Conorte,* fol. 267v) and for the Feast of Saint Major (*Conorte,* fol. 356rv).

3. "Dezidme, señores, ¿avéis visto al que ama la mi ánima?" (*Conorte,* fol. 308v). "Him, whom my soul loves" is the epithet applied to the beloved in the Song of Songs 3:3 ("Have you seen him, whom my soul loveth?").

4. "porque qualquier persona que piensa en Dios e desea gozar de las sus dulçedunbres e consolaçiones divinales es oración muy açeuta e aplazible delante d'El" (*Conorte,* fol. 308v).

5. "muy enbriagada y ençendida de amor sobre el que le tenía en sus faldas, adorándole e abraçándole e besándole muchas vezes con soberana reverençia e amor" (*Conorte,* fol. 308v).

6. The connection between Clare and the symbolic vessel is established as early as the saint's bull of canonization (1255): "nor could a vessel filled with perfume be so hidden that it would not emit its fragrance and suffuse the Lord's house with a sweet aroma" (Clare of Assisi, *Early Documents,* trans. Regis J. Armstrong, OFM Cap. [New York: Paulist Press, 1988], 178). The author of Clare's first biography observes that "as the Spirit working within her . . . formed her into a most pure vase, she became known as a vessel of grace, indeed" (*The Life of Saint Clare,* 8).

7. The Vatican manuscript (fols. 522v–533r) offers an extended version of this gloss, which simply repeats the idea that those who successfully navigate the treacherous waters of this world in search of the precious pearl (God) will, like Saint Clare and the other holy virgins, receive the appropriate heavenly rewards.

8. The topic reappears in the sermon "The Preeminences of Friday," when guardian angels bring before God the souls in Purgatory entrusted to them. The souls have not completed their purgation, first, because of the gravity of their sins, and second, because those on earth who had offered suffrages for their sake had not satisfied all the necessary conditions: "no estavan en tanto estado de graçia ni en tanta linpieza de ánima como devían para que sus oraçiones fuesen açeutas delante el acatamiento divinal. E por quanto tomavan las buldas, no tenían aquellas condiçiones e intinçión caritativa que se requiere para ganar enteramente indulgençia plenaria. E d'esta manera tenían aquellas ánimas grande número de años de penas constituidos que avían de padesçer" (*Conorte,* fols. 238v–239r).

9. "Las conditiones de las bulas . . . es doctrina de todos los sanctos doctores y escolásticos" (*Conorte,* fol. 309v).

10. "se havía de escrevir con letras de oro en estos miserables tienpos" (*Conorte,* fol. 309v).

11. "conmiençó de su ponçoña . . . bulas y purgatorio y luego buenas obras por quedar en todo malo" (*Conorte,* fol. 309v).

12. Edward E. Malone, OSB, *The Monk and the Martyr: The Monk as the Successor of the Martyr* (Washington, D.C.: Catholic University of America Press, 1950), 59–60.

13. Caroline Walker Bynum, *Holy Feast and Holy Fast: The Religious Significance of Food to Medieval Women* (Berkeley and Los Angeles: University of California Press, 1987), 282–294.

14. Mircea Eliade, *Images et symboles* (Paris: Gallimard, 1952), 169–170.

15. "Union ki naist de rusee / E ki en piere est engendree, / Union Jesu signefie, / Piere dunt naist, Sainte Marie; / Union ki naist de rusee / Signefie grace aprestee: / Par grace fut que li fiz Dé / Fut a la virgine presenté, / Par grace en cuillit le salu / E par grace fut cunceü. / Cum la piere ovre senz frainture / E el se juint senz creveüre, / Cum la piere fait la rusee, / Si fut la virgine cunsecree, / Issi cunçut e enfantat / La virgine ki Jesu portat; / Virgine cunçut, virgine enfantat, / Virgine permist e permaindrat" (*Le Bestiaire de Phillippe de Thaün*, vv. 3063–3080, ed. Emmanuel Walberg [Lund: Hj. Möller, and Paris: H. Welter, 1900], III). Likewise, in the *Physiologus:* "The stone which is called the conch is a figure of Holy Mary concerning whom Isaiah prophesied, 'There shall come forth a shoot (*virga*) from the stump of Jesse' [Isa. II:I]. And again, 'Behold, a young woman (*virgo*) shall conceive within her womb and give birth' [Isa. 7:14]. And Holy Mary was called a virgin (*virgo*) because of this shoot (*virga*). In truth, the flower born to Holy Mary is Our Lord God Jesus Christ" (*Physiologus*, trans. Michael J. Curley [Austin and London: University of Texas Press, 1979], 35).

16. Also relevant here is the symbolism of the pearl established in the patristic exegesis of the Gospel parable of the pearl of great price (Matthew 13:45–46). Origen, for example, says that he who would gain wisdom and truth must go beyond the law and the prophets to find the precious pearl that is Christ. See his commentary on the gospel of Saint Matthew in *Patrologiae cursus completus: Series graeca*, ed. J.-P. Migne, 162 vols. (Paris: Migne, 1857–1866), vol. 13, cols. 855, 858.

17. For the association between the pearl and virginity in medieval literature, see C. A. Luttrell, "The Mediaeval Tradition of the Pearl Virginity," *Medium Aevum*, 31 (1962) 194–200.

18. The relation between Saint Clare and the wise virgins appears in the saint's earliest biographies. The narration of the scene in which Saint Clare receives the habit incorporates reminiscences of Luke 12:35–36 and of the parable of the ten virgins: "Igitur domo, civitate et consanguineis derelictis, ad Sanctam Mariam de Angelis festinavit, ubi Fratres, qui in aula Dei sacras observabant excubias, prudentem virginem obviam Sponso cum lampade non vacua procedentem, gestantes et ipsi lucernas ardentes in manibus exceperunt" (Bihl, "Tres Legendae," 41). This passage also formed part of the liturgical office for the Feast of Saint Clare. See, for example, the *Breviarium secundum morem romane curie* (Venice: 1481), n.p.

19. Rabanus Maurus, *Allegoriae in sacram scripturam*, in Migne, *Patrologia Latina*, vol. 112, col. 1011.

20. Saint Hilary, *Commentarius in Evangelium Matthaei*, in Migne, *Patrologia Latina*, vol. 9, col. 1060.

21. The anonymous censor of the *Conorte* crossed out but a single passage in the sermon on the ten virgins: the one relating how the sinners provoke God's anger. Father Torres responds by quoting several canonical examples of divine

anger: the Flood and Sodom (*Conorte*, fol. 387r). Nevertheless, at the end of the sermon Torres pens another marginal note that combines his desire to control the future reception of the text, his praise for Mother Juana's infused knowledge, and a sort of prayer in the name of all the *Conorte*'s readers, who are identified with the wise virgins: "En este capítulo notarás al principio la parábola en estremo bien declarada. Y después en la figura y segunda parte yo seguro que quien con devoción lo mereciere leer que entenderá y gustará bien. ¡Qué dichosos los que son vírgines prudentes!, pues esta simple y idiota tanta sabiduría y tanta dulçura alcançó para sí y para nosotros. Plega a Dios que no seamos vírgines fatuas y sucias y manchadas y descuidadas y desapercevidas para bodas de tal esposo que tan inefables bienes y deleites i dulcedunbres nos tiene, si somos cuerdas vírgines y velamos en cada hora, como si aquella fuese en la que nos a de llamar. El nos dé tal gracia para que nos abra la puerta y le veamos y gocemos en el siglo de los siglos en perpetua unión con El. Amén" (*Conorte*, fol. 388v).

22. A similar trope appears in the Transfiguration sermon: "E que así está el ánima tan ayuntada con El como el niño pequeñuelo quando mama las tetas de la madre" (*Conorte*, fol. 298v).

23. In the sermon for the Feast of Saint Lawrence, when the saint begs the Lord to accept his throne, his marriage bed, and all his other celestial treasures, the Lord answers that He will do so on the condition that He and Saint Lawrence may be seated together on the throne and marriage bed as are husband and wife on the day of their wedding: "A mí me plaze, mi amigo, de te conçeder la petiçión tan justa e amorosa que me demandas. Pero a de ser con una condiçión, que yo e tú juntos estemos asentados en el tálamo e trono alto como están el esposo e la esposa el día de las bodas" (*Conorte*, fol. 271rv).

24. "Notandum vero quod omnes lampades habent, sed omnes oleum non habent, quia plerumque bona in se opera cum electis et reprobi ostendunt, sed soli ad sponsum cum oleo veniunt, qui de his quae foris egerint intus gloriam requirunt. . . . Tunc omnes virgines surgunt, quia et electi et reprobi a somno suae mortis excitantur. Lampades ornant, quia sua secum opera numerant, pro quibus aeternam recipere beatitudinem exspectant. Sed lampades fatuarum virginum exstinguuntur, quia earum opera, quae clara hominibus foris apparuerant, in adventu judicis intus obscurantur. Et a Deo retributionem non inveniunt, quia pro eis receperunt ab hominibus laudes quas amaverunt" (Saint Gregory the Great, *XL homiliarum in Evangelia libri duo*, Homilia XII, in Migne, *Patrologia Latina*, 76, cols. 1119–1120).

25. For an overview of medieval exegesis of the parable of the ten virgins, see Stephen L. Wailes, *Medieval Allegories of Jesus' Parables* (Berkeley and Los Angeles: University of California Press, 1987), 177–184.

26. For example, passages from Saint Gregory's sermon are quoted in Rabanus Maurus's *Commentarium in Matthaeum*. See Migne, *Patrologia Latina*, 107, cols. 1084–1089.

27. A sermon by Saint Augustine on the parable of the ten virgins establishes a similar contrast between admitted and rejected virgins: "For, lo, those *foolish virgins, who brought no oil with them*, wish to please men by that abstinence of theirs whereby they are called virgins, and by their good works, when they seem to carry

lamps. And if they wish to please men, and on that account do all these praise-worthy works, they do not carry oil with them. . . . The lamps of the wise virgins burned with an inward oil, with the assurance of a good conscience, with an inner glory, with an inmost charity. Yet the lamps of the foolish virgins burned also. Why burnt they then? Because there was yet no want of the praises of men. But after that they arose, that is in the resurrection from the dead, they began to trim their lamps, that is, began to prepare to render unto God an account of their works. And because there is then no one to praise, every man is wholly employed in his own cause, there is no one then who is not thinking of himself, therefore were there none to sell them oil" (Saint Augustine, *Sermons on Selected Lessons of the New Testament*, trans. by members of the English Church, 2 vols. [Oxford: John Henry Parker, 1844–1845], 1 : 360).

28. See, for example, Joel T. Rosenthal, *The Purchase of Paradise: Gift Giving and the Aristocracy, 1307–1485* (London: Routledge and Kegan Paul, and Toronto: University of Toronto Press, 1972); and Jacques Chiffoleau, *La Comptabilité de l'au-delà. Les hommes, la mort et la religion dans la région d'Avignon à la fin du Moyen Age (vers 1320 –vers 1480)* (Rome: Ecole Française de Rome, 1980).

29. The economics of salvation and the value of illnesses are underscored in the final lines of the *Canticle of Exhortation to Saint Clare and Her Sisters* (1225), a poem that Saint Francis composed for Clare and her companions: "Those who are weighed down by sickness / and the others who are wearied because of them, / all of you: bear it in peace. / For you will sell this fatigue at a very high price / and each one [of you] will be crowned queen / in heaven with the Virgin Mary" (Clare of Assisi, *Early Documents*, 251).

30. "E si no tenéis azeite de buenas obras, id a quien lo vende, que es Dios, el qual os crió e redimió e tiene méritos e dones que os dar" (*Conorte*, fol. 385r).

31. "Señor Dios nuestro, verdad es que os ofreçíamos todas aquellas cosas, mas vos nos las distes, que nada de todo ello no es nuestro" (*Conorte*, fol. 386r). Cf. "Who am I, and what is my people, that we should be able to promise thee all these things? All things are thine, and we have given thee what we received of thy hand" (I Chronicles 29 : 14). Similarly, in Saint Augustine's sermon on the parable of the ten virgins, the oil in the vessels is a gift from God: "There is the oil, the precious oil; this oil is the gift of God. Men can put oil into their vessels, but they cannot create the olive" (*Sermons* 1 : 360).

32. See Chapter 2, note 12 of this study.

V. Scripture and Scriptures

The end of the Creation sermon, which occupies the final folios of the Escorial manuscript of the *Conorte,* stands out as the place where the book turns its eye upon itself, as it were, to ponder the nature of its own creation—and to shape its readers' reactions to it—in a striking moment of self-consciousness. Here the nuns who wrote out the manuscript reflect upon their task, using what are probably miscellaneous fragments of Mother Juana's visions to ponder the mystery of the revelation and the writing of the sermons. This is not, to be sure, a unique moment, for at various times Mother Juana herself had already paused to consider the miraculous revelation of the sermons. Nonetheless, it is at the end of the manuscript that the process of the book's revelation and of its writing become self-conscious. Through Mother Juana's voice the Lord repeatedly addresses the *Conorte*'s readers or listeners, offering the visionary and her companions one last opportunity to control the reception of the text: the nuns defend the book's divine inspiration, answer the objections of its critics, and seek to convert the unbelieving.

In fact, it is at the end of the Escorial manuscript of the *Conorte* (see Appendix I) that, almost for the first and only time,[1] Mother Juana's companions speak in their own voices, displaying their awareness of their task as scribes, for God Himself has ordered the writing of the book:

Porque tanto quanto estas preçiosas palabras son más eçelentes e altas, tanto an menester las gentes más lunbre e graçia para las entender e conprehender e gustar. Porque son dichas e declaradas por la boca del poderoso Dios, el qual tuvo por bien de dar liçençia para que se escriviesen e dibulgasen por el mundo. (*Conorte,* fol. 452r)

(Because the more excellent and lofty these precious words are, the more people are in need of greater light and grace to understand and comprehend and savor them. Because they are uttered and interpreted by the mouth of God almighty, who saw fit to grant permission for them to be written down and made known throughout the world.)

God's mandate to write down and to spread His word notwithstanding, the nuns had to contend with the problem of authority, for they found themselves caught between two jurisdictions, the one divine, the other earthly. On the one hand, the superiors of their order had commanded that Mother Juana's revelations be written down, probably in order to examine their orthodoxy.[2] On the other hand, God Himself had declared that the world was unworthy to receive such secrets:

E aun dixo e fue fecho assí como prometió que daría lunbre e memoria para se retener y escrevir, suplicándoselo nosotras por quanto fuimos mandadas de algunos perlados que escriviésemos lo que oíamos. Enpero respondió su divina magestad que no hera dino el mundo, conviene a saber, todos nosotros pecadores, los quales somos cada uno de nosotros un mundo de pecados, de oír ni escrevir ni leer tan altas palabras e secretos. E confiando en su gran misericordia, enpeçamos a escrevir algo de lo que oíamos. (*Conorte,* fol. 452r)

(And He even said, and so it was done, since He promised that He would give light and memory to remember and to write, for we had asked it of Him inasmuch as we were ordered by certain prelates to write down what we heard. However, His Divine Majesty answered that the world, that is to say, all us sinners, for each one of us is a world of sins, was not worthy of hearing or writing or reading such lofty words and secrets. And trusting in His great mercy, we began to write down something of what we heard.)

Trapped between speaking and keeping silent, forced to choose between activity and passivity, the nuns decided to obey the more immediate authority and to write down Mother Juana's revelations, thus disobeying the divine prohibition. However, their trust in God's mercy was vindicated when the Lord approved the good intentions that led them to begin to write:

E respondió entonçes su divina magestad a nuestro propósito e intinçión, diziendo que no esperava El otra cosa sino que nos comidiésemos a lo fazer para honra e gloria suya e salvaçión de las ánimas. (*Conorte,* fol. 452r)

(Then His Divine Majesty responded to our resolve and intention, saying that He did not expect anything else than that we would begin to do it for His honor and glory and for the salvation of souls.)[3]

If Mother Juana's companions ended up conforming to the will of God by writing the *Conorte,* they still had to resolve the problem of the text's reception by its earthly readers and listeners. The nuns felt compelled to respond to the criticisms, real or imagined, that had been leveled or could be leveled at the revelations. In particular, they address the question of the novelization of sacred history, a technique that constitutes one of the most salient characteristics of Mother Juana's sermons. The fleshing out of the Scriptures with noncanonical details is especially characteristic of Franciscan spirituality.⁴ Juana is conscious of the problems raised by that technique, and at various moments in the *Conorte* she attempts to justify the inclusion of details and even entire episodes that are not found in the canon of Holy Writ. In the case of the Creation sermon, she finds it sufficient to insist that her amplifications of the Scriptures are divinely inspired. Through Juana, the Lord Himself defends the authenticity of the words of the Holy Spirit, surely a more reliable authority than any earthly writer:

E declaró el Señor, diziendo que no se maraville ninguno porque en este santo libro ay algunas cosas más largamente declaradas o denunçiadas o tratadas que en las otras santas escrituras que acá están escritas, por quanto las dize e declara el Espíritu Santo y el mesmo resollo e virtud de Dios, el qual sabe mejor todas las cosas que ninguno de quantos escrivieron o fizieron las escrituras que acá están escritas. Porque assí como el Espíritu Santo alunbra y enseña de dentro del ánima mayores e más altas e maravillosas cosas que las escrituras le pueden dezir ni mostrar, así por semejante el mesmo Espíritu Santo, el qual fabló e declaró todas estas cosas, las sabe e conoçe mejor que nadie lo puede dezir ni declarar ni manifestar. (*Conorte*, fol. 450r)

(And the Lord declared, saying that no one should marvel that in this holy book there are some things more lengthily explicated or revealed or treated than in the other holy scriptures that are written here on earth, inasmuch as the Holy Spirit and very breath and power of God utter them and gloss them, for He knows all things better than any one of all those who have written or composed the scriptures that are written on this earth. Because just as the Holy Spirit enlightens and teaches from within the soul greater and more lofty and marvelous things than the scriptures can say or show, so likewise the very same Holy Spirit, who spoke and interpreted all these things, knows them better and is more familiar with them than anyone could say or expound or disclose.)⁵

In other cases Juana justifies the revelation in the *Conorte* of details not found in the Bible by attributing certain omissions to the four Evangelists. Indeed, according to Juana, it was simply impossible for the Evangelists to record all of Christ's words.⁶ In the sermon for the Feast of Saint Luke, the Virgin Mary reveals to the saint certain previously unrecorded details regarding the Annunciation. When Saint Luke wonders if he will be capable of transcribing so much information, the Virgin tells him to write down only what is most pertinent to the salvation of humankind:

"Fijo mío Lucas, sea como tú quisieres. Yo todo quisiera que lo escrivieras, mas de muchos granos buenos que yo te doy, escoge los mejores e más provechosos para el provecho de las ánimas." E que así escrevía de cada cosa un poquito e lo mesmo que fizo San Lucas fizieron los otros evangelistas, que de las muchas e altas palabras que Nuestro Señor Jesuchristo fablava (dixo El mesmo) no escrivieron sino unas poquitas. (*Conorte,* fol. 384r)

("My son Luke, be it as you will. I would like you to write down everything, but of the many good kernels that I give you, choose the best and most useful for the benefit of souls." And so he wrote a little bit about everything and the other Evangelists did the same as Saint Luke, for of the many and lofty words uttered by Our Lord Jesus Christ—He Himself said—they only wrote down a few.)

A similar justification is given in the sermon for the Feast of Saint Anne. Christ explains that when He was two or three years old and Saint Anne was carrying Him about in her arms, He revealed certain secrets and mysteries to her and to the Virgin Mary. His mother and grandmother never revealed those secrets to anyone, for it was not their task to do so. Even the four Evangelists, whose duty it was to record Christ's public life, only wrote down one-tenth of what happened:

Enpero que como Santana e Nuestra Señora heran parte, nunca quisieron descubrir a nadie lo que veían e sabían e sentían, por quanto no hera dado a ellas descubrir tales secretos. Que aun de las cosas e maravillas que El fizo siendo honbre de edad perfeta, las quales maravillas fazía públicas e manifiestas, no escrivieron los evangelistas de diez partes la una de lo que pasó. (*Conorte,* fol. 289v)

(Although Saint Anne and Our Lady were privy [to these events], they refused to reveal to anyone what they saw and discovered and experienced, inasmuch as it did not fall to them to reveal such secrets. For even with regard to the deeds and marvels that He performed in His prime, which marvels He performed publicly and openly, the Evangelists wrote down only one-tenth of what occurred.)

The task left unfinished by Saint Anne, the Blessed Virgin, and the four Evangelists has now fallen to Mother Juana, who thus completes the divine revelation. In so doing, Juana not only assimilates her role to that of the four Evangelists but also associates herself with a specifically female channel of revelation.

In the Easter sermon Juana tells how the wounds on Christ's body continued to bleed even after the Resurrection and how the Apostles applied cloths soaked in cold water to His wounds to make the blood disappear. To justify her inclusion of this noncanonical detail, the visionary explains that the Evangelists failed to record the episode because they did not wish to digress from matters pertinent to the salvation of humankind:

E declaró el Señor, diziendo que no se maraville nadie porque los apóstoles y evangelistas no escrivieron de las piedades que le fazían después de resuçitado, viéndole las feridas frescas, porque ellos no quisieron dezir otra cosa sino lo que fazía al caso e convenía para nuestra fe. (*Conorte*, fol. 163r)

(And the Lord declared, saying that no one should marvel that the Apostles and Evangelists did not write about the acts of compassion they did unto Him after He was resurrected, when they saw His fresh wounds, because they did not want to say anything other than what pertained to the matter at hand and was important for our faith.)

The Lord then observes that the omission of this detail by the Evangelists constitutes a lesson in modesty, for they did not wish to praise their own good works, as such deeds should not be performed out of the desire for glory but only to serve God.

The sermon for Wednesday of Holy Week considerably amplifies the episode of the angel who came to the Garden of Gethsemane to comfort Christ (Luke 22:43). According to Mother Juana, various angels appeared to Christ, begging Him not to undergo the Passion. In response, He showed them an allegorical pageant to demonstrate the necessity of the Crucifixion. The Lord explains that He did not wish to disclose the episode at that time, because it was not an appropriate moment for such revelations:

la qual visitaçión e revelaçión nunca El quiso por entonçes dezir ni manifestar a ninguna persona porque aquel tienpo en que El entonçes estava hera más de humilldad e paçiençia e silençio e sufrimiento de injurias e tormentos e llagas e feridas que de dezir ni descubrir secretos ni visiones ni revelaçiones. (*Conorte*, fol. 141v)

(which visitation and revelation He refused to recount or disclose to anyone because the moment in which He then found Himself was a time more for humility and patience and silence and suffering insults and torments and wounds and injuries than for revealing or disclosing secrets or visions or revelations.)

Finally, in the sermon devoted to the Losing of Jesus in the Temple, Juana offers many details not found in the Gospel narrative. The Lord Himself explains that the Evangelists failed to record the event with all the detail that appears in the *Conorte* for two reasons. First, the Evangelists were not eyewitnesses to the events of Christ's childhood nor did they afterward fully learn what had occurred in those times. Second, the Evangelists had the time to record only a small part of such holy mysteries:

E declaró el Señor, diziendo que en este misterio de su santo perdimiento no hablaron los santos evangelistas más largamente ni declararon todas las cosas e secretos e misterios así como aquí en este santo libro El lo fabló e declaró, lo primero porque ellos no lo vieron ni supieron assí tan por entero cómo ello fue e acontesçió en aquel tienpo e niñez suya; lo segundo, porque los mesmos evangelistas no tenían lugar ni espaçio para escrevir d'este misterio e de cada uno de los otros santos misterios sino muy poquito e lo que hazía brevemente a la salvaçión de las ánimas. Por lo qual tuvo por bien su divina magestad (dixo el mesmo Dios e Señor Nuestro Jesuchristo) de lo declarar e manifestar aora en estos tienpos por que viésemos e conosçiésemos quánto ama a las ánimas e desea su convertimiento e salvaçión. (*Conorte,* fol. 112v)

(And the Lord declared, saying that the holy Evangelists failed to speak at greater length of this mystery of His holy Losing in the Temple—nor did they explain all the events and secrets and mysteries—in the way that He spoke and explained it here in this holy book, first, because they did not witness it nor did they learn in such detail how it was and happened at that time during His childhood; second, because the Evangelists themselves had neither the time nor the space to write but a little bit and what was most pertinent to the salvation of souls about this mystery and about each one of the other holy mysteries. For which reason His Divine Majesty—so said the very same God and Our Lord Jesus Christ—saw fit to declare and reveal it now in these times so that we might see and know how much He loves the souls and desires their conversion and salvation.)

Thus, the delayed revelation of such details has been accomplished through Mother Juana, whose role in this process of revelation is implicitly enhanced by the Lord Himself.

The novelization of events that occurred prior to the Nativity, and therefore before the time of the four Evangelists, requires a different sort of justification. In the Creation sermon, for example, the crucial scene in which the Lord creates a beard on the chin of the sleeping Adam is followed by a defense of that episode. God Himself warns that no one should be surprised that the scene is not found in the Scriptures, for at the time of the Creation there was no one present to record such events:

E que no deve ninguna persona dudar ni maravillarse de cómo crió El las barvas a Adán después de le aver criado, aunque no lo fallen en las Santas Escrituras, porque entonçes no avía gentes que escriviesen esto ni otras muchas cosas e secretos que se están oy día en silençio. (*Conorte,* fol. 444v)

(And no one should doubt or marvel at how He created Adam's beard after creating him, even though it is not to be found in the Holy Scriptures, because at that time there was no one to write this or the many other things and secrets that even today remain cloaked in silence.)

What is implicit, of course, is that there *was* an eyewitness to the event, namely, God Himself, who has now chosen to reveal that incident through Juana.[7]

Likewise, Juana's sermon on the creation of the angels and the fall of Lucifer presents a highly novelesque account of events in Heaven. God observes that, while here on earth some things have been written about those happenings, such writings are not as complete as they might be, for their authors were not eyewitnesses to what they recorded.[8] God, of course, was, for He created the angels and vanquished those who sinned against Him:

E declaró el Señor, diziendo que aunque tienen acá en la tierra escritas algunas cosas de la creación de los ángeles e del caimiento e bengança de los malos e sobervios e de la santificación de los ángeles buenos e de los gozos e consolaçiones que El les a dado e da de cada día e dará para sienpre, no está todo tan entero e cunplido como ello fue, porque los que lo escrivieron no lo vieron ni supieron ellos, así como El mesmo que los crió e derribó a los que erraron contra El. (*Conorte*, fol. 362v)

(And the Lord declared, saying that although here on earth some things have been written about the creation of the angels and the fall and the revenge on the evil and proud ones and about the sanctification of the good angels and about the joys and comforts that He gave them and continues to give them every day and forever, it [that writing] is not all as full and complete as it [the actual event] was, because those who wrote about it did not witness it nor did they learn about it, as did He Himself who created them and threw down those who sinned against Him.)

The implication, then, is that in this case Juana's version of the revolt of the bad angels is more accurate than any other account, for it is none other than God's own version of that event. In her role as earwitness to the supreme eyewitness, Juana is not amplifying the Scriptures on her own but is merely completing, through the will and inspiration of God, what the Evangelists were unwilling or unable to reveal. Thus, the visionary not only becomes a sort of latter-day evangelist, but her writings, by completing and complementing the Bible, aspire to the authority enjoyed by the canonical Scriptures.

Mother Juana likewise confers authority on her writings through the establishment of two important dichotomies, one spatial, the other temporal, intended to promote the legitimacy of both the revelation and the writing of *El libro del conorte*. The temporal dichotomy serves to enhance and defend the miraculous nature of the divine revelation that God accomplishes through the mouth of His handmaiden Juana. The spatial dichotomy serves to justify the more detailed narration of sacred history that the

Conorte provides. Thus, the end of the Creation sermon relates the question of the novelization of biblical narratives to the notion of the two spaces, a "here" (*acá*) and a "there" (*allá*), that correspond to earth and Heaven, respectively. Juana locates *El libro del conorte* in both spaces, making it participate in what has been written in both places. On the one hand, the book is assimilated to the other earthly scriptures. Concretely, when Juana refers to "the other holy scriptures that are written here on earth" (*Conorte,* fol. 450r), she appears to associate the *Conorte* with the Bible itself. It must be observed, nonetheless, that the visionary establishes this relationship in an equivocal manner, using to her advantage the ambiguity between generic scriptures and sacred Scriptures. On the other hand, the *Conorte* distinguishes itself from the Holy Scriptures because it affords a more detailed narrative of certain events. Nonetheless, the principal difference between the *Conorte* and the other earthly scriptures arises from the spatial dichotomy that Mother Juana has established, for the words of her book are also written on the walls of the kingdom of Heaven:

E los misterios e secretos d'este santo libro son tan grandes que todas las palabras d'él (dixo el Señor) están escritas en el reino de los çielos, assí como El las dixo e fabló, por las paredes de las calles e alcáçares con letras muy grandes e resplande-çientes e claras que las pueden todos quantos allá están leer. E sale d'ellas tan suave olor que todos los bienaventurados se deleitan en las oler e mirar. (*Conorte,* fol. 452r)

(And the mysteries and secrets of this holy book are so great that all of its words—said the Lord—are written in the kingdom of Heaven, just as He uttered and spoke them, on the walls of the streets and palaces in very large and brilliant and luminous letters that everyone there can read. And from them issues so sweet an odor that all the blessed souls delight in smelling and looking at them.)

This means that the book possesses a heavenly dimension that the other scriptures lack. Thus, not only does Juana justify the more detailed versions of sacred history that the *Conorte* offers, but the *Conorte* gains an authority and prestige that the other scriptures lack. Moreover, as is pointed out later in the sermon, if everything in Heaven is superior to what is on earth, then the words of the *Conorte,* because they are written in Heaven, also participate in that superior state, surpassing any other earthly writing.

The spatial dichotomy "here" and "there" finds its temporal equivalent in the dichotomy "now" (*agora*) and "then" (*entonçes*). The end of the Creation sermon establishes this dichotomy to respond to critics who wondered why God had chosen to manifest Himself by speaking through

Juana's mouth instead of by performing miracles. The visionary answers this objection with an argument based on historical perspective. Miracles are associated only with the time when Christ walked upon this earth and with the time of the Apostles:

avía algunas personas que dezían que pues El dezía que hera Dios e se manifestava por ello, que fiziese miraglos e maravillas para que le conoçiesen e creyesen. E a los pensamientos de los que tales cosas demandavan respondió el mesmo Dios, diziendo que ya hera pasado su día, que un día e otro avía de fazer miraglos e no más, conviene a saber, un tienpo que los fizo El quando vino en el mundo e otro tienpo que los fizieron sus diçipulos. (*Conorte*, fol. 450r)

(there were some people who said that, since He said that He was God and manifested Himself therefore, He should work miracles and marvels so that they would recognize and believe Him. And God answered the thoughts of those who asked for such things, saying that His day was already passed, for one day and the next He was to perform miracles and not more, that is to say, a time when He worked them when He came into this world and another time when His disciples worked them.)

However, the miracles appropriate to Juana's times are of a different nature:

Que los miraglos e maravillas que El agora quería fazer heran en las ánimas, por quanto ellas heran las que le traían e fazían venir a fablar en esta boz, viendo tan gran muchedunbre de ánimas cómo se le pierden continuamente e se van al infierno. E que se tuviesen por çiertos todos los que miraglos e señales demandavan que no les daría ni les mostraría otras sino la graçia e consolaçión que dava a esta bienaventurada sierva suya que le veía e la fe e gozo muy verdadero que dava en los coraçones e ánimas de todas las personas que le oían e creían. (*Conorte*, fol. 450rv)

(For the miracles and marvels that He wished to work now were in the souls, inasmuch as they were what brought Him and made Him come to speak in this voice, seeing how so great a multitude of souls is constantly being lost and going to Hell. And that all those who desired miracles and signs should rest assured that He would neither give them nor show them signs other than the grace and comfort that He gave to this blessed handmaiden of His who saw Him and the faith and true joy that He gave in the hearts and souls of all the persons who heard and believed Him.)

That is to say, the miracle appropriate to Juana's times is the "interior" miracle. Concretely, God refers to His manifestation through Juana, a sign no less visible and valid than the signs of previous times.

Although the question of miracles did not provoke any reaction from the *Conorte*'s anonymous censor, its defender, Father Francisco de Torres, did comment on the passage in question. His annotation underscores the

miraculous nature of both God's revelation through Juana and His interpretation of that revelation. Torres ends with a sort of prayer that warns
against the Devil and expresses the friar's desire to see the book printed:

Y esplicar su magestad el mesmo dicho suyo que El dixo tanbién es milagro, que no
lo pudieron hacer estas vírgenes que lo escrivieron por su sancta gracia ni su esposa y amada Juana no lo supiera pronu[n]ciar si en rapto absorta en éxtasi no lo
dixera. . . . porque el demonio a conocido bien que este libro le a de quitar muchas ánimas, procura con todas sus fuerças destruirlo si pudiese. Mas yo espero
en el Señor y en su Madre y en su sancta que no saldrá con ello. Rabie quanto él
mandare, que muchas a de perder y impr[e]so a de ser. Yo lo vea. Amén. (*Conorte,*
fol. 450rv)

(And for His Majesty to explicate His very own words that He spoke is likewise a
miracle, for these virgins who wrote them through His holy grace were incapable
of doing so, nor would His bride and beloved Juana know how to utter them if she
had not said them while enraptured in a mystical trance. . . . because the Devil has
well recognized that this book is to steal many souls from him, he tries with all his
might to destroy it, if he could. But I trust in the Lord and in His Mother and in
His saint that he will not succeed in that. Let him rage all he wants, for he is to lose
many [souls] and it is to be printed. May I see it. Amen.)

Torres then appropriates Juana's now/then dichotomy as he steers future
readers toward a favorable reception of the text. The friar addresses those
readers in an aggressive tone:

Esto as de entender que a los que le demandavan señales quando hablava en esta su
celestial sierva para que, pues El mismo decía que era el Señor, lo conociesen con
un milagro que hiciese, a estos tales decía que no era servido darles señal porque era
curiosidad judaica, pues tan conocida cosa era y tan visible en la hermosura y alegría de la sancta y en las cosas maravillosas que decía. Y algunas veces hablar en
diversas lenguas y otras responder a los pensamientos de los presentes y continuamente dar consolationes espirituales escesivas y grandes más que de ninguna cosa
terrena podían recevir. Y los que con tan milagrosas cosas no creen y piden más
milagros indinos son de ellos y como judíos tentadores. (*Conorte,* fol. 450v)

(You must understand that to those who demanded signs when He spoke through
His heavenly servant, so that they might recognize Him through a miracle that He
might perform, since He Himself said that He was the Lord, to those He said that
He was not pleased to give them a sign because that would be mere Judaic in-
quisitiveness,[9] for it was such a widely known fact and so evident in the beauty and
joy of the holy woman and in the marvelous things that she said. And [in] sometimes speaking in tongues and other times responding to the innermost thoughts
of those present and constantly giving abundant spiritual comforts greater than
they could receive from any earthly source. And those who in the face of such mi-

raculous things do not believe and ask for more miracles are unworthy of them and are as Jewish tempters.)

Evidently, the way in which the question of miracles is expounded constitutes a significant textual strategy through which Mother Juana justifies her own authority. If God's self-revelation through her is a legitimate miracle, then He thereby authorizes her not only to preach the sermons but also to write them down and therefore to create the *Conorte*. One cannot help observing that the miracle motif appears repeatedly in the sermons. In the sermon for the Feast of the Holy Cross, the Lord underscores the then/now dichotomy, declaring that His preaching through the mouth of His handmaiden is the miracle most appropriate to the times:

E si le pidién miraglos e maravillas, pues que hera Dios verdadero e nos venía a fablar, dixo que El no quería mostrar otros sino los que mostrava, que heran fablar e aconsejar, que pues teníamos luz, que anduviésemos en ella, que harta luz nos avía dexado en sus santos evangelios e predicaçiones e dotrinas. Porque quando El vino en el mundo a encarnar, entonçes truxo poderío del Padre çelestial para fazer miraglos e maravillas. Mas quando El venía a fablar en esta boz por su grande misericordia e piedad, dixo que no venía a otra cosa sino a conbidar a bodas e a dezir que nos alegrásemos e nos gozássemos, que se açercava el reino de los çielos. (*Conorte,* fol. 278v)

(And if they requested miracles and marvels, since He was the true God and came to speak to us, He said that He did not wish to show any others than those which He showed, which were to speak and to give counsel, that since we had the light, we should walk in it,[10] for He had left us sufficient light in His Holy Scriptures and preaching and teachings. Because when He came into the world to be incarnated, He brought at that time the power from the heavenly Father to work miracles and marvels. But when He came to speak in this voice out of His great mercy and compassion, He said that He did not come for any reason other than to invite [us] to nuptials and to say that we should be happy and rejoice, for the kingdom of Heaven was at hand.)

Likewise, at the end of the sermon for the Feast of the Presentation, the Lord anticipates the objections of Mother Juana's critics, extolling His speaking through her as the miracle most suitable to the times:

E dixo su divina magestad que si preguntavan por qué no fazía miraglos e maravillas, pues que dezía que hera Dios, que les dava por respuesta que, porque están las gentes muy çiegas y endureçidas en sus maldades e pecados, no conosçen las maravillas e miraglos que El faze cada hora en nos criar e sostener e sufrir, que no nos hunde e destruye en un momento por los grandes pecados e ofensas que con-

tinuamente le fazemos. E que si dezían que por qué no fazía miraglos públicos e
señalados, que a esto respondía ser ya pasado su tienpo. Que por esto avía El dicho
en el tienpo qu'El andava por la tierra: "Oy e mañana faré miraglos e no más." E
que esto dixo El porque entonçes avía neçesidad de sanar las enfermedades corporales para que le creyesen e conoçiesen, mas que en este tienpo no avía neçesidad de
otra cosa sino de sanar las enfermedades espirituales. E con este deseo venía El e
tañía por esta flauta e órgano de boz para sanar e remediar las ánimas que tan caras
le avían costado. E que esto tenía El por mayor miraglo que otros ningunos de
quantos fizo. (*Conorte*, fol. 428r)

(And His Divine Majesty said that if they wondered why He did not work miracles
and marvels, since He said that He was God, that He answered that, because
people are so blinded and hardened in their wickedness and sins, they do not recognize the marvels and miracles that He works at all hours in creating and sustain-
ing and enduring us, for He does not cast down and destroy us in a single moment
on account of the serious sins and offenses that we constantly commit against Him.
And if they asked why He did not in public perform evident miracles, He answered
to that charge that His time was already passed. For to this effect He had said at the
time when He walked upon this earth: "Today and tomorrow I shall work miracles
and no more." [11] And that He said this because then He needed to cure bodily sicknesses so that they would believe and recognize Him, but that at this time He had
no need of anything other than to cure spiritual infirmities. And with this desire
He came and played this flute and organ of a voice in order to heal and succor the
souls that had cost Him so dearly. And He considered this to be the greatest miracle of all those He had worked.)

Thus, the Lord not only insists on the then/now dichotomy but also exalts
Mother Juana herself as the vehicle for the kind of miracle suitable to
present times. As a channel of divine grace, the visionary gains greater authority for herself and for the work she dictates. Furthermore, Christ
Himself enhances the nun's role, declaring that His speaking through her
is the greatest miracle of all those He performed.

In two cases the miracle of God's revelation through Juana is compared to the way in which He manifests Himself in the Eucharist. In the
sermon for the Feast of the Holy Cross, hearing God speak through Juana
without being able to see Him is associated with His invisible presence in
the consecrated host:

Fablando el Señor en un día de la santa cruz de la batalla, dixo que no se maravillase
nadie ni dudasen por qué El venía e fablava en esta boz, pues tiene poder para fazer
todas las cosas e viene e deçiende en el santo sacramento del altar cada vez que le
llaman por las palabras de la consagraçión. Y estava allí Dios e honbre verdadero
como en el sacramento del altar, que le oyemos fablar e no le podíamos ver. Así
como está en la hostia consagrada, que vemos la hostia e no podemos ver a El,

aunque está metido y ençerrado en ella, Dios y honbre verdadero e poderoso. . . . Porque assí como en el santo sacramento no amuestra ni faze quanto al pareçer muchos miraglos ni maravillas, que assí por semejante no quería fazer, quando venía a fablar en esta voz, otros miraglos ni maravillas sino dezirnos e declararnos todo lo que nos cunplía para nuestra salvaçión e corregirnos e reprehendernos de lo que errávamos e ofendíamos contra su divina magestad. (*Conorte,* fols. 278v–279r)

(When the Lord spoke one day on the Feast of the Triumph of the Cross,[12] He said that no one should marvel nor should they question why He came and spoke in this voice, for He has the power to do everything, and He comes and descends into the Holy Eucharist whenever He is called through the words of the consecration. And He was there, true God and man, as in the Eucharist, for we heard Him speak and could not see Him. Just as He is in the consecrated host, for we see the host and we cannot see Him, even though He is entered and enclosed in it, true and powerful God and man. . . . Because just as in the Eucharist to all appearances He does not display or perform many miracles or marvels, so likewise when He came to speak in this voice, He did not wish to perform miracles or marvels other than to tell us and declare to us all that was necessary for our salvation and to chastise us and reproach us for that we erred and offended against His Divine Majesty.)[13]

The same simile is repeated in the sermon for the Presentation of the Virgin:

E que el que venía en el santo sacramento del altar, escondido y encubierto por nos consolar e recrear e por que merezcamos en le creer e adorar debaxo de aquella muy blanca cobertura de hostia, venía a fablar en aquella boz, no quiriendo mostrar otras ningunas señales sino la boz formada, la qual hera de su virtud e resollo e del soplo de su boca. (*Conorte,* fols. 427v–428r)

(And that He who came in the Eucharist, hidden and invisible, to comfort and restore us and so that we might be deserving in believing in Him and adoring Him under that very white covering of the host, He came to speak in that voice, not wishing to show any signs other than the clearly produced voice, which came from His power and the respiration and the breath of His mouth.)[14]

The invisible presence of God in the Eucharist and His manifestation through Mother Juana are not only associated on a metaphoric level but can also be related implicitly to the spheres of action allotted to each sex. Only priests, that is to say, men, are authorized to "call" the Lord through the words of the consecration. Women are excluded from the priesthood but are allowed to fulfill the more typically feminine role of visionary. When Mother Juana associates the two phenomena, she suggests that they are analogous activities and that the one is no more important than the other. Thus, she enhances her role as visionary by comparing it with the priesthood: the gift of prophecy is revealed to be equal in value to the power to consecrate.

The topic of the equivalence, and even of the equality, of the activities allotted to the two sexes is also raised in the sermon "The Unbelievers Reproached." The Lord begins by exalting His miraculous manifestation through Juana in the face of the incredulity of certain people:

E otra vez hablando el Señor reprehendiendo a todas las gentes de sus incredulidades e dubdas e poca fe que tienen en su misericordia e piedad, dixo que no dudassen ni tuviessen pensamiento ni corasçón duro ningunas de las personas que tienen entendimiento e seso natural ni dixessen que no hera el mesmo Dios el que mostrava estos tan grandes miraglos e maravillas y el que dava el soplo de su sagrada boca de verdad. Con la qual virtud e soplo e resollo se hablaron todos los secretos e misterios contenidos en este santo libro. (*Conorte*, fol. 76v)

(And on another occasion when the Lord spoke, reproaching all the people for their disbelief and doubts and the little faith that they have in His mercy and compassion, He said that no one with understanding and good sense should doubt nor should he have any suspicion or a hard heart nor should he say that He who manifested these great miracles and marvels and He who gave the breath of His truly sacred mouth was not the very same God. Through which power and inspiration and breath were uttered all the secrets and mysteries contained in this holy book.)

The Lord then responds to another criticism leveled at the *Conorte*, namely, that the revelations were manifested through a women. He underscores the arbitrary nature of His behavior even as He associates His own humility with the humility of those creatures through whom He has chosen to reveal Himself:

E que si dubdan e dizen que cómo es posible venir Dios verdadero e desçender del çielo a una muger pobre e pequeña, respondió el mesmo Señor, hablando en esta boz, e dixo que por ser El tan bueno e piadoso no quitava su bondad a ninguno, mas antes le devían dar mayores graçias por quererse El tanto humillar e hazer tan grandes misericordias. E que si El venía e repartía sus tessoros e graçias e dones con quien El quería y era su voluntad, que no tenía ninguno por qué se lo demandar ni El por qué dar qüenta, pues hera Dios e pudié hazer de sí mesmo todo lo que quisiese, y que non negarié ni ascondrié su misericordia a ninguna persona que le amasse e con fervor e perseverança le desease e buscasse como hazié esta su sierva. (*Conorte*, fol. 76v)

(And if they doubt and wonder how it is possible for the true God to come and descend from Heaven to a slight and lowly woman, the Lord Himself answered, speaking in this voice, and said that because He was so good and compassionate He did not deprive anyone of His goodness. On the contrary, He should be thanked for wishing thus to humble Himself and to perform such great works of mercy. And if He came and distributed His treasures and graces and gifts to whoever He pleased and desired, that no one had any reason to protest nor did He have any reason to give an accounting, for He was God and could do of Himself all that He wished, and that He would not withhold or hide His mercy from anyone who loved Him and desired and searched for Him with fervor and perseverance as did this His handmaiden.)

Lastly, God introduces the notion of His divine indifference toward sexual roles, declaring that it matters little to Him whether it is a man or a woman who records His holy words. In so doing, He exalts Juana as the most recent in a series of holy women harking back to the Virgin Mary:

E dixo hera su voluntad que se escriviesen algunos de los secretos e maravillosas cosas qu'El dezía y que no se le dava más que fuesen honbres que mugeres los que escriviessen sus sagradas palabras. Porque tanbién quiso El ser atestiguado de mugeres como de honbres en la su gloriosa Resurreçión, pues fue atestiguado de María Madalena e mostrado a ella antes que a otra alguna persona, salvo a su gloriosa madre. E de Santa Isabel quiso fuese atestiguada su santa Encarnasçión. E de otras bienaventuradas mugeres quiso ser loado e manifestado por Dios e por Señor como lo es. (*Conorte*, fol. 76v)

(And He said that it was His will that some of the secrets and wondrous things that He uttered should be written down and that it mattered little to Him whether it was men or women who wrote down His holy words. Because He wished to be witnessed also by women as well as by men in His glorious Resurrection, for He was witnessed by Mary Magdalene and He showed Himself to her before anyone else, except for His glorious mother. And He wanted His holy Incarnation to be witnessed by Saint Elizabeth. And He wished to be praised and manifested as God and as Lord as He is by other blessed women.)

In this way the Lord Himself sanctions the appropriation of the role of evangelist by Mother Juana and her companions and further justifies this role by associating it with the tradition of holy women who witnessed His miracles. Juana is thus authorized and exalted by her identification with Mary Magdalene, Saint Elizabeth, and the Virgin Mary herself. In addition to fulfilling the typically feminine role of visionary, by divine permission and mandate the nun is also called upon to play the traditionally masculine role of evangelist. God Himself legitimizes the widening of Mother Juana's sphere of action: He allows her to go beyond being simply an instrument of His divine manifestation to participate as well in the writing of those revelations, which, in turn, become a sort of latter-day gospel.

The passage that deals with God's indifference toward the sex of His evangelists failed to attract the attention of the anonymous censor of the Escorial manuscript of the *Conorte*. In contrast, Father Torres saw a splendid opportunity to rise to the defense of women. He begins by deflating the wisdom of Solomon, using the same strategy that Mother Juana herself will use in the Creation sermon, then goes on to praise the divine wisdom revealed through a woman:

Y quien dio la sabiduría a Salamón, varón que tanpoco la sudó, que no le costó sino una breve y descansada petitión, saviendo Dios que havía de desvaratar tanto y más que el más necio de los nacidos, bien se la pudo dar a esta su escogidíssima virgen, que con tantas ansias desde su niñez, con tantos sudores y derramamientos de sangre, lo buscó y se la pidió, haviendo de perseverar asta la muerte en su verdadera adoratión y inflamado amor, tanto y más que sapientíssimos varones. Nota los exenplos de la gloriosa Madalena y Santa Isabel. ¡Qué grandes y eficaces para persuadir el Señor esta verdad presente! No ay otros dos más notables en todas las Sanctas Escripturas, pues los dos más maravillosos y gloriosos misterios de todos quantos el omnipotentíssimo obró estas más que dichosas mugeres los atestiguaron y anunciaron. (*Conorte,* fol. 76v)

(And He who gave wisdom to Solomon—a man who hardly had to work hard for it, for it cost him but a brief and effortless request, since God knew that he would act just as foolish as the dullest of mortals, and even more so—well could give it [wisdom] to this His most chosen virgin, who since childhood with such great desires had sought Him out and asked Him for it with such sweat and loss of blood, having to persevere even unto death in His true adoration and ardent love, as much as and even more than the wisest of men. Note the examples of the glorious Magdalene and Saint Elizabeth. What great and effective [examples] for the Lord to persuade [us] of this present truth! There are no two more notable examples in all the Holy Scriptures, for the two most wondrous and glorious mysteries of all those the Almighty performed were witnessed and proclaimed by these more than blessed women.)

As the annotation proceeds, Father Torres continues his praise of women, emphasizing how Christ Himself was the beneficiary of many stereotypically feminine activities:

Quien dubda sino que eternalmente a Dios de glorificar este devotíssimo sexu y género de las mugeres, pues d'él quiso ser concebido y nacer y ser empañado y reclinado en el pesebre y substentado a sus pechos y nutrido de su leche y del guisado de sus manos y al quiso obedecer viviendo y volver a hablar yendo con cargosa, pesada y intolerable cruz y d'él quiso ser más llorado y plañido en su muerte y más buscado y aconpañado en su sepulcro y finalmente en su Resurrectión a él quiso aun primero que a sus apóstoles parecer para claramente enseñarnos que en las cosas de devotión y de gracia y de gloria, que nos tienen ventaja. Que el mayor trono y la más real y imperial silla después de Dios muger la tiene, en la qual no solo domina y señorea a todos los honbres mas aun sobre los altíssimos choros de los ángeles está sobreexaltada, emperatriz de todo el mundo. Y justíssimamente tiene primado la primogénita hija del Padre eterno, única engendradora de su primogénito Hijo y única esposa del Espíritu Santo, sobre todas las criaturas diníssimamente aventajada y singularíssimamente privilegiada. (*Conorte*, fols. 76v–77r)

(Who doubts but that God must forever glorify this most pious feminine sex and gender, for through it He wished to be conceived and be born and be swaddled and placed in the manger, and nourished at their breasts, and fed with their milk and with the cooking of their hands, and which He wished to obey while He lived, and speak to again while carrying His burdensome, heavy, and unbearable cross. And by that sex He wished to be more mourned and grieved over in His death and more sought out and accompanied at His grave. And lastly, at His Resurrection He wished to appear to that sex even before [appearing] to His Apostles, in order to teach us clearly that in matters of devotion and grace and glory, women have the advantage over us [men]. For the greatest throne and most royal and imperial seat—after that of God—a woman possesses, from which she not only rules and holds sway over all men but is exalted even above the highest choirs of angels, the empress of the entire world. And most justly the first-born daughter of the eternal Father, the one and only engendress of His first-born Son, and the only spouse of the Holy Spirit holds the first place, rightly preferred and most singularly privileged over all other creatures.)

The commentary continues amid still more praises of the Virgin Mary and of Mother Juana herself, ending with repeated exhortations to the reader to believe in the divine inspiration of the visionary's words.

In general terms, the insistence on the divine inspiration of Mother Juana's sermons both justifies the process of novelization of biblical narratives and authorizes the very writing of *El libro del conorte*. Answering critics who required a more visible sign of the divine origin of her revelations, the visionary maintains that God's speaking through her is the type of miracle most appropriate to modern times. But the revelations also provoked other criticisms, which are answered in turn in the final folios of the *Conorte*. Specifically, Mother Juana defends her book against those who wondered how it was possible for there to be animals (and particularly, horses) and worldly delights and pastimes in Paradise. In the Creation sermon the visionary treats but briefly the problem of the presence of horses in Heaven, suggesting that skeptics

creyesen e pensasen, quando los tales pensamientos de dudas les viniesen, cómo Dios, que crió en la tierra para consolaçión e ayuda de los honbres animalias de natura de tierra según El quiso e fue su voluntad, puede tanbién fazer en el çielo animalias de otro espeçie muy más preçioso e oloroso e luzido. (*Conorte*, fol. 450v)

(believe and think, when such doubting thoughts come to them, how God, who for the comfort and succor of mankind created on earth animals of an earthly nature as He desired and according to His will, can also create in Heaven animals of a much more precious and fragrant and splendid kind.)

In fact, despite the brevity of Juana's response here in the Creation sermon, it appears that the horse question was a burning issue for her contemporary critics, for at various moments in the *Conorte* she feels obliged to defend the presence of those animals in Heaven. In the sermon for the Feast of Saints Peter and Paul, for example, the Lord insists on winning through a kind of horse race the sheep that the Apostles wish to offer Him. Christ Himself then raises the horse question in a passage designed to anticipate the incredulity of certain readers or listeners:

E dixo el Señor que no deve nadie dudar que ay en el çielo cavallos ni maravillarse d'ello. Porque en aquella palabra que está escrita en la Santa Escritura que dize "que ni ojo vio ni oreja oyó ni en coraçón de honbre subió lo que El tiene aparejado para los que le sirven e aman" se ençierran todas las cosas. Porque si El crió en este mundo (el qual dixo que puede ser llamado, en conparaçión de su santo reino, establo lleno de estiércol muy fidiondo de pecados e maldades) tantas e tan fermosas e olorosas e ricas cosas, que más razón hera que las criase en su santo reino más ricas e preçiosas para su serviçio e para consolaçión de los bienaventurados que El tiene consigo. . . . E declaró el Señor, diziendo que tan grande es la humilldad que los santos ángeles tienen, que ellos mesmos le ruegan se quiera servir d'ellos, mandándoles tomar cuerpos de cavallos. (*Conorte*, fol. 278r)

(And the Lord said that no one should doubt or marvel that there are horses in Heaven. Because in that verse in the Holy Scriptures that says "that eye hath not seen, nor ear heard, neither hath it entered into the heart of man, what things God hath prepared for them that serve and love Him"[15] are contained all things. Because if He created in this world—which He said can be called, in comparison with His holy kingdom, a stable full of manure most foul-smelling with sins and wickedness—so many beautiful and fragrant and precious things, it was fitting that He should create them in His holy kingdom more lovely and more precious for His use and for the comfort of the blessed that He has with Him. . . . And the Lord spoke, saying that the holy angels have such great humility that they themselves beg Him to make use of them, commanding them to take the form of horses.)[16]

In the sermon for the Feast of Saint Lawrence, Christ and the saint appear on horseback. Once again the Lord warns that no one should doubt that there are horses in Heaven:

E dixo el Señor que no deve ninguna persona dudar aver en su santo reino cavallos muy preçiosos e olorosos, que escrito es en el Apocalipsi que vido San Juan salir del çielo cavallos. E aun en la tierra an visto al glorioso Santiago algunas personas venir en cavallo a socorrer a los que con fe e amor le llaman en tienpo de neçesidad. (*Conorte*, fol. 305r)

(And the Lord said that no one should doubt that there are most precious and fragrant horses in His holy kingdom, for it is written in the Book of Revelation that Saint John saw horses come out of the heavens.[17] And even on earth people have seen glorious Saint James come on horseback to help those who summon him with faith and love in time of need.[18])

Mother Juana employs here two kinds of arguments. First, she appeals to the authority of the Bible, that is to say, of "the other holy scriptures." Then, she appeals to the authority of the venerable traditions of her fatherland, for every loyal Castilian believed in the legendary-historical apparitions of the apostle Saint James at critical moments in the history of her people.

In the Creation sermon the defense of games and other pastimes in Heaven relies mostly on a quotation from the Sermon on the Mount, a quotation placed in the mouth of Christ Himself: "Blessed [are] those that weep, for they will laugh in the kingdom of Heaven."[19] The Gospel text is misquoted here, apparently on purpose, in order to defend Mother Juana's revelations, for Matthew 5 : 5 actually says that those who weep will be consoled: "Blessed are they that mourn, for they shall be comforted." Thus, Mother Juana has Christ Himself modify the Gospel text in order to confound the critics of her sermons.[20]

Up to now attention has been given to the ways in which Mother Juana deals with the problems raised by the past reception of her book: she attempts to overcome the incredulity of her readers and to defend the novelization of sacred history. But at other times the visionary deals not with the text's past reception but with its future reception and with ways of controlling it. Juana begins by employing a gustatory image, postulating two kinds of readers, one kindly disposed, the other hostile. The reader who is "sick" with sins and therefore whose palate is perverted will find that the book tastes bitter:

Porque así como la persona que está enferma e mal dispuesta tiene el gusto de la boca muy amargo e todo quanto come, por dulçe e bien guisado que sea, le amarga e le sabe mal, que así por semejante qualquier persona que tuviere el ánima enferma de pecados y el gusto amargo de incredulidad e dureza e maliçia y enbidia e otros pecados semejantes no le sabrá bien esta santa escritura porque quanto ella es más eçelente, tanto menos la sabrán gustar los malos. (*Conorte*, fols. 451v–452r)

(Because just as the person who is sick and indisposed has his sense of taste embittered and all that he eats, no matter how sweet and well prepared it may be, tastes bitter to him and tastes bad, so likewise to anyone whose soul is sick with sins and whose sense of taste is bitter with incredulity and obstinacy and malice and envy and other such sins this holy scripture will not taste good, because the more excellent it is, the less people who are evil will know how to savor it.)

On the other hand, the book will taste delicious to the good and the virtuous:

Enpero que así como el que está sano e bien dispuesto tiene el gusto de la boca bueno e le sabe bien lo que come, así por semejante qualquier persona que tuviere su ánima sana e bien dispuesta sin ninguna enfermedad de pecado e tuviere el gusto bueno e sabroso para con Dios le sabrá muy bien esta santa escritura e le pareçerá en su paladar más dulçe que el panar de la miel. (*Conorte*, fol. 452r)

(However, just as he who is healthy and well has a fine sense of taste and what he eats tastes good to him, so likewise to anyone whose soul is healthy and well, without any sickness of sin, and whose sense of taste is fine and capable of savoring God, to him this holy scripture will taste good and to his palate it will seem sweeter than honeycomb.)

The gustatory image is traditional and would seem to be ultimately derived from the Bible. Thus, Psalm 118:103 praises the sweetness of the words of the Lord: "How sweet are thy words to my palate! more than honey to my mouth." But more specifically, the notion of literally eating a sacred text appears in two biblical passages: "And he said to me: Son of man, thy belly shall eat, and thy bowels shall be filled with this book, which I give thee. And I did eat it: and it was sweet as honey in my mouth" (Ezechiel 3:3); "And I took the book from the hand of the Angel, and ate it up: and it was in my mouth, sweet as honey" (Revelation 10:10). Mother Juana's strategy consists of juxtaposing the biblical image of the book that tastes sweet and its opposite, the book that tastes bitter, thus establishing two categories of "eaters"/readers. This amounts to a sort of blackmail: if the book will taste good only to the reader who is neither a sinner nor a disbeliever, then the reader who does not wish to be associated with sinners is obliged to accept as true the *Conorte*'s divine inspiration.[21]

The topic of the two kinds of readers (or listeners) also appears in the sermon "The Unbelievers Reproached":

E dixo el Señor que las personas devotas que tuvieren algún amor con El o algunos gustos de sus dulçedunbres conosçerán luego cómo todas estas palabras son divinales e dichas por su sagrada boca. E los que tuvieren el ojo de la intinçión dañado que no sabrán gustar a Dios ni conosçer sus verdaderas palabras e dulçedunbres. (*Conorte,* fols. 76v–77r)

(And the Lord said that the pious who love Him or have tasted of His sweetness will recognize therefore how all these words are divine and uttered by His holy mouth. And those whose will is damaged will not know how to taste God or to recognize His true words and sweetness.)

Here, Mother Juana uses a gustatory image similar to that in the Creation sermon, for knowing God is equivalent to tasting God. Once again there is a sort of blackmail in her strategy that is as simple as it is ingenious: if the good recognize that Juana's words are of divine origin, but those with malice in their hearts disbelieve, this implies that those who believe in the divine inspiration of her sermons can consider themselves God's friends, but those who doubt that God speaks through her must be numbered among the evil.

The Creation sermon goes even further in extolling the effects of the *Conorte* on its readers and listeners. So great is the book's power that even though the reader may be in a state of mortal sin when he begins to read, by the time he has finished he will be in a state of grace:

E dixo el Señor que con tanto amor e fervor e devoçión e fe lo puede alguna persona leer que, aunque al prinçipio esté en pecado mortal, quando acabe esté en estado de graçia. (*Conorte,* fol. 452r)

(And the Lord said that a person can read it with such great love and fervor and devotion and faith that, although at the beginning he may be in mortal sin, when he finishes he will be in a state of grace.)

In this case the book does not seem to derive its powers from its contents as such. Rather, it is a question of the spiritual disposition of the reader and the very act of reading the text. There has been a kind of transfer of power: the miracle of God's speaking through Mother Juana has been transmitted to the book she has dictated. Both the process of revelation and the book itself, as a physical object, are miraculous. Indeed, the supernatural powers ascribed to the *Conorte* can be verified in other sources. The manuscript that gathers together various traditions of the convent of Santa María de la Cruz praises the book's power over storms and the Devil:

Púsole el Señor este título de *Conorte* y concedióle el Señor muchas bendiciones y virtudes contra los demonios y tempestades. Y mandó el santo ángel que quando alguna estubiesse en pasamiento, le pusiessen algo de la lectura d'este libro para defensa del demonio. Y en las tempestades manda la prelada saquen el santo libro o sus traslados, y se ha visto cesar la tempestad muchas vezes. (*Casa,* fol. 20v)

(The Lord gave it the title of *Conorte* and granted it many blessings and powers against demons and storms. And the holy angel ordered that when any [of the nuns] was on her deathbed, they read to her from this book to protect her from the Devil. And during storms the mother superior orders the book or copies of it to be brought out and often the storm has been seen to abate.)

Thus, the manuscript itself became a talisman.[22]

The value of the *written* text of the *Conorte* is also evident in another passage from the final folios of the Creation sermon:

Enpero que guay de los incrédulos e dudosos en tan gran benefiçio e alunbra- miento para las gentes. Porque la tal escritura e secretos puede ser dicho d'ella ser nueva luz en el mundo para los sapientes en gustar e conoçer a Dios e para los inorantes que no saben qué cosa es Dios ni sus dulçedunbres e deleites. Por lo qual declaró el Señor, diziendo que no ay tilde ni letra ni palabra de quantas en este preçioso libro están escritas ni de quantas El mesmo fabló que no sea una perla e una piedra preçiosa e una joya muy rica e una flor muy olorosa para todos los bienaventurados que moran en el reino de los çielos e para qualquier ánima fiel que con fe e amor e devoçión lo leyere e oyere. (*Conorte,* fol. 452r)

(However, let the disbelievers and the doubters of such great benefits and illumina- tion for people beware. Because such a scripture and secrets can be said to be a new light in the world for those versed in savoring and knowing God and for the igno- rant who know neither what God is nor His sweetness and delights. On account of which the Lord spoke, saying that there is not a single tittle or letter or word of all those written in this precious book or of all those He Himself uttered that is not a pearl and a precious stone and a very valuable jewel and a very fragrant flower for all the blessed who dwell in the kingdom of Heaven and for any faithful soul that reads and hears it with faith and love and devotion.)

This passage attracted the attention of Father Esparza when he examined *El libro del conorte* as part of Juana's beatification process in the seventeenth century. The censor objects to Mother Juana's reference to her book as "precious": "Vocat istum suum librum pretiosum" (*Reparos,* fol. 43r). The criticism is probably due to his belief that the adjective can be fittingly applied only to the canonical Scriptures. Or, perhaps, he reacts against what he considers spiritual arrogance in general. In any case, in responding to Esparza's objections, Father Coppons bases his defense of the *Conorte* on the correction of a misunderstanding. According to him, it is not Juana herself who calls the book precious but the companions who transcribed what she dictated. Moreover, Coppons insists that it is not the defender's task to examine what the other nuns say on their own. Therefore, there is no need for further commentary, since he is only interested in the words of Mother Juana herself (*Reparos,* fols. 53v–54r).

Indeed, the textual self-consciousness of the final folios of the *Conorte* goes beyond concern for the book's reception by the general reader to confront the problem of its possible censorship by a specific group of readers, the ecclesiastical hierarchy. In order to protect herself against official censorship, Mother Juana employs a textual strategy that combines audacity and modesty. Although there is no reason to doubt the orthodoxy of the words of the *Conorte,* God asks that the text be examined by learned men. He does this not because the book contains anything objectionable, but rather to offer an example of humility:

> Enpero que en todo lo sobre escrito en este libro de Luz Norte El lo pone en mano de buenas personas, en espeçial de buenos honbres e letrados e buenos christianos. E dixo más su divina magestad que no encomienda estas palabras e santo libro a otras ningunas personas ni a ereges malos infieles sino a los buenos cristianos verdaderamente creyentes en la santa fe católica. E que a ellos dize e ruega e manda, como a hermanos e fijos, que lo esaminen e miren. Porque quiere que aun las cosas que El dize las esaminen los honbres buenos de su santa iglesia, y esto que lo faze El por nos dar enxenplo de humilldad para que no presumamos nosotros que todo lo que hablamos e dizimos es perfeto e que no es menester que nadie lo retraiga o reprehenda. Comoquier que dixo que en las cosas d'este santo libro no avía ninguna cosa que dudar ni reprehender, porque El avía dado su Espíritu Santo así para las dezir por el estrumento como para las escrevir los oyentes. (*Conorte,* fol. 453r)

(However, all the aforegoing in this book of *Luz Norte* [*Pole-star*[23]] he places in the hands of good people, especially good and learned men and good Christians. And His Divine Majesty said further that He does not entrust these words and holy book to evil disbelieving heretics or to anyone else save to true Christians, true believers in the holy Catholic faith. And to them He says and He begs and orders them as to brothers and sons that even the things that He utters should be examined by good men of His holy Church, and that He does this to offer us an example of humility lest we presume that everything we speak and say is perfect and it is not necessary for anyone to criticize or reproach it. Inasmuch as He said that there was nothing to doubt or reproach in the words of this holy book, because He had sent His Holy Spirit both to speak them through His instrument and to have them written down by their audience.)

True to this injunction, in the prologue of the Escorial manuscript Mother Juana's companions appropriate this divine "challenge" to the ecclesiastical authorities and ask that the *Conorte* be examined, just as the Lord had ordered:

El qual libro otrosí se pone debaxo de la correçión de los católicos y devotos christianos sabios y discretos, entendidos y sentidos en las cosas de Dios. Y si en este dicho libro o libros que d'él se pueden hazer fuere alguna cosa que parezca no bien dicha, no se a de echar la culpa al mesmo sapientísimo Espíritu Santo, el qual dize y haze y enseña todas las cosas muy perfetamente, sino a quien lo escrivió. Porque pudo la péndola errar o la memoria en algo trastordarse [*sic*]. (*Conorte*, fol. 1)

(Furthermore, this book is submitted to the judgment of Catholic and devout Christians, both wise and prudent, knowledgeable and experienced in the things of God. And if in this book or the copies that may be made of it there is anything that seems inaccurate, it must not be blamed on the most wise Holy Spirit Itself, who utters and does and teaches everything perfectly, but on whoever wrote it. Because the pen could slip or memory confuse something.)

Nonetheless, there is a significant difference between the prologue and the corresponding passage from the end of the Creation sermon. In the sermon the Lord maintains that the Holy Spirit inspired both the words that Mother Juana spoke and the transcription of those words by her companions. In contrast, the prologue dissociates the book's writing from its revelation, declaring that the Holy Spirit inspired its revelation but not necessarily its composition. Despite this clarification, the question of the *Conorte*'s divine inspiration provoked yet another criticism from Father Esparza. He calls attention to the fact that the nuns to whom *El libro del conorte* was dictated compare themselves to the Evangelists who wrote the Holy Scriptures. These nuns, says the censor, boldly (*audacter*) appropriate the certitude that belongs only to the canonical Scriptures (*Reparos*, fol. 43r).

In his defense of the *Conorte*, Father Coppons begins by quoting (in Latin translation) the passage from the book's prologue in which the text is submitted for examination to the ecclesiastical authorities. That passage, says Coppons, distinguishes between the sermons' revelation and their writing: the Holy Spirit inspired the revelation but not necessarily the writing, which is always liable to slips of the pen and of memory. Mother Juana's companions, says Father Coppons, wished to emphasize their role as witnesses to God's revelation. Therefore, when they are compared to the four Evangelists, the nuns are not attempting to claim the certitude that belongs only to the Bible. Rather, they are merely calling attention to the fact that, like the Evangelists, they were witnesses to what they recorded (*Reparos,* fol. 54rv).

The final folios of *El libro del conorte* also consider the topic of Mother Juana's prophetic voice. The notion is first introduced in the context of the traditional image of the visionary as a musical instrument played upon by God:

Enpero que [a] los tales vernán días e tienpos en que sabrán claramente cómo estas cosas fueron dichas por boca de Dios mientras le plugo de enbiar su Espíritu Santo en aquella persona por cuyo estrumento estas cosas fabló, que así lo dezía El mesmo que no las quería dezir sin medianería de algún estrumento o órgano. Así como el tañedor quando quiere fazer algún son, agora sea baxo, agora sea alto o triste o alegre o de gozo e bien sonante, busca algún estrumento con que tanga e cante e denunçie algunas cosas de su coraçón a los oyentes que quiere que las sepan. (*Conorte,* fol. 452v)

(However, there will come a time and season to such [skeptics] when they will know clearly how these things were uttered by the mouth of God while it pleased Him to send His Holy Spirit to that person through whose instrument He spoke these things, for thus He Himself said that He did not wish to utter them without the mediation of some instrument or organ. Just as the musician, when he wishes to make some sound, be it low, be it high or sad or happy or joyful and sonorous, seeks out some instrument with which he may play and sing and reveal some things of his heart to those listeners that he wants to know them.)

It has already been pointed out (see Chapter 3) that the musical simile was traditionally used to describe the Old Testament prophets: they are but the passive instruments through which the Lord speaks. Here, the motif reveals the underlying tension in Mother Juana's voice. Just when she appears to call attention with the greatest insistence to the extraordinary powers that are being manifested through her and through her book, she insists on her lack of responsibility for what she says. Nonetheless, the emphasis on her status as a mere vehicle for the words of God is both a display of modesty and a strategy of self-exaltation, for it underscores the fact that it is she, and no one else, through whom God has chosen to reveal Himself.

The relation between Juana and the Old Testament prophets recurs in another passage in the Creation sermon in which a parallel is established between the divine inspiration of the nun's words and the words uttered by Solomon. Once again, it is a question of self-exaltation, for Juana cannot lose by associating herself with the illustrious Solomon. In a sense she even outshines the Old Testament king. The *Conorte* (fol. 452v) points out that the Holy Spirit spoke through the king while he was in a state of grace. Nonetheless, if Solomon was a great prophet, he was also a great sinner: his love affairs with his pagan concubines led him to adore false gods, thus incurring the wrath of God (I Kings 11 : 1–13). Since Juana was never guilty of such great sins, it is therefore implied that, despite the fact that she and Solomon share the gift of prophecy, she surpasses him in moral rectitude.

The prophecy motif is actualized at the end of the *Conorte* in a series of concrete predictions. The Lord foretells certain calamities so frightening that it will seem that the end of the world is at hand:

E dixo el Señor que porque estavan hordenadas çiertas cosas muy espantosas sobre el mundo que avían de acaeçer no dende a mucho tienpo que este libro se acabasse de fazer, en las quales cosas las gentes serían muy espantadas e atemorizadas e angustiadas en manera que les pareçería ser ya la fin del mundo en algunas partes e lugares de la tierra, que por eso quiso El que, antes que estas cosas acaeçiesen, declarar estas cosas por que las gentes se aprovechasen d'ellas e se enmendasen de sus pecados e le sirviesen. (*Conorte,* fol. 453r)

(And the Lord said that because certain very frightening things were decreed with regard to the world that were to happen not long after this book was finished, on account of which things people would be very frightened and terrified and anguished in such a way that it would seem in certain areas and places on earth that it was the end of the world. And for that reason He desired, before these events should happen, to reveal these things so that people might profit by them and turn from their sins into the right way and serve Him.)

Although the text only says that it will *seem* that the end of the world is at hand, a relation is nonetheless suggested between Mother Juana's prophetic voice, the end of the world, and the completion of the writing of *El libro del conorte*. The passage insinuates that the end of the world is near and that the *Conorte* is at once the voice prophesying that end and the appropriate remedy to ensure the salvation of its readers and listeners.

The Creation sermon is not the only occasion when the apocalyptic dimension of Mother Juana's prophetic voice is manifested. The sermon on the Last Judgment begins, not unsurprisingly, with a warning concerning the proximity of the end of the world:

Fablando el Señor reprehendiendo a todo el humanal linage de sus viçios e pecados, dixo que es tan grande la maldad e abominaçión que ay en todas las gentes que le provocan a muy grande ira y enojo. Porque viendo cómo se viene la fin del mundo e cómo andamos fuera de hera, dizen los que tienen poco amor e temor de Dios: "Pues ya andamos fuera de hera e no sabemos qué tanto biviremos, gozémonos todos e alegrémonos." (*Conorte,* fol. 434r)

(When the Lord spoke, reproaching the human race for its vices and sins, He said that the evil and abomination in all people are so great that they provoke His ire and anger. Because, seeing how the end of the world is approaching and how we are beyond our time, those who love and fear God but little say: "Since we are already living beyond our time and we know not how much longer we will live, let us all rejoice and make merry.")

In another revelation Mother Juana's guardian angel insists that the end of the world is approaching rapidly and that all must repent:

"No pienses que estas cosas son sin misterio divinal, porque te hago saber que después que se acabó la era del año de mill y quinientos acá, el Señor, por ruegos de Nuestra Señora la Virgen María y de muchos santos, determinó de alargar algún tiempo más el curso del mundo. Lo uno por que se acabassen de inchir las sillas del cielo. Y lo otro por esperar las gentes a penitencia y conversión." (*Casa,* fol. 58v)

("Do not think that these things do not have a divine hidden meaning, because I inform you that when the era [delimited by] the year 1500 ended, the Lord, at the insistence of Our Lady the Virgin Mary and many saints, decided to prolong the course of the world a while longer. First, so that the heavenly thrones might be completely filled. And second, to give hope to people for penitence and conversion.")

That is to say, if the end of the world had been postponed beyond the year 1500,[24] by the year 1509, which saw the completion of the *Conorte,* the final days must have seemed imminent; whence the urgency with which the book reiterates the benefits to be derived from its reading. The predictions extend even to Mother Juana herself, for God will not spare His handmaiden future tribulations:

"E tú tanbién no quedarás sin penas corporales y espirituales, ca tiempo verná que serás enferma e aborresçible en alguna manera o maneras de algunas gentes, en manera que les pareçerá no aver visto en ti la graçia de mí, tu Dios e Criador, aunque de otras serás muy querida e muy amada. Y esto será e se cunplirá quando fuere la mi voluntad." (*Conorte,* fol. 454r)

("Neither will you be left without spiritual and corporal sufferings, for the time will come when you will be ill and hateful in some way or ways to some people, in such a way that it will seem that they have not seen in you the grace of your God and Creator, although you will be much loved and cherished by others. And this will come to pass and will be fulfilled when such is my will.")

The prophecy would seem to refer either to the episode of painful paralysis that preceded the guitar vision (see Chapter 3) or to the episode of the benefice of Cubas that resulted in Juana's dismissal as abbess (see the Introduction), or to both events.

The prophecy regarding Juana's future tribulations and the divine benediction that follows are the last of the Lord's words to be recorded. The end of the book is approaching, as are the fulfillment of its prophecies and therefore the end of the world. Once again Mother Juana's companions speak in their own voice to assert their certainty that it is God Himself who spoke through Juana and to emphasize their own role as witnesses to what the Lord revealed through her:

Y El fablava con ella todas las cosas susodichas, las quales oíamos claramente las que lo escrevimos, que por nuestros oídos lo [o]ímos quando el Señor lo dezía. E veíamos cómo aquella sierva del Señor no hera ella la que fablava quando el Señor fablava, porque assí se pareçían claras las palabras del Señor, e cómo El le dava a ella la salutaçión e soplo del Espíritu Santo. (*Conorte,* fol. 454rv)

(And He spoke to her all the aforementioned things, which those who wrote heard clearly, for through our [own] ears we heard it when the Lord said it. And we saw how it was not she, that handmaiden of the Lord, who spoke when the Lord spoke, because so clear did the Lord's words seem, and how He gave her the greeting and inspiration of the Holy Spirit.)

But the repeated declarations of the *Conorte*'s divine inspiration failed to achieve the desired effect, for a crucial series of readers was not convinced. The Escorial manuscript was harshly censored by an anonymous examiner, who crossed out numerous passages and even whole pages. Then, in the seventeenth century the unfavorable opinions of Cardinal Bona and Father Esparza were the principal reason for the negative outcome of Juana's beatification process.[25] Specifically, Bona recommended that the beatification process be suspended if the *Vida* and the *Conorte* were indeed authentic works of Mother Juana (*Reparos,* fol. 2v). In effect, in 1678 the Congregation of Sacred Rites asked the pope to impose perpetual silence on the cause. The pope agreed in a brief of December 4 of the same year.[26]

The only recourse left to Mother Juana's supporters was to deny her authorship of writings so damaging to her cause. This occurred in 1731, when the beatification process was reopened. First, it was held that the writings sent to Rome were not the original manuscripts but copies. In 1729–1730 a search for the originals in Spain had been fruitless. It was therefore requested that as long as the original manuscripts were unavailable, the writings examined by the censors not be considered as belonging to Mother Juana. Second, it was argued that in any case Mother Juana herself was not the author of the works, for her companions had written the *Conorte* and her confessor (or, at least, it was so alleged) had written the *Vida*. Therefore, Juana could not be held responsible for their contents, and that damaging evidence should be discarded. In the face of the failure to find the original manuscripts, it was requested that the Congregation proceed with all due haste with the consideration of the miracles.[27] These maneuvers failed, and the beatification process was suspended. It was reopened in 1986.

If the world did not end, as the Lord had predicted, with the completion of the writing of the *Conorte,* His apocalyptic prophecies were fulfilled in quite a different sense: the world Mother Juana had known ended. In fact, after the golden age presided over by Cardinal Cisneros, in which extraordinary religious phenomena were allowed to flourish, Spain's spiritual climate changed rapidly. The persecution of the Erasmists, the abdication of Charles V, and the fear of the Protestant menace[28]—all seemed to conspire to devalue the kind of unmediated experience of the divine that is represented by Mother Juana's revelations.[29] Female visionaries in particular suffered a cruel fate, for the Inquisition ended up branding them as deluded, thus completely discrediting their religious experiences.[30] By the time Juana's beatification process was opened in the seventeenth century, the Counter-Reformation had made it more difficult than ever to enter the company of the saints. Moreover, the eccentricity of some of Juana's visions turned out to be excessive even for the baroque religious sensibility.

The well-intentioned but unsuccessful attempts by Mother Juana's supporters to dissociate her from her writings ultimately manifested the strong link between visionary and visions, for the revelations constituted the core of her experience of the sacred. Mother Juana did all she could to create her own authority and to defend her book, anticipating the criticisms of her detractors and attempting to control the reception of the text. If her efforts had a limited success and eventually failed, such success and failure do not detract from her courage in seeking to defend her right to have extraordinary religious experiences and to communicate those experiences.

Notes

1. Aside from the prologue, the only other occasion when the "we" of Mother Juana's companions is manifested appears to be a passage in the sermon for the Feast of the Holy Cross: "E que aunque El estava fablando con nosotras en esta boz, o tañendo con aquella flauta, que hera Dios todopoderoso que está en todo lugar. E todos los çielos e la tierra están llenos d'El, que no ay rincón ni lugar, por escondido que sea, en que El no esté" (*Conorte*, fol. 279r). The nuns go on to relate an incident they witnessed concerning the gift of tongues: "E como en este tienpo que El visitava esta casa de su preçiosa madre se ganase la çibdad de Orán e tru- xesen algunos moros de la dicha çibdad captivos a Castilla e unas personas devotas ofreçiesen a Nuestra Señora unas esclavas, el Señor, por su gran bondad, quando venía a fablar en esta boz, las fablava tanbién a ellas en su lenguage algunas palabras muy provechosas para su convertimiento e salvaçión. Y ellas le entendían e no nosotras, porque hera arávigo muy çerrado. El Señor, quando las avía fablado, nos declarava en nuestro lenguage las cosas que les dezía, las quales heran muy altas e provechosas para salvaçión de sus ánimas" (*Conorte*, fol. 279r).

2. In an analogous case the visionary receives a revelation concerning the be- neficent properties of certain "blessed knots" shaped like the girdle of the Franciscan order, whose knots represent the lashes of Christ's Passion. At first, Juana does not wish to disclose this revelation, but her angel orders her to write it down: "La qual dicha sierva de Dios quería callar, que no le curaba de lo dezir. Y fuele mandado por ciertas vezes que escribiesse la dicha revelación por el santo ángel y las palabras que en ella avía oído" (*Casa*, fol. 55v). Later, the text is turned over to the superiors of her order: "Y la dicha sierva de Dios que esto escrivió dixo que ella se ponía en manos de sus prelados y de Dios primeramente y de las personas doctas que deven conocer las cosas espirituales. Porque ella no se sentía digna de saber examinar la tal revelación" (*Casa*, fol. 56r).

3. This passage elicited Father Torres's exhortation to the reader to believe in the divine inspiration of Mother Juana's sermons: "Nota bien todas estas cosas y créelas, que si te encomiendas a Dios de coraçón y lees en estos divinos sermones con humildad y devotión, Dios te hará merced que lo entiendas y que lo veas ser así más claro que el sol" (*Conorte*, fol. 452r).

4. The late-thirteenth-century *Meditationes vitae Christi* is probably the proto- type of this Franciscan tradition. In his prologue the anonymous author demon- strates his awareness that not all the episodes he will invite his readers to contemplate are to be found in the Bible: "However, you must not believe that all things said and done by Him on which we may meditate are known to us in writing. For the sake of greater impressiveness I shall tell them to you as they occurred or as they

might have occurred according to the devout belief of the imagination and the varying interpretation of the mind" (*Meditations on the Life of Christ: An Illustrated Manuscript of the Fourteenth Century,* ed. Isa Ragusa and Rosalie B. Green [1961; Princeton: Princeton University Press, 1977], 5). For the *Meditationes* as an archetypically Franciscan work, see John V. Fleming, *An Introduction to the Franciscan Literature of the Middle Ages* (Chicago: Franciscan Herald Press, 1977), 242–251.

5. At the beginning of this passage a hand that is not that of Father Torres has written in the margin: "Esto se mire mucho." Torres addresses the reader in turn with the following rather lapidary warning: "Esto creo yo muy bien ser así y así lo creerán los que tuvieren sano entendimiento. Y el que no lo creyere es infiel o no lo entiende" (*Conorte,* fol. 450r).

6. Saint John the Evangelist (21:25) himself observed: "But there are also many other things which Jesus did which, if they were written every one, the world itself, I think, would not be able to contain the books that should be written."

7. Father Torres writes alongside the quoted passage the following annotation: "En escripturas canónicas como en el Génesis no quiso el Señor que se escriviese, como no quiso que otras muchas y inumerables más importantes no se escreviesen, pues otros auctores que los que después por espíritu divino las escrivieron, como Moisés, David, Salomón, Job, etc., no los tenemos ni creo que los huvo, ni aun savemos que alguien de aquel principio del mundo escriviese. Y si lo supo alguien hacer, sería Adán mejor que nadie, porque fue más savio que sus hijos y que sus descendientes, al qual le dotó Dios en gran sabiduría y en todas las cosas. Mas no ay notitia de que sola una letra escriviese. Aunque por voz puso nonbre a todas las cosas, no savemos que por escripto nonbrase sola una. Mucho devemos a esta sancta, pues nos hiço Dios saver por ella cosas que por nadie las supimos. D'El sepamos todo lo que ella supo, que fue más que lo que aquí se escrive" (*Conorte,* fol. 444v).

8. For the authority accorded to the eyewitness narrator in medieval historiography, see Jeanette M. A. Beer, *Narrative Conventions of Truth in the Middle Ages* (Geneva: Droz, 1981), 23–34.

9. Father Torres seems to allude to I Corinthians 1:22 ("For both the Jews require signs, and the Greeks seek after wisdom").

10. Cf. "Walk whilst you have the light, that the darkness overtake you not" (John 12:35).

11. This is probably a reminiscence of Luke 13:32 ("Behold I cast out devils, and do cures to-day and to-morrow, and the third day I am consummated").

12. The feast (July 16) commemorates the decisive Christian victory over the Muslims at Las Navas de Tolosa in 1212.

13. The comparison between the Eucharist and God's revelation through Juana was lightly crossed out by the anonymous censor. Father Torres's commentary has its own corrections, for as he himself recounts, at first he misread the passage in question: "Esto que he dicho en esta glosa d'este capítulo a la letra lo dixe de la cruz en que Dios murió, que es possible que Dios obre en ella todas las maravillas. Y fue la causa que me engañé, que entendí mal que Nuestro Señor havía venido a hablar a sus bienaventurado [*sic*] en su misma cruz en vez d'estar en ella como en el sancto sacramento, mas después lo entendí mejor, que no hablava sino

de su amada Juana de la Cruz, la qual podemos llamar cruz biva del Señor. No padeció en ella, mas padesció y murió por ella. Y cosa llana es que, pues recevía el sancto sacramento y Dios se le dio en manjar y así se da en todo fiel que recive la altíssima Eucharistía, bien le es possible estarse en su sierva como en la sancta hostia y venir a ella y hablar en ella como es verdad que de hecho lo hiço" (*Conorte,* fol. 278v). Thus, Torres emphasizes that not only is God present in Juana *sacramentalmente* but, as in the case of the guitar vision, Juana is at once the cross and Christ.

14. The anonymous examiner crossed out this passage. Father Torres answers that all the cross-outs should be stricken.

15. Cf. I Corinthians 2:9.

16. The anonymous censor did not react at all to the justification of the presence of horses in Heaven, but he did cross out the passage in which the angels offer to become horses.

17. Cf. Revelation 6:1–8.

18. The anonymous censor crossed out this passage. In defending the *Conorte,* Father Torres declares that the celestial horses are healthy and sweet-smelling as is everything else in Heaven (*Conorte,* fol. 305r). His commentary perhaps explains why some considered the presence of horses a jarring note: the animal's lack of cleanliness and foul smell would ill suit the perfection of Paradise.

19. "Bienaventurados los que lloran, que ellos reirán en el reino de los çielos" (*Conorte,* fol. 450v).

20. It appears that this was a burning issue. An anonymous fifteenth-century treatise contains a chapter entitled "Cómo en paraíso ay juegos e bailes e risos," which is intended to justify, according to the appropriate authorities, the presence of such pastimes in Heaven. See *Tractado muy devoto e provechoso a todos aquellos que lo bien estudiaren e acataren bien a las cosas en él contenidas,* Biblioteca Nacional, Madrid, MS 5626, fols. 57v–59r. The said chapter coincides nearly word for word with chapter XXVI ("Que la nostra anima se deu promoure a desijar la gloria de paradis per los balls, iochs e ris qui en ella son") of Book III of the *Scala de contemplació* of Antoni Canals (1352–1418). See the edition by Juan Roig Gironella, S.J. (Barcelona: Fundación Balmesiana, 1975), 184–185. It is probable that both texts are derived from chapter CCCXCI ("Qui ensenya con, en Paradís, ha cants e bals e jochs e ris") of *Lo libre de les dones* by Father Francesc Eiximenis (1330/35–1409). See the edition by Frank Naccarato, 2 vols. (Barcelona: Universitat de Barcelona and Curial Edicions Catalanes, 1981), 2:567–568.

21. The passage that follows, which insists on the divine inspiration of Mother Juana's sermons, was crossed out by the anonymous censor. In his marginal annotation Father Torres accuses his predecessor of not heeding the divine warning regarding the two types of readers: "Havíase de correr mucho de dar las rayas el que acabava de leer la conparatión que el Señor pronunció." Torres goes on to speak of the miraculous nature of the revelation and of the writing of the sermons, contrasting the book-learning of men with the infused knowledge of women: "Y yo prometo que ninguno de los nacidos que no los apruebe diga de súpito y sin estudiar tales y tan graves y tan estrañas y tan subidas cosas ni las escriva y que ninguno de los que viven en el mundo con cien años de estudio dixera muchas y inumerables cosas que aquí están, sino por revelación de Dios, que por libros, pues

no estás en ellos, mal las aprendiera. Anda, véncete y, si no eres protervo, confiesa que Dios enseñó a esta sancta y habló en esta sancta y escrivió en estas sus siervas. Así sea en nosotros. Amén. Amén. Amén" (*Conorte,* fol. 452r).

22. This is not the only such case of magical powers being ascribed to a religious text. In his *Cantiga* 209 Alfonso the Wise relates how placing the manuscript of the *Cantigas de Santa María* upon him cured a painful illness. See John E. Keller and Richard P. Kinkade, "Iconography and Literature: Alfonso Himself in *Cantiga* 209," *Hispania,* 66 (1983) 348–352. A fifteenth-century Catalan manuscript that contains a narration of the death and Assumption of the Virgin Mary purports to protect its reader or bearer against the Devil and other enemies: "Así comensa lo espasament de la verge maria e lo reculliment de aquella e diu que tota persona quil dirá hol fará dir ho ab si hol portará ab bona deuoció ni remembrança, no li cal hauer pahor del diabbla, ni de neguna cosa qui mala sia o no li cal tembre de sos enemichs que no li poran fer mal ni dan, ni de yra de senyor" (Francesch Carreras y Candi, "Lo passament de la Verge María. Llibret talismán del segle XV," *Boletín de la Real Academia de Buenas Letras de Barcelona,* 10 [1921] 215). And a *Devocionario castellano del siglo XV* specifies that a certain prayer to the Virgin will protect both he who says it and he who carries it with him: "E sepa cada una persona que la rezare o la traxere consigo con buena voluntad e devoción que non podrá morir mala muerte e sin confessión" (Real Academia de la Historia [Madrid], MS 9/5809, fol. 27r).

23. This is the alternate title that was occasionally given to *El libro del conorte.* The corresponding passage in the Vatican manuscript (fol. 729r) refers to the book as the *Conorte.*

24. For apocalyptic notions in Italy regarding the year 1500, see André Chastel, "L'Apocalypse en 1500. La fresque de l'Antéchrist à la Chapelle Saint-Brice d'Orvieto," *Bibliothèque d'Humanisme et Renaissance,* 14 (1952) 124–140. The *Libro del antichristo,* translated by Martín Martínez de Ampiés and published at Zaragoza in 1496, warns that the Last Judgment will not be long in coming, given the evils of the times (fol. 35r).

25. *Toletana beatificationis et canonizationis Ven. Servae Dei Joannae de Cruce . . . Positio super dubio an stante non reperitione assertorum opusculorum originalium possit ad ulteriora in causa procedi. Relatio Reverendissimi Fidei Promotoris super statu causae* (Rome: Typis Reverendae Camerae Apostolicae, 1731), 7.

26. *Toletana beatificationis et canonizationis . . . Relatio,* 6.

27. *Toletana beatificationis et canonizationis Ven. Servae Dei Joannae de Cruce . . . Positio super dubio . . . Restrictus facti et juris. super dubio an stante non reperitione assertorum opusculorum originalium, possit ad ulteriora in causa procedi* (Rome: Typis Reverendae Camerae Apostolicae, 1731), 3–17.

28. For Philip II's efforts to protect Spain from what he perceived to be dangerous outside influences, see Juan Ignacio Gutiérrez Nieto, "La discriminación de los conversos y la tibetización de Castilla por Felipe II," *Revista de la Universidad Complutense de Madrid,* 22 (1973) 99–129.

29. Barely three years after Mother Juana's death, the anonymous Franciscan author of the *Excelencias de la fe* (Burgos, 1537) harshly criticized the interpretation of the Scriptures by women: "La mujer, por sabia que sea, en los misterios de la fe

y de la Iglesia ponga un candado de silencio a su boca. Pues es cierto lo que dijeron los antiguos, que la joya que más alinda a la hembra es el candado del silencio a las puertas de sus labios para todas pláticas, y particularmente para los misterios de santidad y para no ser maestra de doctrinas de Escripturas Santas. . . . El sentido literal dellas [Saint Paul's epistles], cuánto más el espiritual, es muy dificultoso a los sabios; cuánto más a la señora beata e a la mujercilla que se olvida de la rueca por presumir leer a San Pablo" (quoted in Melquíades Andrés, *La teología española en el siglo XVI*, 2 vols. [Madrid: Biblioteca de Autores Cristianos, 1976–1977], 2:558).

30. See Claire Guilhem, "L'Inquisition et la dévaluation des discours féminins," in *L'Inquisition espagnole, XVe–XIXe siècle*, ed. Bartolomé Bennassar (Paris: Hachette, 1979), 197–240.

Appendixes

Appendix A

MADRE JUANA DE LA CRUZ: *EL LIBRO DEL CONORTE*

Capítulo LXXII. *Que trata de la creaçión de los çielos e la tierra e de todas las cosas que en ellos son e del honbre a imagen e semejança de Dios* [Selections]

[fol. 444r] Fablando el Señor del gozo que ovo toda la Santíssima Trinidad quando ovo criado todas las cosas çelestiales e terrenales e infernales, dixo que se levantó Dios en su entendimiento y en su voluntad y en su magestad y en su sapiençia y virtud y en su palabra e crió los çielos e las moradas e sillas e abitaçiones d'él. Los quales son tan grandes e anchos que cada uno de los bienaventurados que en ellos moran tiene más anchura e lugar para él solo que todo el universo mundo. E dixo su divina magestad que después que El ovo criado todos los çielos, hízolos tan luzidos e claros e preçiosos que son todos más que de oro e cristal e piedras preçiosas con todos sus arreos. E ansimesmo crió la tierra e todas las cosas que en ella son.

E como criase el çielo e la tierra, crió luego los ángeles, los quales provó luego en obediençia. E como no los falló fieles a todos, crió luego el honbre a imagen e semejança suya para reparar las sillas de los que cayeron. Porque ésta es la voluntad de Dios, que si uno se pierde y es malo, otro posea su silla e lugar en nonbre de bueno, si lo es e faze las obras. E después que ovo criado el honbre, sacóle del mesmo la muger. E después que los huvo criado e vido cómo tenían entendimiento e ingenio tan bivo, gozóse e alegróse mucho. E más se alegró cuando vido que estavan en puridad e inoçençia e amor el uno con el otro en aquel huerto tan deleitoso, florido e tenplado, conviene a saber, en el paraíso terrenal, en el qual avíamos todos de estar en grandes gozos e deleites, si Adán e Eva no pecaran.

E que estando ellos en esta inoçençia, enpeçaron entramos a jugar, e luego enpeçó a reinar en ellos la maliçia y el desamor. E como nuestra madre Eva veía que Adán la amava tanto e se iva en pos d'ella dondequiera que iva, atrevíase en alguna manera e feríale e fazíale mal. E viendo Adán cómo la muger le fería e le dolía cuando le dava, después de se lo aver sufrido algunas vezes por el grande amor que le tenía, no podía acabar con su coraçón de ferirla ni fazerle mal. Enpero, quexávase al Señor, diziendo: "O Señor Dios todopoderoso, mira la conpañera que me diste, que me fiere e me faze mal." E dixo el Señor que le respondía El: "Pues, si ella te fiere a ti, fiérela tú tanbién a ella, que iguales e conpañeros sois." E que Adán le dezía: "Señor, ámola tanto que en ninguna manera la puedo ferir ni fazer ningún mal." E tornando Adán otras vezes a ella, fablándola e jugando con ella, por semejante le tornava a ferir e fazer mal. Y él tornávase a quexar, diziendo cómo le fería sienpre e le fazía mal. Y el poderoso Dios (dixo El mesmo) le respondía: "Pues, si la muger te fiere, apártate d'ella e no vayas tú adonde ella está." E Adán dezía: "O Señor, eso de pena se me haze, que aunque me fiere, en ninguna manera me querría apartar d'ella." Y el Señor le dixo: "Pues, no te quieres apartar d'ella, déxame e no me digas esas cosas. Anda, ve, échate a dormir, que yo te faré de manera que te tema / [fol. 444v] e aya miedo de llegar a ti e que tú seas señor sobre ella e no ella sobre ti." E luego Adán (dixo el Señor), cunpliendo su mandamiento, se echó a dormir e a reposar. E así como fue dormido, le crió El e le puso barvas en el rostro.

E que no deve ninguna persona dudar ni maravillarse de cómo crió El las barvas a Adán después de le aver criado, aunque no lo fallen en las Santas Escrituras, porque entonçes no avía gentes que escriviesen esto ni otras muchas cosas e secretos que se están oy día en silençio.

E dixo el Señor que cuando Adán recordó e se vido con barvas, que se maravilló mucho e se fue adonde estava Eva con gran deseo de la ver e fablar. E cuando ella le vido, como tenía barvas, ovo muy gran miedo d'él e fuyó. E que viendo Adán que Eva fuía d'él, angustiávase mucho e iva en pos d'ella, llamándola a grandes bozes e diziendo: "Ven acá, amiga. Ven acá, hermana, que no te faré ningún mal." E cogía de las mançanas e flores e de las otras frutas que tenían los árboles e iva corriendo, conbidándola e diziendo: "No fuigas de mí, hermana, que ningún mal te faré. Toma estas flores e frutas que traigo para ti." E dixo el Señor que, viendo Adán cómo en ninguna manera quería Eva venir adonde él estava, entristeçíase e iva a su divina majestad, diziendo: "O Señor Dios todopoderoso, ¿qué es esto que me diste, que fuye la muger de mí e no me quiere ver ni llegarse a mí? Quítamelo, que estoy con ello muy angustiado." E que El le dixo: "Calla, Adán, que bien estás assí, que mi voluntad es que todos los varones tengan lo mesmo e sean señores sobre las mugeres."

E declaró el Señor, diziendo que tuvo El por bien de dar e fazer nasçer las barvas [a] Adán e a todos los honbres por que fuesen señalados y estimados e acatados e temidos, por cuanto el honbre sinifica e representa a la persona del Padre çelestial. Porque así como el honbre tiene esta propiedad, que es fuerte e señor sobre la muger e sobre todas las cosas criadas en la tierra, enpero que si es prudente e discreto tanbién es piadoso e manso e amoroso, que así por semejante la persona del Padre es muy fuerte e poderosa, porque en El está todo el poder e fortaleza e puede destruir e matar y es señor sobre todos los çielos e la tierra. Enpero, si le aman e sirven e obedeçen e temen, es misericordioso e manso e humillde e piadoso.

E la muger es figurada e significa a la persona del Fijo, porque así como la muger es más humillde e obediente e piadosa e mansa que el honbre, así la persona del Fijo fue tan humillde e obediente al Padre que fasta la muerte de la cruz le obedeçió. E tan grande fue su piedad e mansedumbre que nunca respondió palabra a cuantas injurias le dixeron, mas antes estando en la cruz, rogava al Padre por los que le cruçificaron. E que así como las mugeres, si son discretas, son naturalmente mansas e piadosas e perdonan las injurias antes que los honbres, así Nuestro Señor Jesuchristo perdona muy presto las injurias que le son fechas y es contino perdonador e abogado de todo el humanal linage. E assí como la muger tiene ingenio e agudeza, así por semejante Nuestro Señor Jesuchristo es la sabiduría del Padre. . . .

[fol. 445v] . . . dixo el Señor que como Eva fuía de Adán, que iva Adán en pos d'ella e la traía por fuerça algunas vezes e otras vezes la traía con halagos e con amor e la fazía llegar a él. E que por todo esto que fazían, no se enojava El con ellos, mas antes le plazía que se amasen entramos. E dixo su divina magestad que quando Adán comió la mançana que le dio Eva, que lo fizo por el desamor que Eva le tenía e por que no se apartase d'él e se fuesse fuyendo como otras vezes solía fazer. De manera que la discordia e poca paz e desamor que entre entramos avía fue causa e raíz e prinçipio del pecado tan grande en que cayeron. E cunplióse en ellos la palabra que El mesmo dixo en el evangelio, que todo reino entre sí diviso será destruido. . . .

[fol. 451r] Dixo el Señor que quando El crió [a] Adán, que aunque le formó e fizo luego honbre de perfeta edad en quanto al cuerpo e le crió cabellos en su cabeça y en las otras partes de su cuerpo e le vistió e cubrió de vestidura, según El quiso e fue su voluntad, a él e a nuestra madre Eva, enpero que en quanto a la faz entramos la tenían de una manera e no avía diferençia del uno al otro, porque quando El crió a Adán e después a Eva, a entramos les fizo las fazes como de ángeles muy fermosas. Porque assí como el niño quando naçe, aunque es varón, no se le pareçe en el rostro ni tiene diferençia de la muger, aunque en el cuerpo y en los mienbros la tiene. E que assí como el honbre, quando creçe y es formado, le cría El las barbas en el rostro, assí por semejante quando El crió a Adán, le fizo como mançebo joven en la faz. Enpero, por quanto la muger le quería sojuzgar e no le quería tener por igual sino por menor que ella, permitió El que le naçiesen a Adán barvas en el rostro por que fuese tenido en veneraçión.

Appendix B

MORISCO LEGEND

Kuando haleqó Allāh a Adam, no tenía qabellos Adam en la barba, i Hawa no lo respetaba mucho, qomo le beía de sin qapellos. I ansí por esto no resbetan tanpoqo a los onbres quando no tienen parbas. I adurmióse Adam i Hawa, i qonpuso Allāh en la qara de Adam su parba muy larga i muy onrada. I desbertóse Adam, i quando se bio akella parba, marabillóse mucho de akello. I kuando se desbertó Hawa i bio a Adam kon akella barba larga, marabillóse d'ella Hawa. I d'allí adelante tubo mucho resbeto i bergüensa Hawa a Adam i lo respetó mucho d'allí adelante. I ansí son resbetados todos los haleqados bor la barpa i bor las kanas. I ansí fue Ibrahim.

(When Allah created Adam, Adam had no beard, and Eve did not respect him much, as she saw him hairless. And so for this reason are men not respected either when they have no beards. And Adam and Eve fell asleep, and Allah made on Adam's face a very long and honorable beard. And Adam awakened, and when he saw that beard, he was greatly amazed. And when Eve awakened and saw Adam with that long beard, she marvelled at it. And from then on Eve was very respectful and modest before Adam and respected him greatly from then on. And so are all men respected for their beards and for their white hairs. And likewise was Abraham.)

Appendix C

Nach dem Adam und Eva werd
Gingen auff diser Erd,
Eines tags der Herr kam
Rüffet und sprach: Adam,
Sag mir, förcht dich dein Weibe?
Adam saget: o Herre, nein.
Von Ir leid ich vil pein.
Dann wann sie zornig wirt,
Sie mich grausam vexirt,
Greifft mir nach meinem leibe.
Und der Herr sprach:
Kum, folg mir nach.
Zu einem bach
Det er denn Adam füren.
Der Herr sprach: thu dein Hand ins
    Wasser rüren.
Weiter saget der Herre frum:
Fahr umb dein maul herum.
Und Adam was nit faul,
Fuhr mit der hand umbs Maul.
Der Herr sprach: dich wol reibe.

Zuhand wuchs Im ein langer bart
Gar rauch zotiger art.
Der Herr sprach: Adam, sich,
Dein Weib wirt förchten dich,
Wenn sie dich wirt ansehen.
Do nun Adam heim kam zu hauß,
Floh Weib und Kind hinauß,
Sie förchten sich vor Ihm.
Als Eva hört sein stim,
Det sie sich zu Im nehen.
Sprach mit begir:
Adam, sag mir,
Von wann kumpt dir
Doch umb dein Maul das Hare?
Adam der sprach: der Herr erst bei
    mir ware,
Fürt mich zu einem Wasser klein,
Mein hand stieß ich darein.
Mit der so fuhr ich auch

After Adam and Eve came to walk
upon this earth, the Lord arrived one
day, called, and said: "Tell me, Adam,
does your wife fear you?" Adam said:
"No, O Lord. On account of her I suffer great pain, for when she becomes
angry, she annoys me terribly and she
grabs me all over my body." And the
Lord spoke: "Come. Follow me." He
brought Adam to a brook. The Lord
said: "Dip your hand into the water."
Then said the good Lord: "Stroke
your jaw with it." Adam didn't hesitate
one bit; he touched all around his jaw
with his hand. The Lord said: "Rub
it well."

Immediately, there grew on him a long
beard, quite hairy and shaggy. The
Lord spoke: "Look, Adam, your wife
is going to fear you when she looks at
you." When Adam came home, his
wife and child fled, for they were
afraid of him. When Eve heard his
voice, she drew near him. She spoke
with eager desire: "Tell me, Adam.
Where did you get that hair around
your jaw?" Adam said: "Just now the
Lord was with me; He led me to a
small river; I dipped my hand in it.
When I passed it over my chin, I became all hairy. As I verily tell you."

Umbs Maul, do ward ich rauch,
Thu ich mit Warheit jehen.

Eva höret Im fleissig zu.   Eve listened diligently. Early the next
Des andren tages fru   morning, she secretly left the house.
Ging sie heimlich hinauß,   She looked for the water and ap-
Spehet das Wasser auß,   proached the brook all alone. She
Kam zu dem Bach aleine.   wished to test the water's powers, to
Wolt probieren des Wassers art,   see if it would make hair and beards
Ob es Brecht Har und Bart,   grow. She dipped her hand into it, but
Ir hand sie darein stieß.   at that moment a bumblebee bit her
In dem ein Humel biß   between her legs. She prudently with-
Sie zwischen Ire Beine.   drew her hand and struck the bee with
Ir hand sie klug   her wet hands. Thereupon, she became
Auß dem Bach zug   hairy, as are still all women in that very
Und nach Ir schlug   place. Thus the beard originated with
Mit Iren nassen Henden.   Adam, and Eve likewise, who became
Do ward sie rauch, wie dann ann   hairy out of an excess of curiosity, as is
    selben Enden   still common among women.
Noch sind die Weiber alesam.
So kamen von Adam
Die Bert, und Eva auch,
Die wart durch fürwitz rauch,
Ist bei In noch gemeine.

Appendix D

VIDA Y FIN DE LA BIENABENTURADA VIRGEN SANCTA JUANA DE LA CRUZ

Capítulo 21. De la gran caridad con que esta bienaventurada rogó al Señor por la salvaçión de la religiosa que havía sido causa de su persiguimiento, a la qual tenía por abadesa [Fragment]

[fol. 99v] Quando le hera mostrado a esta sancta virgen por la voluntad de Dios algo de las penas que las ánimas por sus peccados padesçen, si le fuera dada liçençia de Dios, ella tomara las penas sobre sí por que ellas tuvieran descanso, aunque son muy insufribles. Lo qual hiço esta bienaventurada muchas veçes, dándole Dios para ello liçençia y esfuerço caridoso, que suplicándole ella a Nuestro Señor huviese piedad de las ánimas que ella havía visto en tan grandes penas y tormentos y le hiçiese a ella tan gran merçed que pudiese ayudarles a padesçer sus penas, aunque fuese acreçentándole a ella sus dolores, aunque los tenía muy grandes y a su paresçer insufribles. Todo lo padesçería por la consolación y quitamiento de penas de las ánimas de purgatorio. Y si para otorgarle su divina magestad esta merçed, le quiere dar nuevas enfermedades, que con su graçia e ayuda ella estava aparejada para todo. Y continuando esta bienabenturada en su oraçión e ayudándola a rogar su sancto ángel, fuele otorgada su petiçión de caridad exerçitada en los próximos vivos y difuntos. La qual ella exerçitó muy enteramente todos los días de su vida.

Y exerçitando esta caridad con las ánimas, le acaesçió una cosa por donde se le descubrió un secreto açerca de las ánimas de purgatorio. Y fue en esta manera. Que teniendo esta sancta virgen a causa de sus enfermedades los miembros fríos, paresçióle a ella que unos guijarros caliente[s] entre la ropa de su cama le darían algún refrigerio en aquella neçessidad que tenía. Rogó que se los buscasen, si los havía en el monasterio. Y haviendo traído para una obra que haçían en la casa una carretada d'ellos muchos tiempos antes de sus enfermedades y de estas guijarros havía algunos por la casa. Y buscándolos a su pedimiento, hallaron uno muy grande a una puerta de una cueva, con el / [fol. 100r] qual havían molido muchas vezes pez. Y llevándole a esta bienabenturada, dixo que hera muy bueno y mandó allí en su presençia le calentasen en un brasero de lumbre. Deque fue empeçado a calentar y calentado, empeçó a oír unos muy dolorosos gemidos formando manera de palabras en las quales deçía: "¿Ay crueldad tan grande?" Y esto no lo oía ninguna de las monjas que allí estavan sino la sancta virgen que dende su cama lo mirava e oía. E le paresçía ser ánima de purgatorio. Y mirando con su entendimiento de dónde salían aquellos gemidos e palabras, sintió salían del guixarro que a la lumbre estava. Y no diçiendo por entonçes la causa d'ello, mandó aprisa no le calentasen más y le quitasen luego, y enbuelto en un paño, se le pusiesen sobre sus manos. Y deque le tuvo allí, le dixo en silençio: "Anima, yo te ruego me perdones la pena que he sido causa resçivas. E dime cómo as venido a estar aquí." El ánima le respondió: "Ruégote no mandes calentar más este guijarro donde estoy por mandado de Dios, que si quisieres calor, yo te le daré y también frío. Y a lo que preguntas cómo estoy aquí, ya te he dicho que es voluntad de Dios. Mas primero que a este monasterio me truxesen, estava en un río que se llama Taxo, e las bestias con sus pies me sacaron d'él e los hombres peccadores me truxeron a esta casa." La bienabenturada le dixo: "¿En guijarros y en piedras están y penan ánimas?" Respondióle: "Sí, que muchas están en piedras y en guijarros y en aquel río adonde yo estava, havía gran número de ánimas metidas en guijarros. Y ellas y yo a muchos años que estamos allí." Díxole la sancta virgen: "Ruégote, amiga, me digas tu neçessidad y me pidas el ayuda que quisieres." El ánima le respondió lo que Dios le dio liçençia.

E deque la bienabenturada vido a su sancto ángel, díxole: "Señor, muy / [fol. 100v] maravillada estoy de una cosa que he savido, que las ánimas penan en guijarros y en piedras y en cosas semejantes." E diziéndole en qué manera lo había savido, díxole el sancto ángel: "¿De eso te maravillas, criatura de Dios? Bien puedes creer que muchas son las que de esa manera padesçen y penan porque Nuestro Señor les diputó por hospital cada piedra e lugar donde las ánimas están por voluntad del mesmo Dios. Una cosa te hago saver, que después que el poderoso Dios te otorgó que pudieses ayudar a pagar a las ánimas de purgatorio lo que por sus culpas y peccados mereçen, heres estableçida y hecha por la voluntad de Dios hospital de las ánimas que tienen penas. Y esto se entiende las que su sancta voluntad quisiere y diere liçençia o quien yo y tú pidiéremos a su poderosa misericordia. Porque ansí como el hospital se haçe para los pobres e neçessitados e día y noche los resçiven, así tú resçivirás día y noche las ánimas que Dios por su voluntad te embiare para que las ayudes e alibies sus travajos con los tuyos. E mira que acaeçe ban los pobres al hospital unos con sed, otros con ambre y otros con demasiada calor e otros con demasiado frío e con otros muchos géneros de neçessidades causados por las diversas enfermedades que consigo traen. Ansí te digo, criatura de Dios, bendrán a ti muchas ánimas con demasiados calores de fuegos y fríos entolerables y con otras diversas penas que por sus peccados mereçen. Y tú, hospital por la voluntad de Dios y por tu consentimiento, las resçivirás con mucha caridad y las [MS : los] aposentarás sobre tus miembros y coyunturas muy dolorosas y descoyuntadas de las neçessidades que traen. Y ellas serán allí recreadas y consoladas de las neçessidades que traen en la cantidad y manera que fuere la voluntad de Dios. Y tú, sierba suya, esfuérçate en la paçiençia y / [fol. 101r] caridad, que mucho as de partiçipar y sentir las penas d'estas ánimas. E sábete estás tan sujeta por la voluntad de Dios a padesçer por las ánimas, que aunque agora te faltase la caridad para padesçer esto de grado, por fuerça lo padesçerías porque ansí lo quiere el Señor Dios, pues tú lo pediste con tanto afinco." Respondió la bienabenturada al sancto ángel, diziendo: "Señor, muy gran merçed me a hecho vuestra gran hermosura con su habla e aviso. Yo me tengo por dichosa de cumplir la voluntad de Dios y suplico a vuestra señoría le ruegue me dé graçia para ello."

Y de aí adelante rogava a las religiosas le traxesen los guijarros que por el monasterio hallasen. Y ellas con mucho cuidado lo haçían, aunque no savían para qué hera. E quando alguno le traían, mandavan que se le pusiesen en la cama. Y teniéndole allí, conoçia si tenía dentro algunas ánimas, e los [MS : las] más tenían una y muchas. Y los [MS : las] que no tenían ninguna mandávalos sacar de su çelda. Y no contenta ni satisfecha de caridad con los que en el monesterio estavan, rogó que le hiziesen traer algunos de un río que ella señaló, del qual traxeron muchos. Y todos venían con muchas ánimas de dentro de sí, de manera que siempre tenían en el hospital de sus caridosos miembros bastamiento de ánimas. E por la voluntad de Dios y con su poder siempre venían ánimas (y vinieron a esta sancta virgen hasta en fin de sus días) a ser ayudadas por su oración y méritos.

Quando ella las vía venir, dezíales que tomasen por lugar en que estuviesen los guijarros donde estavan las otras que antes que ellas havían venido por la voluntad de Dios. Y aunque en cada una de aquellas piedras estavan muchas ánimas, cada una tenía la pena en sí propia que por sus peccados mereçía, diferentes unas de otras. Y como esta bienabenturada no tenía manos con que poner sobre sus miembros las piedras, de neçessidad preguntándoselo las religiosas, les descubrió el secreto e les rogó que todas las vezes que ella s[e] los pidiese, se los diesen / [fol. 101v] e pusiesen donde ella les dixese. Las religiosas, mucho maravilladas de saver tal secreto, le dixeron que lo harían de voluntad. Y dende entonzes empezó esta bienabenturada a poner sobre su persona y miembros aquellas piedras e por su desseo y voluntad ayudarles a padesçer sus penas, ofreçiendo sus dolores y pidiendo a Nuestro Señor se le acreçentasen por que aquellas ánimas que consigo tenía fuesen recreadas y alibiadas las penas y por su piadosa misericordia y sancta Passión fuesen libres de todas ellas. Aunque havían sido peccadoras, hera mayor su piadad para las perdonar y haçer merçedes. Y que allí estava su cuerpo doloroso y tullido para pagar por ellos lo que su divina magestad mandase. Y puniéndose esta sancta virgen estas piedras alrededor de su cuerpo y miembros, sentían mucha consolaçión e alibiamiento de penas las ánimas que dentro d'ellas estavan.

Y acaesçía elevarse, y esto muy contino, teniendo contino mucha de esta compañía. Y aunque los guijarros heran grandes y sus miembros muy delicados, no se los osaban quitar las monjas hasta que Nuestro Señor la volvía en sus sentidos. Hera muy grande admiraçión y causa de mucha devoçión verla estar ansí de esta manera quando unas ánimas havían acabado de purgar sus peccados mediante la sancta Passión de Nuestro Señor e ayuda de la sancta madre iglesia y de todas las otras cosas que su divinal clemençia tiene otorgadas para estos remedios y por los méritos de esta bienabenturada. Ibanse estas ánimas libres de penas y venían otras con la mesma liçençia de Dios. La cantidad de las ánimas que iban y venían heran muchas, según dezía la sancta virgen. Cada vez que venían mucho número de ánimas juntas, no heran todas d'ellas aún libres, porque unas estavan más tiempo que otras, según tenían la neçessidad. Muchas cosas veían manifiestamente todas las religiosas del monasterio açerca de este secreto e caridad que Nuestro Señor haçía mediante la oraçión y méritos de esta bienabenturada.

Y como las ánimas viniesen tan llenas de penas y fuegos y fríos, todo muy ensufrible, e con otros muchos tormentos, luego las tomava ella e las juntava con sus dolorosos miembros, a cuya causa partiçipava en mucho grado de las penas que ellas traían, quedándole sus miembros / [fol. 102r] con muy acreçentados y grandes dolores y con tan reçios fuegos que le pareçía estar ella metida en los mesmos fuegos de purgatorio, tanto que de neçessidad muchas vezes le haçían aire e otras le ponían paños mojados en agua fría sobre sus quebradas coyunturas. Y en tiempo de calores le heran tan rezios de sufrir estos dolores y fuegos que la haçían dar muy grandes gemidos y gritos, pidiendo ayuda a la magestad divina para poder llevar tan insufribles y reçios tormentos. Y en este travajo estava muchos días junto sin tener alivio día ni noche ni tomando cosa con que se pudiese substener.

Estando muy fatigada con estos demasiados fuegos en el mes de henero, no osando ella pedir a las religiosas algunas cosas frías que por lo ser el tiempo se las defendían, pensando que le heran dañosas para la salud corporal, embió a llamar secretamente una religiosa de pequeña hedad y díxole el secreto: "Ruégoos vos vais al alberca de la huerta y me trayáis un pedazo del yelo que en ella está, envuelto en un paño de lienzo, y no le vea nadie." Y la religiosa, yendo con voluntad amorosa, tomó una piedra y quebró con fuerça el yelo, el qual estava grueso, ansí de ser mucha el agua como de haver muchos días y algunos que estava detenida y haver quaxado muchas noches. Y tomando un gran pedaço, envolvióle en un paño y llevóle a la zelda de la sancta virgen. Y díxole en secreto cómo le traía más que hera tan grueso como dos dedos. Ella respondió: "Bueno es. Alzá la ropa de la cama y ponedle junto a mi lado. Y de aquí a un poco tened cuidado de volver acá." Y dende a media hora volvió y díxole la bienabenturada: "Buscad, amiga, el paño que truxistes con el yelo y llevadle y no digáis esto a nadie que havemos hecho yo y bos." Y buscándole, hallóle junto con las carnes de la sancta virgen y el yelo no halló ninguna cosa, ni tenía mojada la ropa de la cama ni la túnica que tenía bestida ni sus carnes. El paño en que estava enbuelto el yelo estava un poco liento, de lo qual la religiosa se mucho maravilló y no le osó preguntar qué se havía hecho el

yelo. Y saviéndolo las religiosas dende algunos días, se lo preguntaron. Y la bienaventurada / [fol. 102v] les respondió que él se havía gastado y se gastara otro que
fuera mayor en los grandes fuegos que las ánimas tenían, de los quales ella partiçipava, teniéndolas sobre sus miembros e coyunturas. Y ellas y ella juntamente de
lo sano penavan.

E ansí como las ánimas traían pena de crueles fuegos, ansí otras vezes traían de
frío muy insufrible y le davan tanta fatiga y travaxo de padesçerlo como en la pena
del calor, porque ninguna cosa le dava calor ni descanso, aunque acaesçía tenerle
puesto alrededor de su cuerpo tres o quatro cosas llenas de brasas muy ençendidas.
Y con los demasiados fríos que las ánimas partiçipaban le creçían todos sus dolores
en mucho grado y le causaron enfermedad en las hijadas y estómago de muy creçidos dolores y en toda la oquedad de su cuerpo. Y tanto hera el travajo y dolores
que padeçía, que dava doloros[os] gritos e gemidos. Y estos travajos y tormentos
acaesçía algunas vezes durarle un mes y otras vezes quinze días y más y menos,
según hera la voluntad de Dios. Tenía ansimismo muy gran dolor de caveza, que le
durava el dolor sin ningún alivio algunas vezes seis y siete días e otras veçes más y
menos, según hera la voluntad de Dios y la neçessidad de las ánimas por quien
padesçía havía menester. Y quando este dolor tenía, no hablava palabra, porque el
dolor no la dexava, ni comía ninguna cosa si no hera de vever un poco de agua. Y
assí como ponía los guijarros sobre los miembros de su persona e junto a su lado,
por semejante hazía que se los pusiesen sobre las almoadas junto a su dolorosa
caveza. Quando assí estava, leían algunos ratos en su çelda, porque ella lo tenía
dicho para esfuerzo de sus travajos, liçión spiritual y en la Passión de Nuestro Redemptor Jesuchristo.

Y quando ya sus travajos se le aliviavan, aunque quedava muy enflaquezida,
permitía Nuestro Señor se elevase para dalle consolación y mostrarle el fauto de sus
dolores. Y supieron esto las religiosas a causa que, tornando ella en sus sentidos,
traía gran hermosura y alegría, que paresçía no haver padesçido ningún mal. Y en-
portunándola les dixese de qué tornava tan alegre, díxoles con mucho amor e
agradeçimiento / [fol. 103r] de lo que por ella hazían: "Señoras, no podría yo dezir
con mi lengua las grandes merçedes que de la magestad divina resçivo, por las
quales se muda mi rostro y esfuerça mi gran flaqueza para vivir y padesçer otra vez y
vezes los dolores que Dios me mandare. Mi alegría es que en el secreto y gloria me
fueron mostradas aquellas ánimas que yo vi muy atormentadas y padesçer conmigo, las quales havía muchos años que padesçían en penas, y tantos que algunas
d'ellas havía quinientos años e otras treçientos e otras menos. Y todas heran tan
solas, que no havía quien d'ellas se acordase para les hazer bien sino el que la sancta
madre iglesia haze en general por todos los difuntos. Y viendo yo estas ánimas en la
gloria y descanso que Dios por su misericordia les a querido dar mediante su sancta
Passión, es tan grande el alegría y gozo espiritual que mi ánima resçive, que no lo
podría comparar."

Quando esta bienabenturada quería que la llevasen al coro o a otra parte de la
casa, quando las religiosas la sentavan en el lugar donde havía de estar, poniéndole
bien la ropa que llevava bestida, topavan con los guijarros que llevava pegados a sus
coyunturas, los quales no havían visto hasta entonçes. Iban asidos unos devajo de
las corbas y otros de los pies. Ellas, muy maravilladas de ver el milagre, probavan a
quitarlos y nunca podían despegarlos, aunque ponían fuerça. La sancta virgen, so-

corriéndose, les dezía: "Dexadlas estar donde Dios les dio liçençia que estuviesen, que con su poder están esas ánimas que ay haún." Y esto se vido muchas vezes de la más parte del convento e algunas de todo.

Appendix E

VIDA Y FIN DE LA BIENABENTURADA VIRGEN SANCTA JUANA DE LA CRUZ

Capítulo 22. De una revelación qu'esta bienaventurada vido estando enferma [Fragment]

[fol. 107r] Estando esta bienaventurada en su cama enferma de calenturas, demás de todas las enfermedades que tenía, vino a ella el padre nuestro el glorioso Sant Françisco muy glorioso y acompañado de muchos sanctos bienaventurados. E saludóla y convidóla, diziéndole que se fuese con él al paraíso si pudiese y tiene esfuerzo para ello. Y si no podía por su mucha enfermedad, se estuviese en su cama, la qual le havía dado el Señor por nido como a páxaro o gallina que está enpollando sus huebos por que d'ellos nazcan páxaros vivos o pollitos de colores salidos de los huebos, los quales se crían pasçiendo en las yerbas buenas. Y diziéndole esto, le hechó con sus benditas manos en la cama tres dozenas de huevos, unos tan grandes como de abestruz e otros medianos e otros más pequeños. Los quales huevos heran muy blancos y claros y limpios, que pareçían de nácar o aljófar. Y la sancta virgen les resçivió de muy buena voluntad y la bendiçión que el glorioso Sant Françisco le dio. E le rogó por toda su orden de frailes e monjas, en espeçial por sus hermanas y compañeras, les diese su bendiçión. Y bendiziendo a las religiosas, despidióse el glorioso padre. Y la bienabenturada en el despedimiento besóle sus sanctos pies y él a ella en la caveça, diziendo: "Quiero yo besar los dolores del mi Señor Jesuchristo en ti, filia mea, por su misericordia transformados."

Dixo esta bienabenturada que le dio a entender el glorioso Sant Françisco que los pajaritos bivos y las pollitas de colores salidas de los huevos que se exían pasçiendo en las buenas yervas eran las ánimas que mediante la Passión de Nuestro Señor Dios y los dolores que ella padesçía heran ayudadas y remediadas. Y los huevos que le dio heran ánimas (que le traía por la voluntad de Dios para ser ayudadas d'ella) de personas que, viviendo en los cuerpos, havían sido devotas del glorioso Sant Françisco.

Appendix F

MADRE JUANA DE LA CRUZ: EL LIBRO DEL CONORTE

Capítulo LIX. Que trata de cómo nuestro redentor Jesuchristo fabló en un día del seráfico e alférez suyo San Françisco, diziendo e declarando los secretos e misterios siguientes [Selections]

[fol. 369v] Fablando el Señor en un día del glorioso San Françisco, dixo que estando El ençerrado en el seno del Padre, viendo cómo se perdía la iglesia militante, fabló al Padre, diziendo: "Padre mío poderoso, graçias te fago porque ascondiste tus escondidos e altos secretos a los letrados e sabios e los revelaste a los sinples e despreçiados e humilldes. E si me preguntas, Padre mío, porqué lo feziste, dígote que porque fue tu voluntad de lo fazer / [fol. 370r] e te plugo d'ello. E pues que así lo fazes, Padre mío, ruégote que me des una gallina morenita que está en la tierra, la qual es de muy sinple e reta intinçión, para que repare la mi iglesia que se quiere caer." Y el Padre le preguntó, diziéndole: "Fijo mío muy amado, ¿quién es ese que me pides?" Y el Fijo le respondió: "Padre mío, es uno que, aunque al pareçer es algo feo e no muy fermoso quanto al cuerpo, mas es muy fermoso en el ánima e de muy buena e sinple intinçión." E el Padre le respondió: "Fijo mío, yo te le otorgo, e tómale para ti."

E dixo el Señor que luego apareçió El a San Françisco e le fabló en un cruçifixo que estava en una iglesia derribada e muy vieja. E declaró el Señor, diziendo que llama El a San Françisco la gallina morenita porque así como la gallina se trabaja por sacar los huevos que le echan, aunque no los a ella puesto e son de otras gallinas, y está por sacarlos en penitençia fasta que se para amarilla e muerta de hanbre, e quando los a sacado, dexa ella de comer por darlo a los pollos, así por semejante fizo el glorio[so] San Françisco, que estuvo en penitençia fasta que se paró muy amarillo y enfermo por traer muchas ánimas a Dios, aunque no heran sus fijos carnales. E por dar e ofreçer a Dios gran manada de ánimas, estava sienpre en lloro, e dexando de comer manjares corporales por darles a ellos enxenplo que lo fiziesen así e se fartasen e deleitasen más de los manjares espirituales que de los corporales. E por darles exenplo que continuamente deven llorar e lagrimar e trabajar por ofreçer a Dios muchas manadas de ánimas. E que por esto le llama El algunas vezes, aunque está en su santo reino muy triunfante e gozoso, la gallina morenita. Porque el glorioso San Françisco resçibe d'ello muy grande honra e consolaçión. E responde a su divina magestad, diziendo: "O Dios mío e Señor mío, a ti me conparas, que aun tú dizes, Señor: 'O Jerusalén, así te deseo meter debaxo de mis alas como la gallina faze a los pollos por guardarlos del vilano tragador.'" E dixo el Señor que llama El a San Françisco gallina morenica con gran sobramiento de amor e jugando e aviendo plazer con él, a manera de padre muy piadoso que juega con el fijo que mucho ama e le pone nonbre como le plaze y es su voluntad. E tanbién porque sienpre deseó allegar muchas manadas de ánimas para ofreçer a Dios. E no solamente lo deseó estando en la tierra, mas aún lo desea agora estando en el çielo, continuamente rogando a Dios por los de su horden e por todos sus devotos.

E que como el bienaventurado San Françisco fuese este mesmo día a le ofreçer todos los de su horden e a rogarle por todos los de la tierra, que iva muy aconpañado de muchas proçesiones de bienaventurados, así de otras órdenes como de la suya. Entre las quales (dixo el Señor) la suya hera la que más luzida y clara e resplandeçiente iva, porque ellos son luz del mundo, en quanto siguen la dotrina del santo evangelio e traen en el reino de los çielos todas las vestiduras claras como espejos, en las quales se pareçían muchas ánimas muy fermosas, así como niños e niñas. A sinificaçión que por la horden de San Françisco se salvan muchas ánimas, así de honbres como de mugeres, por muchas maneras. Unos por tener devoçión con el ábito, por quanto es figura e semejança de la su / [fol. 370v] cruz, e porque en persona que tenía tal ábito enprimió El las sus llagas. Esto fue en el glorioso San Françisco, el qual debaxo de aquel ábito las truxo por espaçio de dos años ascondidas, por lo qual tiene tantas indulgençias e perdones. E que otros se salvan porque tienen devoçión de morir en este santo ábito. E otros porque tienen devoçión con el mesmo San Françisco más que con otro ningún santo del çielo. E otros porque fazen bien a sus frailes. E otros porque fazen y edifican monesterios de su horden. E dixo el Señor que a acontezido [a] algunas personas ser tan malas, que estavan ya condenadas para el infierno, e por solo fazer una limosna a los frailes de San Françisco o por reçebir uno d'ellos en su casa e darle a comer o ençenderle un poco de lunbre, salvarse e fazerlo con tanto fervor e caridad que en aquella ora le son perdonados todos sus pecados.

E dixo el Señor que como San Françisco subió delante d'El, le llamó, diziéndole: "Ven acá, mi amigo seráfico e alférez mío. Muéstrame tus tetas." E que él le respondió, diziendo con mucho gozo: "Mis tetas, Señor, helas aquí, que éstos que aquí traigo comigo fueron las tetas de mis deseos." Y el Señor (dixo El mesmo) le tornó a fablar, diziéndole: "Amigo, muéstrame tu manto." El qual le estendió luego, que le traía sobre sí lleno de muchas joyas muy resplandeçientes. E los ángeles tomaron de los cabos del manto e le estendieron. Y era tan grande su anchura que cubría todo el mundo. A sinificación que su horden está desparzida por todo el mundo.

E dixo el Señor que después que El ovo coronado e dado muy grandes premios e gualardones a todos los bienaventurados que ivan con el glorioso San Françisco, le llamó a El, diziéndole: "Ven acá, tú, mi hermano e mi mártir. Siéntate en mi trono a par de mí e resçibe muy grandes premios por tus trabajos." E que le llama El hermano porque le remedó e llevó las pisadas de su vida e sig[u]ió la dotrina del santo evangelio. E que le llama su mártir porque los otros mártires fueron martirizados de mano de los infieles e San Françisco de la suya, imprimiéndole El las sus çinco llagas. E porque estando él en el monte, le apareçió cruçificado así como serafín muy ençendido e inflamado. Y entre otras palabras que le fabló le dixo: "Dime, amigo San Françisco, si quieres ser mi muger e si te quieres huñir e ayuntar comigo." E San Françisco le respondió: "Sí, Señor Dios mío, de buena voluntad estaré yo sugeto e obediente a todo lo que tú quisieres e mandares, así como faze la muger que está sugeta e obediente a su marido. E de buena voluntad me ayuntaré contigo, así como la esposa se ayunta con el esposo." E Nuestro Señor Jesuchristo le tornó a dezir: "Amigo, pues súfreme un dolor o dolores que agora te daré, pues con tantas lágrimas me lo as pedido e demandado a sentir los dolores de la mi Pasión. E yo te daré después por ello infinitos gozos e deleites mayores que son los dolores, por fuertes que sean e por mucho que te duelan." E dixo el Señor que, viendo El la respuesta tan humillde del glorioso San Françisco e la grande obediençia con que le tornava a responder, que a todos los dolores que El mandase estava aparejado a resçebir por su amor. E que así fue tan ayuntado con el en aquella hora que le inprimió las sus çinco llagas de / [fol. 371r] la manera que las resçibió en la cruz.

. . . [fol. 372v] E va luego el glorioso San Françisco alunbrando con sus llagas todo el purgatorio. E saca e libra todas las ánimas que es voluntad de Dios que

saque. E llévalas todas alrededor de sí, así como la gallina quando lieva gran manada de pollos. E dixo el Señor que como le veen los demonios ir así tan çercado de
ánimas, se levantan e van en pos d'él por se las arrebatar todas e despedaçarlas entre
sus uñas con muy gran crueldad, así como faze el vilano quando lieva los pollos. Y
el glorioso San Françisco toma todas las ánimas e las recoge y encubre, así como
faze la gallina a los pollos, que los anpara debaxo de sus alas para los defender del
vilano.

Appendix G

VIDA Y FIN DE LA BIENABENTURADA VIRGEN SANCTA JUANA
DE LA CRUZ

Capítulo XI. De çiertos avisos que el sancto ángel dio a esta
bienabenturada [Fragment]

[fol. 58v] "Hablando yo una vez con mi sancto ángel, vile muy triste e se le
mudaron a deshora las bestiduras resplandeçientes e claras e fermosas en manera de
un romero pobre de los que demandan por amor de Dios. E preguntéle por qué se
le havían mudado tan súpitamente las bestiduras e respondióme: 'La tristeza que
ves que traigo e la mudanza de mi persona todo es por ti sola, que ha dado Dios,
Nuestro Señor, una gran sentençia sobre ti de muchas penas e travajos, los quales
tú sentirás y verás antes de mucho tiempo. E como yo te quiero tanto, he acordado
andar en este ábito pidiendo limosna a los sanctos y a Nuestra Señora que todos
rueguen por ti a Dios, que lo has mucho menester. E yo también rogaré e tú ruega
por ti e por las ánimas e personas bienhechoras que tienes [a] cargo y heres obli-
gada. E pregunta a tus hermanas las religiosas qué es lo que dixo el Señor la
postrera vez / [fol. 59r] que habló en ti, pues saven [que] no a hablado después acá
en aquella manera que solía, estando tú elevada.'"

E preguntando esta bienabenturada a las religiosas lo que el sancto ángel le
mandó, respondiéronle diziendo: "Nosotras no savemos si es postrera vez o no la
plática que oímos al Señor pocos días a, que pareçía profetiçava, e las profeçías
heran rezias con palabras de amor e otras de reguridad. En las de amor dezía
querría hazer una prueba en su esposa querida e amada." E amostrava a las que la
oían [que] de ninguna cosa se maravillasen ni escandaliçasen ni pensasen en sus
coraçones [que] hazía Dios aquella prueba o castigo en aquella persona por peccados que en ella huviese ni porque El estuviese enojado con ella. Por ninguna cosa
más de quererlo El haçer e lo haría porque le plaçía y hera su voluntad de quebrar
aquel órgano o trompeta en qu'El hablava e le quería mudar e trasmudar en otro
estado que pareçiese muy menospreçiado y enfermo y muy lastimado e doloroso e
quexoso, que casi no pareçiese el que solía. E hablava con la mesma, diziendo:
"Juanica, tú heres este órgano que digo, que quiero que seas despreçiada e abilitada
e gravemente atormentada por probar tu paçiençia. Yo me apartaré de ti por algún

tiempo y çesará mi habla e convertírsete an los gozos en dolores y las risas en gemidos e tristeza, en quanto a lo corporal. Que en quanto a lo espiritual, la enfermedad enfortaleza la fee, e la virtud del ánima no está en fuerça de brazos ni de miembros corporales."

E todo esto que el Señor dezía e profetiçava no lo entendían las personas que lo oían hasta que después dende a pocos días veían a esta bienabenturada tullirse toda, en tanto grado que no le quedaron fuerças ningunas ni miembro sano ni coyuntura en su cuerpo que no estuviesen desparçidos los huesos unos de otros, hasta los dedos / [fol. 59v] de las manos e pies, que no se podía encubrir ni sus dolores sin gemido sufrir. Tenía muy gran conformidad e paçiençia en su larga e grande enfermedad e increíbles dolores, sugetándose a la voluntad del poderoso Dios con gran desseo de padesçer siempre por su amor. Encogiéronsele las rodillas, que nunca más las estendió. E los brazos e manos por semejante teníalas tan tullidas y los dedos bueltos e quebradas las coyunturas de manera que no podía comer con sus manos ni las podía menear si no se las meneavan, ni volverse de ninguna parte si no la volvían, ni comer ni vever si no se lo davan por mano agena. Ningún miembro de su persona podía menear si no hera la lengua. Dixo esta sancta virgen a sus monjas: "Supliqué a mi sancto ángel me dixese qué hera este mal tan reçio que unos dizen uno e otros, otro; en ninguna cosa de quantas manda hacer para remedio mío aprovechan. Respondióme diziendo: '¡Qué maravilla que sea agora por amor de las gotas sanguíneas [que] quien no holgó de tener las mayores perlas e joyas tenga ésas! Esto digo por las llagas que rogaste a Dios te quitase. A determinado su divina magestad de imprimir en [ti] sus dolores e sentimiento de su sancta Passión, como lo verás.'

"E ansí se cumplió como él me lo dixo, que estando yo elevada un día de viernes, víspera de los diez mill mártires, veía en espíritu que haçían remembranza de la Passión de Nuestro Señor Jesuchristo, como si fuera Viernes Sancto. Esto hera en un campo. Y veía ansimismo allí a los sanctos mártires cuya fiesta e día hera, e cómo los matavan e cruçificavan y a Nuestro Señor Jesuchristo con ellos, confortándolos y El ansimismo cruçificado. E deçíales: '¡Ea, mis amigos, que yo esa muerte morí por vosotros e justa cosa es [que] vosotros la paséis por mí, que el amor no se pagó con amor ni la muerte si contra muerte, que no tiene ninguno mayor amor que poner la vida por su amigo! Yo soy vida y resurecçión e gloria. Consolaos conmigo e acompañáme, que abierto está el paraíso y vuestras coronas delante de cada uno la tiene su ángel / [fol. 60r] propio.' E yo, muy espantada de estas cosas que veía, pregunté a mi sancto ángel, que estava delante de mí: '¿Qué cosa es ésta que Nuestro Señor Jesuchristo está aquí cruçificado y ansimesmo estos otros muchos que le acompañan?' Respondióme: 'Muchos compañeros tiene Dios después que resçivió la sancta humanidad en el vientre virginal de Sancta María. E tú, que esto vees, apáréjate, que partiçipar tienes de esta cosa, que ansí lo quiere Dios, que para eso te truxe yo a ver esta remembranza que se haçía este día en memoria de la Passión de Nuestro Señor y de sus siervos.'

"Y estando mi sancto ángel diziéndome estas palabras, voló a deshora Nuestro Señor Jesuchristo e vile delante de mí. Preguntó a mi sancto ángel: '¿Qué estás aquí platicando con esta persona?' Y él, arrodillado en tierra, dixo: 'Señor, está maravillada de los misterios que aquí pasan.' Entonçes miróme el Señor y dixo:

'¿Quieres tú gustar de esta fruta?' Yo respondí: 'Señor, quiera vuestra sancta voluntad e no más ni menos.' Entonçes abrazóme el Señor y puso sus pies en mis pies y sus rodillas en mis rodillas—todo las alimpió—e sus palmas en las mías e su caveza e cuerpo todo junto con el mío. Y quando esto hizo, fue tanto lo que sentí que me parezía entravan en mí muchedumbre de clavos muy agudos e ardientes. E sonava estruendo enrededor a manera de quando hazen la remembranza de Nuestro Señor, dando martilladas. Inchávase con la presencia suya e con el gusto y dulçor de su amor.

"Aunque heran muy grandes los dolores que padeçí, no heran tan crueles como los que sentí después que fui tornada en mis sentidos e naturaleza corporal. Parézeme veo todos los miembros e benas e coyunturas de mi cuerpo hechas como a manera de cuerdas e teclas o clavijas de vihuela e a Nuestro Señor tocarlas con sus sacratíssimas manos, atañer con ellas a manera de instrumento o vihuela e azer muy dulçe e suave son de armonía. E quando su divina magestad apresura el son e le haze más alto, entonzes tengo muy grandes e creçidos dolores, e quando / [fol. 60v] avaja el son, no solamente no los tengo grandes mas muy menores. Oigole cantar quando tañe palabras formadas e muy preçiosas e saludable[s] para las ánimas."

Appendix H

MADRE JUANA DE LA CRUZ: *EL LIBRO DEL CONORTE*

Capítulo XLVI. *Que trata de las fiestas e solenidades que el poderoso Dios fizo a la gloriosa virgen Santa Clara en el reino de los çielos*

[fol. 308r] Fablando el Señor en un día de la gloriosa Santa Clara, dixo que como fueron oídas en el çielo los loores e fiestas que en la tierra se fazían d'ella, que mandó fazer llamamiento con las tronpetas, las quales dezían: "Salgan todas las vírgines e vengan delante el Señor a le ofreçer sus vasos." E El deçendió del seno del Padre e se asentó en medio de una muy fermosa plaça en un tálamo muy adornado y enriqueçido de muchas e muy preçiosas joyas. E delante del tálamo estavan puestas muy lindas mesas y El çercado de muchas conpañas de bienaventurados, los quales le fazían muchas adoraçiones e serviçios, tañendo e cantando delante d'El con grande dulçedunbre e melodía.

E que estando así todos con El, vinieron todos los coros de las vírgines, trayendo cada una d'ellas su vaso muy preçioso e oloroso en sus manos. E fincadas todas de finojos delante el su tálamo, le ofreçía cada una su vaso con gran reverençia e acatamiento. Y el Señor (dixo El mesmo) tomava cada uno de aquellos vasos e metía la mano dentro e sacava muy olorosos licores e muchas rosas e flores d'él. E las olía El mesmo e después las dava a oler a los otros, diziéndoles: "Mirad, amigos, cómo huelen los licores d'estos preçiosos e fermosos vasos." E que después que El los ovo resçebido e olido e tomado en sus preçiosas manos, los puso en las mesas que estavan delante de su preçioso tálamo. E como los vasos heran de oro muy fino e llenos de muy preçiosos licores e muy finas rosas e flores, davan de sí tan grande resplandor e olor que subían los fumos e claridad d'ellos fasta la Santísima Trinidad. A sinificaçión que todas las santas vírgines nunca ensuziaron los vasos de sus cuerpos ni de sus ánimas con ningún amor ni deleite carnal ni terrenal, mas sienpre fueron puestos sus pensamientos e deseos e amor con solo Dios. E que por eso subían los olores de sus buenas obras delante de la Santísima Trinidad, así como fumo de ençienso e de perfumes muy olientes. E dixo el Señor que como la gloriosa Santa Clara viniese en medio de las otras vírgines, que la llamó El, diziéndole: "Sal tú acá, amiga mía Clara, que bien me entenderás que digo a ti, que aunque aya otras en mi santo reino que se llaman claras, / [fol. 308v] pocas son e no tan señaladas como tú." E que esto dezía El porque pocas personas ay que se llaman claras. E dixo su divina magestad que oyendo Santa Clara cómo El la llamava, salió luego de entre las otras e fuese muy apriesa para El a le ofreçer su vaso. E viendo El el deseo e amor que ella traía, a desora se le desapareçió delante de sus ojos, que no le pudo ver. Y esto fizo El por que ella le buscase con mayor afinco e fervor, e quando le fallase, se gozase e alegrase más con El.

Y andándole ella a buscar con muy grande afeçión e amor e deseo, preguntando a todos e diziendo: "Dezidme, señores, ¿avéis visto al que ama la mi ánima?" Dixo el Señor que después que ovo andado Santa Clara por una parte e por otra buscando e mirando e preguntando, se asentó en medio de una muy grande e fermosa plaça, mirando e pensando e deseando quándo le vería. E este pensar e mirar e desear que ella fazía hera horar, porque qualquier persona que piensa en Dios e desea gozar de las sus dulçedunbres e consolaçiones divinales es oraçión muy açeuta e aplazible delante d'El.

E que estando ella así mirando, a desora vido en sus faldas una concha grande e muy fermosa e resplandeçiente e salían d'ella fumos muy olorosos e suaves. E viendo ella cosa tan fermosa e olorosa sintió muy grande alegría e consolaçión e dezía: "O, si viese ya a mi amado, ésta le daría e ofreçería, que es muy linda e perteneçiente para El." E diziendo ella estas cosas, a desora vido abrir la concha e salir d'ella al Señor (dixo El mesmo) muy poderoso e fermoso e resplandeçiente. E con el grande gozo e dulçedunbre que sintió de verle, cayó sobre su faz muy enbriagada y ençendida de amor sobre el que le tenía en sus faldas, adorándole e abraçándole e besándole muchas vezes con soberana reverençia e amor. Y El le dixo: "Levántate, amiga mía, e muéstrame tu vaso." E que ella le respondió: "Dios mío e Señor mío, hele aquí, que nunca en ningún tienpo me encubrí ni ascondí de ti."

E dixo el Señor que la tomó El en sus braços, y estando ella así, a desora le salió de los pechos fazia la parte del coraçón un caño de oro como de órgano muy resplandeçiente, e le tañía El con su preçiosa boca e con sus manos tañía en el vaso que estava de la otra parte. E fazía muy dulçes e suaves e deleitosos sones e melodías. E que con los preçiosos e castos tañimientos que El fazía a la bienaventurada Santa Clara, reçebía ella tan grandes dulçedunbres e consolaçiones e gozos açidentales, que se caía a una parte e a otra muy enbriaga y ençendida en amor divinal, algunas vezes no sintiéndose dina de estar ayuntada con El e otras vezes dándole graçias por tan grandes benefiçios e consolaçiones a ella dados e otorgados.

[fol. 309r] E dixo el Señor que estando El con la gloriosa Santa Clara coronándola e dándole grandes gualardones, trayeron los santos ángeles unas ánimas que estavan en purgatorio e avían salido por ruego de Santa Clara aquel día aver alguna recreaçión, aunque no heran del todo libradas ni avían acabado de purgar. E que por semejante le rogavan muy humillmente todos los santos que las acabase de librar e les perdonase lo que les quedava de purgar por que no bolviesen más a purgatorio. Dixo su divina magestad que les respondió El: "Bien vedes, mis amigos, que no es justiçia eso que me pedís, que harto bien les fize en no condenarlas según los grandes pecados que ellas tenían."

E que oyendo aquellas ánimas la respuesta que El dava a los bienaventurados, se fincaron de finojos muy humilladas delante d'El e le dixeron: "Bien conoçemos nosotras que mereçíamos el infierno por nuestras maldades, mas pues Tú nos quesiste salvar por sola tu misericordia, acuérdate que tomamos algunas buldas e anduvimos algunas romerías y estaçiones quando estávamos en el mundo." Dixo el Señor que les respondió El, diziendo: "¿Tuvistes vosotras todas las condiçiones que se requieren en las bulas e indulgençias? Que no ay ningún santo padre que sea tan inorante que quando a de otorgar bulas e indulgençias que primero no saca condiçiones e partido comigo, diziendo: 'Señor, si Tú eres servido e fuere tu voluntad de otorgar estas indulgençias que yo conçedo, dalas e otórgalas, e si no, sea como Tú mandares, que yo con tu voluntad las do e las otorgo.'" E dixo el Señor que oyendo las ánimas la respuesta que El les dio, que se hallaron muy confusas e callaron, que no osaron más rogarle.

E que viendo los santos ángeles e los otros bienaventurados cómo estavan aquellas ánimas más confusas e avergonçadas, rogávanle, diziendo: "Señor, aunque ellas no tuvieron las condiçiones que avían de tener para ganar las indulgençias, baste tu misericordia para las acabar de salvar de las penas." Y El les dixo: "Juzgaldo vosotros e contad. Por tal bula quitaldes tantos años e por tal romería o estaçión quitaldes tanbién tantos. E por tal oraçión rezada a mi Passión o a mi madre Santa María quitaldes por semejante tantos. E veréis vosotros cómo con todo esto no acaban aún de pagar ni cunplir. Y en esto les fago misericordia en soltarles lo que les suelto, aunque vayan acabar de pagar lo que deven, e quando estén allá, yo les soltaré algo de lo que an de pagar."

E dixo el Señor que después que los santos ángeles o-/ [fol. 309v] vieron tornado aquellas ánimas a purgatorio, coronó El e dio muy grandes gualardones a muchos santos e ánimas bienaventuradas que avía poco tienpo que avían salido de purgatorio. E las llevó consigo a su trono real e las ofreçió al Padre con grande gozo e alegría por quanto el su gozo e consolaçión es ofreçer al Padre çelestial ánimas salvas, porque por las redemir e salvar padeçió El con muy grande amor la muy cruda e amarga Passión.

E declaró el Señor, diziendo que fallarle la gloriosa Santa Clara en la concha metido y ençerrado e después abrirse la mesma concha e salir El de dentro d'ella e darle tan grandes consolaçiones e gozos fue sinificaçión que la mesma virgen Santa Clara e todas las otras vírgenes le fallaron ençerrado y escondido por fe e por graçia e amor en la concha de la mar de las tribulaçiones e angustias e trabajos e persecuçiones e martirios. Porque así como la margarita preçiosa se busca e se falla en las aguas muy fondas de la mar con grandes trabajos e peligros, que así por semejante le fallaron las gloriosas vírgenes en la mar d'este mundo, guardando su virginidad e linpieza e padeçiendo grandes persecuçiones e trabajos.

Appendix I

Capítulo LXXII. *Que trata de la creaçión de los çielos e la tierra e de todas las cosas que en ellos son e del honbre a imagen e semejança de Dios* [Selections]

[fol. 450r] E declaró el Señor, diziendo que no se maraville ninguno porque en este santo libro ay algunas cosas más largamente declaradas o denunçiadas o tratadas que en las otras santas escrituras que acá están escritas, por quanto las dize e declara el Espíritu Santo y el mesmo resollo e virtud de Dios, el qual sabe mejor todas las cosas que ninguno de quantos escrivieron o fizieron las escrituras que acá están escritas. Porque assí como el Espíritu Santo alunbra y enseña de dentro del ánima mayores e más altas e maravillosas cosas que las escrituras le pueden dezir ni mostrar, así por semejante el mesmo Espíritu Santo, el qual fabló e declaró todas estas cosas, las sabe e conoçe mejor que nadie lo puede dezir ni declarar ni manifestar.

En lo qual no deve nadie dudar, porque quando el mesmo Dios venía a fablar e declarar los misterios e secretos e maravillas que en este santo libro están escritas, avía algunas personas que dezían que pues El dezía que hera Dios e se manifestava por ello, que fiziese miraglos e maravillas para que le conoçiesen e creyesen. E a los pensamientos de los que tales cosas demandavan respondió el mesmo Dios, diziendo que ya hera pasado su día, que un día e otro avía de fazer miraglos e no más, conviene a saber, un tienpo que los fizo El quando vino en el mundo e otro tienpo que los fizieron sus diçipulos. Que los miraglos e maravillas que El agora quería fazer heran / [fol. 450v] en las ánimas, por quanto ellas heran las que le traían e fazían venir a fablar en esta boz, viendo tan gran muchedunbre de ánimas cómo se le pierden continuamente e se van al infierno. E que se tuviesen por çiertos todos los que miraglos e señales demandavan que no les daría ni les mostraría otras sino la graçia e consolaçión que dava a esta bienaventurada sierva suya que le veía e la fe e gozo muy verdadero que dava en los coraçones e ánimas de todas las personas que le oían e creían.

E dixo el Señor que los que por estas cosas no quisieren creer ni por esta santa escritura no se quisieren convertir, que El no les faze fuerça, porque El nunca la fizo ni la faze a nadie para que le crean. Enpero que si no lo creen, no dexan de pecar en ello e ofenderle a El mesmo, pues siendo Dios, venía e lo fablava para consolaçión de los fieles e amantes a El. E que los que dezían que cómo hera posible aver en el çielo danças ni bailes ni juegos ni plazeres ni cavallos, que respondió El a las tales personas, diziendo que, porque se maravillavan ni dudavan aver estas cosas en el çielo, que creyesen e pensasen, quando los tales pensamientos de dudas les viniesen, cómo Dios, que crió en la tierra para consolaçión e ayuda de los honbres animalias de natura de tierra según El quiso e fue su voluntad, puede tanbién fazer en el çielo animalias de otro espeçie muy más preçioso e oloroso e luzido.

E que lo que dizen de las cosas de juegos e plazeres, que miren y entiendan los que lo mereçieren entender cómo está escrito en el evangelio que trata de las bienaventuranças aquella palabra que dize: "Bienaventurados los que lloran, que ellos reirán en el reino de los çielos." E declaró el Señor, diziendo que pues dize el evangelio que an de reír en el reino de los çielos, que se sigue que de sobramiento de gozo e deleites e gloria e plazer e juegos será la risa, porque ¿en dónde más creçidas e cunplidas e verdaderas risas e deleites que en el çielo, donde mora Dios, que es gozo e alegría de los justos e donde moran los justos que mereçen gozar de todos los deleites e plazeres cunplidos? Por quanto los juegos e plazeres e bailes e danças e tañeres e cançiones que se fazen en el çielo, todo es sin pecado y en gran gloria e alabança de Dios y en gloria e mereçimiento d'ellos mesmos. E que por tanto todos los bienes e deleites e riquezas e consolaçiones e plazeres que pueden ser dichos e pensados todos juntos están en el çielo para honra e gloria de Dios e consolaçión de los bienaventurados que con El moran. Porque si en la tierra tienen por costunbre de aparejar e adornar la casa e fazer los mayores plazeres e juegos e aparejos que pueden para resçebir algunos grandes señores que aí an de ser aposentados o estar allí algún tienpo, que quanto más pudo e fizo e aparejó El en sola su palabra en sus altísimos çielos para en que abitase El e morase, que lo vale e lo mereçe todo, e para que aposentase e / [fol. 451r] resçibiese a todos los bienaventurados que allá están e a los que mereçieren subir de aquí a [*sic*] al día del juizio, que escrito es que mayores son e más cunplidos e abastados los gozos del çielo que los de la tierra, por quanto son tan grandes que por una cosa muy pequeña que acá dexemos por amor de Dios, allá lo pagan çiento doble.

. . . [fol. 451v] E declaró el Señor, diziendo que esta santa escritura es tan grande e maravillosa e provechosa que no la podrá entender ni gozar ni gustar la persona que no amare ni gustare las dulçedunbres de Dios. Porque así como la persona que está enferma e mal dispuesta tiene el gusto de la boca muy amargo e todo quanto come, por dulçe e bien guisado que sea, le amarga e le sabe mal, que así por semejante qualquier persona que tuviere el ánima enferma de pecados y el gusto amargo de incredulidad e dureza e maliçia y enbidia e otros pecados semejantes no le sabrá bien esta santa escritura / [fol. 452r] porque quanto ella es más eçelente, tanto menos la sabrán gustar los malos. Enpero que así como el que está sano e bien dispuesto tiene el gusto de la boca bueno e le sabe bien lo que come, así por semejante qualquier persona que tuviere su ánima sana e bien dispuesta sin ninguna enfermedad de pecado e tuviere el gusto bueno e sabroso para con Dios le sabrá muy bien esta santa escritura e le pareçerá en su paladar más dulçe que el panar de la miel.

E dixo el Señor que con tanto amor e fervor e devoçión e fe lo puede alguna persona leer que, aunque al prinçipio esté en pecado mortal, quando acabe esté en estado de graçia. Porque tanto quanto estas preçiosas palabras son más eçelentes e altas, tanto an menester las gentes más lunbre e graçia para las entender e conprehender e gustar. Porque son dichas e declaradas por la boca del poderoso Dios, el qual tuvo por bien de dar liçençia para que se escriviesen e dibulgasen por el mundo. E aun dixo e fue fecho assí como prometió que daría lunbre e memoria para se retener y escrevir, suplicándoselo nosotras por quanto fuimos mandadas de algunos perlados que escriviésemos lo que oíamos. Enpero respondió su divina magestad que no hera dino el mundo, conviene a saber, todos nosotros pecadores, los quales somos cada uno de nosotros un mundo de pecados, de oír ni escrevir ni leer tan altas palabras e secretos. E confiando en su gran misericordia, enpeçamos a escrevir algo de lo que oíamos. E respondió entonçes su divina magestad a nuestro propósito e intinçión, diziendo que no esperava El otra cosa sino que nos comidiésemos a lo fazer para honra e gloria suya e salvaçión de las ánimas.

Enpero que guay de los incrédulos e dudosos en tan gran benefiçio e alunbramiento para las gentes. Porque la tal escritura e secretos puede ser dicho d'ella ser nueva luz en el mundo para los sapientes en gustar e conoçer a Dios e para los inorantes que no saben qué cosa es Dios ni sus dulçedunbres e deleites. Por lo qual declaró el Señor, diziendo que no ay tilde ni letra ni palabra de quantas en este preçioso libro están escritas ni de quantas El mesmo fabló que no sea una perla e una piedra preçiosa e una joya muy rica e una flor muy olorosa para todos los bienaventurados que moran en el reino de los çielos e para qualquier ánima fiel que con fe e amor e devoçión lo leyere e oyere. E los misterios e secretos d'este santo libro son tan grandes que todas las palabras d'él (dixo el Señor) están escritas en el reino de los çielos, assí como El las dixo e fabló, por las paredes de las calles e alcáçares con letras muy grandes e resplandeçientes e claras que las pueden todos quantos allá están leer. E sale d'ellas tan suave olor que todos los bienaventurados se deleitan en las oler e mirar. E ansimesmo dixo el Señor que sobre las cosas escritas en este / [fol. 452v] libro mirarían algunas personas, e a unos les pareçerían muy bien e las tomarán para su salvaçión e provecho e les aprovecharán mucho para sus ánimas e devoçión, si la tuviesen. E que otras avría que no aprovecharían tanto en sus ánimas porque les faltará la devoçión e conoçimiento y el crédito. Enpero que [a] los tales vernán días e tiempos en que sabrán claramente cómo estas cosas fueron dichas por boca de Dios mientras le plugo de enbiar su Espíritu Santo en aquella persona por cuyo estrumento estas cosas fabló, que así lo dezía El mesmo que no las quería dezir sin medianería de algún estrumento o órgano. Así como el tañedor quando quiere fazer algún son, agora sea baxo, agora sea alto o triste o alegre o de gozo e bien sonante, busca algún estrumento con que tanga e cante e denunçie algunas cosas de su coraçón a los oyentes que quiere que las sepan.

E dixo más el Señor que si en la tierra no ay ninguna cosa hordenada ni fecha que por su mano e por su voluntad no sea permitida ni consentida o mandada e criada y ingeniada[?] con entendimiento que a dado a las gentes e sentido a las animalias en este mundo e fechas e criadas del espeçie d'esta tierra, que ¿cómo es inposible en el su santo reino çelestial que tenga y edifique e críe si quiere las mesmas cosas en otra mayor perfeçión o de otras más preçiosas espeçies e calidades muy a su voluntad e perteneçientes para en tan luzido reino e lugar como es donde El tiene su asiento e morada? E delante su trono todas las cosas son más luzidas que oro ni plata ni perlas e piedras preçiosas e más olorosas e ricas que sedas ni perfumes e finos matizes e tinturas fermosas, que no son como los d'este mundo ni son fechos por mano y engenio de honbre.

E dixo más su divina magestad que aun las animalias e aves e qualesquier cosas de diversas maneras que son en los çielos, siquiera perezcan [Vat., fol. 728v: parezcan] por breve tiempo, siquier por tiempo que algo dure, todo es muy linpio e oloroso e tan preçioso que es gran deleite verlo e mirarlo. E que por eso nos venía El a denunçiar algunas cosas de las del çielo e tanbién a declarar las figuras que ay de nosotros algunas vezes en el valle que es dicho de las sinificaçiones del mundo e de las gentes d'él.

E dixo el Señor que por amor que tenía e tiene todavía al humanal linage, quiso e tuvo por bien su divina magestad de nos fazer partiçipantes de algunas de las cosas de su santo reino. Porque así como El está ya en su santo reino glorificado e alegre, así nos querría alegrar e dar muy grande esperança de su glorioso e preçioso reino e mostrarnos sus gloriosas dulçedunbres e amor que con nosotros pecadores sienpre a tenido e tiene.

E dixo el Señor que todas las cosas d'este santo libro heran dichas e fabladas por el Espíritu Santo, assí como en otro tienpo fueron fabladas muchas cosas por Salomón mientras estuvo en estado de graçia e mientras El le dio la sabiduría e prudençia del Espíritu Santo, la qual le dio El quan- / [fol. 453r] do le plugo e se la quitó quando le plugo. E ansimesmo a otros profetas por cuya boca El fabló muchas vezes y enseñó buenos consejos como todopoderoso e puede dezir e fazer todas las cosas que a El le plaze e muchas más podría fazer de las que podríamos nosotros alcançar a conprehender. Enpero que muchas d'ellas dexa de fazer e las encubre de nosotros pecadores porque no somos dignos de ver sus miraglos.

Enpero que en todo lo sobre escrito en este libro de Luz Norte El lo pone en mano de buenas personas, en espeçial de buenos honbres e letrados e buenos christianos. E dixo más su divina magestad que no encomienda estas palabras e santo libro a otras ningunas personas ni a ereges malos infieles sino a los buenos cristianos verdaderamente creyentes en la santa fe católica. E que a ellos dize e ruega e manda, como a hermanos e fijos, que lo esaminen e miren. Porque quiere que aun las cosas que El dize las esaminen los honbres buenos de su santa iglesia, y esto que lo faze El por nos dar enxenplo de humilldad para que no presumamos nosotros que todo lo que hablamos e dizimos es perfeto e que no es menester que nadie lo retraiga o reprehenda. Comoquier que dixo que en las cosas d'este santo libro no avía ninguna cosa que dudar ni reprehender, porque El avía dado su Espíritu Santo así para las dezir por el estrumento como para las escrevir los oyentes.

E dixo el Señor que porque estavan hordenadas çiertas cosas muy espantosas sobre el mundo que avían de acaeçer no dende a mucho tienpo que este libro se acabasse de fazer, en las quales cosas las gentes serían muy espantadas e atemorizadas e angustiadas en manera que les pareçería ser ya la fin del mundo en algunas partes e lugares de la tierra, que por eso quiso El que, antes que estas cosas acaeçiesen, declarar estas cosas por que las gentes se aprovechasen d'ellas e se enmendasen de sus pecados e le sirviesen por que El tuviese por bien de salvar sus ánimas e de rebocar por sus ruegos d'ellos e por sus mereçimientos algunas sentençias que no se cunpliesen y esecutasen tan crudamente sobre las gentes, vençido El por los ruegos piadosos. E tiniendo las gentes las sus palabras en reverençia, de las quales es dicho que salió el senbrador a senbrar su simiente e solamente lo que cayó en buena tierra aquello aprovechó. E lo que cayó en el camino y en piedra aquello no aprovechó. E guay de los que a mal recaudo ponen sus ánimas, que después en el infierno no hallan ni un solo momento de descanso. E darían por él todos los bienes del mundo, si fuesen suyos, e aun los del çielo darían tanbién, si algo tuviesen en él. Enpero que por ser ya tan tarde, no les puede aprovechar ninguna cosa que den ni fagan, que ya no pueden alcançar ni un solo momento de descanso. E que los bienaventurados que van a la gloria del paraíso, que son muy privillijados e libertados después que el Señor santíssimo los a ya santificado. Es tanta su santidad e juventud sin vejez e sanidad e fermosura e fidalguía que an cobrado e cobran por

ser fijos de Dios e / [fol. 453v] santos de su corte, que ninguna cosa que fagan ni
digan, aunque sean en plazeres e juegos e donares honestos e discretos, no les es
pecado e que ésta es la libertad e previllejo de los santos de Dios. E por el contrario,
los que estamos en este mundo estamos captivos por el pecado de nuestros pri-
meros padres de todas las cosas que fazemos, aun de las que son serviçio de Dios.
Porque no obramos perfetamente, aunque sean de juegos e plazeres e otras qualesquier cosas, todas las más son con pecado. Esto por nuestra sugeçión e captiverio
por quanto aun no somos verdaderos fijos de Dios por conoçimiento suyo e paçi-
fico amor de solo El e de su honra e gloria por cuyo amor avían de ser todos los
gozos e las alegrías. E por semejante todas las tristezas por conpassión de su Passión e de las ofensas fechas a El más que por nuestras propias pérdidas e angustias e
tribulaçiones y enfermedades. E dixo el Señor que los que vivimos en este mundo
no podemos ser verdaderos fijos de Dios e tener estos previllejos fasta que le ame-
mos mucho e por propios mereçimientos alcançaremos que El nos quiera e tome
por suyos. E que para esto avemos de echar de nosotros todo pecado e toda maliçia
e todo desagradeçimiento e toda blasfemia e toda ipocresía e vanagloria e ira y enbidia contra nuestros próximos y ermanos e de todos los viçios que la iglesia santa
amonesta que no tengamos. E que los despidamos e desechemos de nos como a
malos e tomemos las virtudes e amonestamientos santos por la santa iglesia como
buenos e como a escaleras para subir al reino de los çielos.

E dixo el Señor que dizen acá algunas personas que en el reino de los çielos no
hablan ni comen. Que no es assí todo tienpo, que algunas vezes fablan, enpero no
vanidades ni murmuraçiones sino alabándole a El, assí como quando uno dize:
"Dios me a fecho a mí muchas merçedes por su bondad." E respondiesen otros,
diziendo: "Tanbién le devo yo mucho a su gran magestad, tantas que no se las sé
servir ni agradesçer jamás." E otros, como quando uno dize: "Dios sea loado." E
responde otro: "Por sienpre." E que estas cosas e otras muchas que se pueden dezir
se dizen en su alabança e cantares muy suaves. E dixo el Señor que comen en el
reino de los çielos quando El les da manjares muy preçiosos de sí mesmo e de sus
dulçedunbres divinales, de los quales El los farta en muchas maneras de deleites e
suavidades sin cuento e les da savor sin fastío e voluntad e deseo e fanbre quando le
plaze e fartura e cabal contento quando le plaze. E que los manjares de acá son los
que enbaraçan y fastían y es pecado husar de demasiada fartura d'ellos. Enpero que
los del çielo, mientras más comen e gustan, más se les acreçienta la gloria e los que
los gustan se contentan e fartan sin desear otra ninguna cosa e sin que vayan en-
baraçados / [fol. 454r] ni enfastiados de la dulçedunbre resçebida, aunque sea el
gusto contino e sin çesar. Y ansí de las otras cosas e gozos e glorias que ay en el su
santo reino de los çielos.

E dixo el Señor que aunque por çierto tienpo avía acostunbrado a fablar las
cosas susodichas, como están en este santo libro fabladas e dichas e conçertadas,
que no las avía de fablar contino ansí por esta manera e conçierto, enpero que
fablaría como le pluguiesse dende adelante el tienpo que asinado por El se cun-
pliesse. E que no quería contarnos contino de las figuras del çielo e misterios de lo
alto, porque si dezía de las cosas escritas, dezíamos que aquello bien lo sabíamos. E
si nos dezía de las cosas del çielo, que dizíamos que que [*Vat.*, fol. 731r: que no]
sabíamos si heran verdaderas e que las dudávamos por no tener entero amor de

Dios ni conoçimiento de las cosas suyas. E lo mesmo fazíamos en las de la santa fe
católica, aunque sabíamos claramente que es muy verdadera e confirmada por infinitos miraglos.

E dixo el Señor que tuvo El por bien de fablar en esta manera e por çierto
tienpo por mostrar el amor que nos tiene aun oy día e porque nos vee apartados
d'El por muchas e diversas maneras. E nos querría consolar e fazer merçedes e
mostrarnos sus misericordias para que tuviésemos amistad con El, como El la tiene
con nosotros, aunque somos pecadores. E que quando nos açota e da angustias, lo
faze porque son medeçinas del alma, aunque a nosotros no nos pareçe assí, que
pensamos que lo faze e permite por nuestro daño e pena, que aun sobre las criaturas santas e de buena vida permitía El angustias e tribulaçiones e congoxas espirituales e tenporales e corporales e persecuçiones por que no piensen los otros que a
solos ellos da las penas.

E dixo el Señor, fablando a la mesma a quien El dava estas graçias e por cuya
boca fablava las cosas susodichas: "E tú tanbién no quedarás sin penas corporales y
espirituales, ca tienpo verná que serás enferma e aborresçible en alguna manera o
maneras de algunas gentes, en manera que les pareçerá no aver visto en ti la graçia
de mí, tu Dios e Criador, aunque de otras serás muy querida e muy amada. Y esto
será e se cunplirá quando fuere la mi voluntad." E assí acabó su divina magestad sus
santas palabras, horas convidándonos a la gloria con sus dulçes falagos e mani-
festándonos su reino, horas reprehendiéndonos e declarándonos las penas infernales. E la bendiçión que El dava en acabando su sermón es ésta que se sigue: "La
bendiçión del Padre mío çelestial e de mí su fijo Jesuchristo e la del Espíritu Santo
consolador que sea contigo e con la conpaña, que me voy, mas no del coraçón de
quien bien me quisiere e me amare." Y esto dezía El porque Nuestro Señor Jesuchristo en la humanidad santa es el que apareçía [a] aquella persona en quien Dios
mostrava estas maravillas.

Y ella fablava con El, según las señales que se pareçían. Y El fablava con ella
todas las cosas susodichas, las quales oíamos claramente las que lo escrevi- / [fol.
454v] mos, que por nuestros oídos lo [o]ímos quando el Señor lo dezía. E veíamos
cómo aquella sierva del Señor no hera ella la que fablava quando el Señor fablava,
porque assí se pareçían claras las palabras del Señor, e cómo El le dava a ella la
salutaçión e soplo del Espíritu Santo. E por eso dava el Señor la bendiçión en nonbre de toda la Trinidad, Padre e Fijo y Espíritu Santo, que son tres personas e un
solo Dios, a quien adoramos, a quien bendezimos, a quien glorificamos e damos
graçias, el qual nos amenaza si le ofendemos e nos falaga e ama si le servimos e
amamos. Y en El esperamos e por amor d'El de todo pecado nos apartamos, por lo
qual nos promete la gloria con muy infinitos gozos e bienaventuranças e riquezas e
gloriosos deleites çelestiales en su santo reino. Deo graçias. Escrivióse este santo
libro en el año de mill e quinientos y nueve años.

Index

University of Pennsylvania Press

MIDDLE AGES SERIES

Edward Peters, General Editor

Edward Peters, ed. *Christian Society and the Crusades, 1198–1229*. Sources in Translation, including The Capture of Damietta by Oliver of Paderborn. 1971

Edward Peters, ed. *The First Crusade: The Chronicle of Fulcher of Chartres and Other Source Materials*. 1971

Katherine Fischer Drew, trans. *The Burgundian Code: The Book of Constitutions or Law of Gundobad and Additional Enactments*. 1972

G. G. Coulton. *From St. Francis to Dante: Translations from the Chronicle of the Franciscan Salimbene (1221–1288)*. 1972

Alan C. Kors and Edward Peters, eds. *Witchcraft in Europe, 1110–1700: A Documentary History*. 1972

Richard C. Dales. *The Scientific Achievement of the Middle Ages*. 1973

Katherine Fischer Drew, trans. *The Lombard Laws*. 1973

Edward Peters, ed. *Monks, Bishops, and Pagans: Christian Culture in Gaul and Italy, 500–700*. 1975

Jeanne Krochalis and Edward Peters, ed. and trans. *The World of Piers Plowman*. 1975

Julius Goebel, Jr. *Felony and Misdemeanor: A Study in the History of Criminal Law*. 1976

Susan Mosher Stuard, ed. *Women in Medieval Society*. 1976

Clifford Peterson. *Saint Erkenwald*. 1977

Robert Somerville and Kenneth Pennington, eds. *Law, Church, and Society: Essays in Honor of Stephan Kuttner*. 1977

Donald E. Queller. *The Fourth Crusade: The Conquest of Constantinople, 1201–1204*. 1977

Pierre Riché (Jo Ann McNamara, trans.). *Daily Life in the World of Charlemagne*. 1978

Edward Peters, ed. *Heresy and Authority in Medieval Europe*. 1980

Suzanne Fonay Wemple. *Women in Frankish Society: Marriage and the Cloister, 500–900*. 1981

Edward Peters. *The Magician, the Witch, and the Law*. 1982

Barbara H. Rosenwein. *Rhinoceros Bound: Cluny in the Tenth Century*. 1982

Steven D. Sargent, ed. and trans. *On the Threshold of Exact Science: Selected Writings of Anneliese Maier on Late Medieval Natural Philosophy*. 1982

Benedicta Ward. *Miracles and the Medieval Mind: Theory, Record, and Event, 1000–1215*. 1982

Harry Turtledove, trans. *The Chronicle of Theophanes: An English Translation of* anni mundi *6095–6305 (A.D. 602–813)*. 1982

Leonard Cantor, ed. *The English Medieval Landscape*. 1982

Charles T. Davis. *Dante's Italy and Other Essays.* 1984

George T. Dennis, trans. *Maurice's Strategikon: Handbook of Byzantine Military Strategy.* 1984

Thomas F. X. Noble. *The Republic of St. Peter: The Birth of the Papal State, 680–825.* 1984

Kenneth Pennington. *Pope and Bishops: The Papal Monarchy in the Twelfth and Thirteenth Centuries.* 1984

Patrick J. Geary. *Aristocracy in Provence: The Rhône Basin at the Dawn of the Carolingian Age.* 1985

C. Stephen Jaeger. *The Origins of Courtliness: Civilizing Trends and the Formation of Courtly Ideals, 939–1210.* 1985

J. N. Hillgarth, ed. *Christianity and Paganism, 350–750: The Conversion of Western Europe.* 1986

William Chester Jordan. *From Servitude to Freedom: Manumission in the Sénonais in the Thirteenth Century.* 1986

James William Brodman. *Ransoming Captives in Crusader Spain: The Order of Merced on the Christian-Islamic Frontier.* 1986

Frank Tobin. *Meister Eckhart: Thought and Language.* 1986

Daniel Bornstein, trans. *Dino Compagni's Chronicle of Florence.* 1986

James M. Powell. *Anatomy of a Crusade, 1213–1221.* 1986

Jonathan Riley-Smith. *The First Crusade and the Idea of Crusading.* 1986

Susan Mosher Stuard, ed. *Women in Medieval History and Historiography.* 1987

Avril Henry, ed. *The Mirour of Mans Saluacioune.* 1987

María Rosa Menocal. *The Arabic Role in Medieval Literary History.* 1987

Margaret J. Ehrhart. *The Judgment of the Trojan Prince Paris in Medieval Literature.* 1987

Betsy Bowden. *Chaucer Aloud: The Varieties of Textual Interpretation.* 1987

Michael Resler, trans. *EREC by Hartmann von Aue.* 1987

A. J. Minnis. *Medieval Theory of Authorship.* 1988

Uta-Renate Blumenthal. *The Investiture Controversy: Church and Monarchy from the Ninth to the Twelfth Century.* 1988

Robert Hollander. *Boccaccio's Last Fiction: "Il Corbaccio."* 1988

Ralph Turner. *Men Raised from the Dust: Administrative Service and Upward Mobility in Angevin England.* 1988

David Anderson. *Before the Knight's Tale: Imitation of Classical Epic in Boccaccio's Teseida.* 1988

Charlotte A. Newman. *The Anglo-Norman Nobility in the Reign of Henry I: The Second Generation.* 1988

Joseph F. O'Callaghan. *The Cortes of Castile-León, 1188–1350.* 1989

William D. Paden, ed. *The Voice of the Trobairitz: Essays on the Women Troubadours.* 1989

William Chester Jordan. *The French Monarchy and the Jews: From Philip Augustus to the Last Capetians.* 1989

Edward B. Irving, Jr. *Rereading* Beowulf. 1989

David Burr. *Olivi and Franciscan Poverty: The Origins of the* Usus Pauper *Controversy.* 1989

Willene B. Clark and Meradith T. McMunn, eds. *Beasts and Birds of the Middle Ages: The Bestiary and Its Legacy.* 1989

Richard C. Hoffmann. *Land, Liberties, and Lordship in a Late Medieval Countryside: Agrarian Structures and Change in the Duchy of Wrocław.* 1990

J. M. W. Bean. *From Lord to Patron: Lordship in Late Medieval England.* 1990

Mary F. Wack. *Lovesickness in the Middle Ages: The* Viaticum *and Its Commentaries.* 1990

Robert I. Burns, S.J., ed. *Emperor of Culture: Alfonso X the Learned of Castile and His Thirteenth-Century Renaissance.* 1990

E. Ann Matter. *The Voice of My Beloved: The Song of Songs in Western Medieval Christianity.* 1990

Patricia Terry, trans. *Poems of the Elder Edda.* 1990

Ronald E. Surtz. *The Guitar of God: Gender, Power, and Authority in the Visionary World of Mother Juana de la Cruz (1481–1534).* 1990